Brain Signal Analysis

Brain Signal Analysis

Advances in Neuroelectric and Neuromagnetic Methods

edited by Todd C. Handy

The MIT Press
Cambridge, Massachusetts
London, England

MIT Press books may be purchased at special quantity discounts for business or sales promotional use. For information, please email special_sales@mitpress.mit.edu or write to Special Sales Department, The MIT Press, 55 Hayward Street, Cambridge, MA 02142.

This book was set in Stone Sans and Stone Serif by SNP Best-set Typesetter Ltd., Hong Kong. Printed and bound in the United States of America.

Library of Congress Cataloging-in-Publication Data

Brain signal analysis : advances in neuroelectric and neuromagnetic methods / edited by Todd C. Handy.
   p. cm.
Includes bibliographical references and index.
ISBN 978-0-262-01308-6 (hardcover : alk. paper)
1. Electroencephalography. 2. Magnetoencephalography. 3. Cognitive neuroscience–Methodology. I. Handy, Todd C.
QP376.5.B735   2009
616.8′047547—dc22
                                                            2008044258

10 9 8 7 6 5 4 3 2 1

Contents

Contributors

Denis Brunet
EEG Brain Mapping Core
Center for Biomedical Imaging of
Lausanne and Geneva
Geneva, Switzerland
&
Denis Brunet
Functional Brain Mapping Laboratory,
Biomedical Imaging Center
Neuroscience Department
University of Geneva
Geneva, Switzerland

Douglas Cheyne
Program in Neurosciences and Mental
Health
Hospital for Sick Children
Toronto, ON, Canada

Marzia De Lucia
EEG Brain Mapping Core
Center for Biomedical Imaging of
Lausanne and Geneva
Lausanne, Switzerland

Sam M. Doesburg
Department of Psychology
University of British Columbia
Vancouver, BC, Canada

John J. Foxe
Program in Cognitive Neuroscience
City College of the City University of
New York
New York, NY, USA

Karl J. Friston
The Wellcome Trust Centre for
Neuroimaging
University College London
London, UK

Marta I. Garrido
The Wellcome Trust Centre for
Neuroimaging
University College London
London, UK

Sara L. Gonzalez Andino
Electrical Neuroimaging Group
University Hospital of Geneva
Geneva, Switzerland

Rolando Grave de Peralta Menendez
Electrical Neuroimaging Group
University Hospital of Geneva
Geneva, Switzerland

Jessica J. Green
Department of Psychology
Simon Fraser University
Burnaby, BC, Canada

Todd C. Handy
Department of Psychology
University of British Columbia
Vancouver, BC, Canada

Anthony T. Herdman
Department of Psychology
Simon Fraser University
Burnaby, BC, Canada

Stefan J. Kiebel
The Wellcome Trust Centre for
Neuroimaging
University College London
London, UK

Edmund C. Lalor
Trinity College Institute of Neuroscience
Trinity College Dublin
Dublin, Ireland

Theodor Landis
Neurology Department
University Hospital of Geneva
Geneva, Switzerland

Teresa Y. L. Liu-Ambrose
Department of Physical Therapy
University of British Columbia
Vancouver, BC, Canada

John J. McDonald
Department of Psychology
Simon Fraser University
Burnaby, BC, Canada

Christoph M. Michel
Functional Brain Mapping Laboratory,
Neuroscience Department
University of Geneva
Geneva, Switzerland

Marla J. S. Mickleborough
Department of Psychology
University of British Columbia
Vancouver, BC, Canada

Micah M. Murray
EEG Brain Mapping Core
Center for Biomedical Imaging of
Lausanne and Geneva
Lausanne, Switzerland
&
Neuropsychology and
Neurorehabilitation Service and
Radiology Service
Centre Hospitalier Universitaire Vaudois
and University of Lausanne
Lausanne, Switzerland

Lindsay S. Nagamatsu
Department of Psychology
University of British Columbia
Vancouver, BC, Canada

Barak A. Pearlmutter
Hamilton Institute
National University of Ireland,
Maynooth
Maynooth, Co. Kildare, Ireland

Durk Talsma
Department of Cognitive Psychology
Vrije Universiteit
Amsterdam, the Netherlands

Gregor Thut
Department of Psychology
University of Glasgow
Glasgow, Scotland, UK

Anne-Laura van Harmelen
Department of Cognitive Psychology
Vrije Universiteit
Amsterdam, the Netherlands

Lawrence M. Ward
Department of Psychology
University of British Columbia
Vancouver, BC, Canada

Preface

With the rise of functional magnetic resonance imaging in the 1990s, it was not uncommon to hear the opinion that cognitive electrophysiology was now doomed to obsolescence. In looking back now, however, it seems that if anything, the advent of fMRI actually *stimulated* growth in ERPs/EEG and MEG, as they have proved to be complimentary methods to fMRI rather than redundant ones. As a consequence, not only have these measures been taken up by ever greater numbers of researchers, but the tools and techniques of data acquisition and analysis have been evolving at an accelerating pace. The advances being made in this latter regard have been considerable, and thus, only a few years on since editing a volume on the basics of ERP methodology, it seemed that a new book was warranted to capture and disseminate these broader developments in cognitive electrophysiology.

In introducing the book's material, perhaps what the contributions here highlight best is the increasing overlap in EEG and MEG analytic techniques. For example, chapters by Kiebel et al. and Ward and Doesburg concern dynamic causal modeling of evoked responses (chapter 6) and phase synchrony analysis (chapter 7) respectively, both of which are equally applicable to EEG or MEG data. Likewise the beamformer approach to source localization was originally applied to MEG data as discussed by Herdman and Cheyne (chapter 5), yet it has now also been developed for use with EEG signals as well, as detailed by Green and McDonald (chapter 4).

The book begins with a set of chapters speaking to new advances being made in ERP/EEG-related analyses. Among these are Lalor and colleagues' presentation of a novel visual-evoked potential based on reverse correlation methods designed to surmount inherent limitations of the classic visual-evoked potential (chapter 1), Murray and colleagues' new approach to topographic mapping using reference-independent spatial information in high-density electrode montages (chapter 2), and Grave de Peralta Mendez and colleagues' novel method for estimating local field potentials via a newly developed solution for the neuroelectromagnetic inverse problem (chapter 3).

Following chapters 4 through 7 on interrelated EEG/MEG techniques, the book concludes with a pair of chapters that speak to the latest thinking on design aspects of EEG/MEG studies: Talsma and van Harmelen discuss how the signal-to-noise ratio of event-related data can be optimized via experimental design considerations (chapter 8), while Handy and colleagues present the latest statistical developments for maximizing power and accuracy when analyzing event-related data via repeated-measures ANOVAs (chapter 9).

That the book has come to fruition is due chiefly to the chapter authors, and I warmly thank each for accepting my email solicitation out of the blue and agreeing to put together a contribution. Of course, the book would also not be possible without the MIT Press, and I am indebted to Barbara Murphy, Susan Buckley, and Robert Prior for their time and patience as the volume has moved from concept to reality. Finally, on a more personal note, I owe my own background in cognitive electrophysiology to the fine guidance and training of George R. Mangun. To Ron, thanks for a strong foundation in this ever-evolving field.

1 Reverse Correlation and the VESPA Method

Edmund C. Lalor, Barak A. Pearlmutter, and John J. Foxe

The traditional method of obtaining event-related potentials (ERPs) typically involves the repeated presentation of discrete stimulus events and extraction from the ongoing neural activity using signal averaging techniques. Assuming a sufficiently high sampling rate, this technique allows for the determination of a response whose individual components are clearly resolved in time, allowing for a temporally detailed analysis of sensory and cognitive processes. While this method has led to tremendous advances in our understanding of the brain, both healthy and otherwise, it has a number of intrinsic limitations. These include the inability to adequately resolve responses to more than one stimulus at a time, the nonenvironmental and somewhat aversive nature of suddenly onsetting stimuli, particularly in the visual domain, and the lengthy acquisition time resulting from the incorporation of a sufficient delay between stimuli to allow the neural activity to return to baseline.

In this chapter we describe a method for obtaining a novel visual ERP known as the VESPA (for visual evoked spread spectrum analysis) that seeks to address the limitations of the standard visual evoked potential (VEP). This method involves the recording of neural activity during the presentation of continuous, stochastically modulated stimuli and the use of reverse correlation to determine the transfer function of the human visual system, that is, the function that converts the presented stimulus into the recorded neural activity. First, we introduce the broader reverse correlation technique that has seen widespread use in the analysis of many physiological systems. We follow this introduction with a description of the VESPA method itself, including a discussion of the differences between the standard VEP and the VESPA, and some proposed applications and extensions.

Analysis of Physiological Systems Using Stochastic Stimuli

In order to gain some useful understanding of complex physiological systems, especially considering the inherent difficulty of accessing the inner details of such systems as they function, one must first make some simplifying assumptions. This allows one to infer models of the system based on observations of its behavior under certain conditions. One approach that has met with some success is the application of system identification methodologies to the analysis of physiological systems. That is to say, one can attempt to obtain a mathematical expression for the system functional, $S(\bullet)$, that converts a given input, x, into a measured output, y, even in the presence of measured noise, w, and unmeasured noise z (see figure 1.1). This is usually accomplished in two steps. First, given all prior knowledge of the system, an appropriate model is chosen. Then, in the second step, the parameters of this model are estimated based on the output of the system corresponding to particular inputs.

The most widely studied and well understood class of dynamical systems considered in practice and in the system identification literature are so-called linear time-invariant (LTI) systems. Study of these systems involves the assumption that the output depends linearly on the input and entails estimation of the impulse response of the system. Despite the obviously unrealistic assumption about the real life processes they represent, the approximations employed are often reasonable and the linear models obtained often lead to useful results. However, a considerable amount of research has also been done extending this methodology to the modeling of nonlinear time-invariant systems. Most of this work is based on the mathematics of the Volterra–Wiener approach. The Volterra series was first studied by Vito Volterra around 1880 as a generalization of the Taylor series of a function. Norbert Wiener (1958) used the Volterra series to model the input–output relationship of a nonlinear system. This technique allows one to define a set of discrete Volterra *kernels* that completely characterize the nonlinear system under investigation. It does so by using a Gaussian time function as an input that allows for the estimation of a set of Wiener kernels that can then be used to determine the model's Volterra kernels. Lee and Schetzen (1965) described a practical method for determining the Wiener kernels by cross-correlating the system response with its white Gaussian input. Schetzen (1981) provides a good review of nonlinear system modeling based on the Wiener theory.

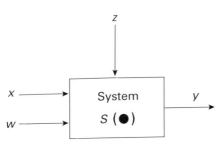

Figure 1.1
System with output y, input x, measured noise w, unmeasured noise z, and system functional $S(\bullet)$.

The primary application of this type of nonlinear system modeling based on the Wiener theory is in the experimental identification of physiological systems (Hung and Stark 1977; Marmarelis and Marmarelis 1978; Marmarelis 2004). As mentioned, linear assumptions can often lead to useful information about a system. However, it is clear that physiological systems are highly nonlinear and that their function is often critically dependent on those nonlinearities. One important consideration in physiological modeling is the type of input that is used to estimate the model of the system. The white noise approach (deBoer and Kuyper 1968; Marmarelis and Marmarelis 1978) proposes utilizing widely varying input–output data in order to span the full dynamic operating range of the system rather than simplified, less natural data that may ignore large parts of this range. By employing spectrally and temporally rich input signals such as white noise to explore the behavior of the system, one maximizes the amount of power being used to drive and thus interrogate the system under investigation.

Several successful examples of the use of nonlinear modeling have been reported across different physiological domains (Marmarelis and Naka 1972; for review, see Marmarelis 2004). In particular, a large number of studies of the visual system have utilized quasi–white light stimulation in order to derive a model of the behavior of cells, from photoreceptors through to simple V1 cells (Marmarelis and McCann 1977; Sakai and Naka 1987; Meister et al. 1994; Jones and Palmer 1987; DeAngelis et al. 1993). At a more macroscopic scale, the Volterra–Wiener approach has been applied to EEG and, in particular, the visual evoked potential (Coppola 1979). In recent work (Lalor et al. 2006) we have revisited this idea and developed a method for evoking a novel ERP known as the VESPA that seeks to harness the technique of reverse correlation and, in so doing, address various limitations of the traditional VEP approach.

The VESPA Method

Following the white noise approach, and unlike the traditional VEP technique, the VESPA is elicited using continuous, stochastic input to the visual system. This is accomplished by rapidly modulating either the contrast or mean luminance of a visual stimulus using a precomputed signal with Gaussian distribution. For example, one can generate a number of checkerboard images of different contrasts and then present a different one on every refresh of a computer monitor as determined by the precomputed signal. Because there is not much EEG or MEG power above 30 Hz, a refresh rate of 60 Hz seems sensible and works well. The modulation signals used to elicit the VESPAs shown in the present chapter had their power spread uniformly over the 0 to 30 Hz range. The fundamental difference between the VEP and VESPA stimulation is illustrated in figure 1.2.

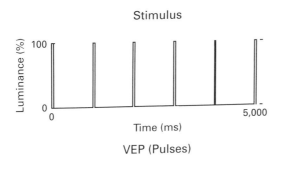

VEP (Pulses)

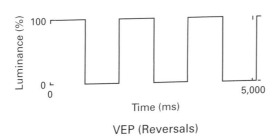

VEP (Reversals)

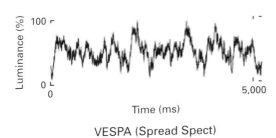

VESPA (Spread Spect)

Figure 1.2
Basic difference between VEP and VESPA stimuli. Pulsed and pattern-reversal VEP stimuli modulated from 0 to 100 percent in discrete jumps isolated in time. The VESPA stimulus smoothly but stochastically modulates across the range 0 to 100 percent with many intermediate values. A Gaussian distribution for this modulating signal works well.

As shown in figure 1.3, the VESPA model assumes that the EEG or MEG response, $y(t)$, consists of a convolution of this stochastic input signal, $x(t)$, with an unknown impulse response waveform $w(\tau)$, plus noise,

$$y(t) = x(t) \bullet w(\tau) + \text{noise}. \tag{1}$$

Given the precomputed stimulus waveform, $x(t)$, and the measured EEG or MEG signals, $y(t)$, we can estimate the values of the impulse response function, $w(\tau)$, using linear least squares estimation (for details, see appendix A). The impulse response $w(\tau)$ is known as the VESPA. The EEG or MEG can be thought of as the superposition of many impulse responses (i.e., VESPAs), one per frame, each scaled by the associated input value (see figure 1.3).

The VESPA is plotted in μV on a time axis that indicates the relationship between the (normalized; see appendix A) incoming stimulus signal and the output EEG a certain time later. For example, the 0 ms time point of a VESPA waveform indicates the relationship between the input stimulus and the EEG at exactly the same time, which should be zero given that the response to a stimulus does not propagate through the visual system in 0 ms! Typically the VESPA is nonzero in an interval from around 50 to 250 ms indicating that each input stimulus affects the EEG across a range of time 50 to 250 ms later, which was already known from use of the standard VEP.

Comparison to VEP

The similar morphologies of the VESPA and VEP are clearly seen in figure 1.4. While these responses show a high degree of correlation ($r = 0.91$, $p < 10^{-28}$), the within subject correlations between responses that make up the group averages are typically much lower (Lalor et al. 2006). This suggests that the VESPA and VEP give largely similar information across a group, but that they may give complementary information on an individual basis.

In fact it can be argued that the VESPA method is a strict generalization of the VEP technique. In the special case of the VEP the stimulus, $x(t)$, consists of a set of widely spaced impulses which, when processed using the VESPA analysis described herein, leads to a straightforward averaging procedure. The more general VESPA analysis allows for the incorporation of a whole range of stimulus classes such as on/off discontinuities, periodic bursts, and changes in temporal frequency, and thus for a much more thorough investigation of the properties of the visual system than discrete stimulation alone.

Another advantage of the VESPA is illustrated in figure 1.5, which shows a plot comparing the signal-to-noise ratios (SNRs) achieved by the VESPA and VEP using the same basic checkerboard stimulus at electrode location Oz. The SNR was calculated at 5,000 ms intervals by defining the noise as the mean of the squared values in the

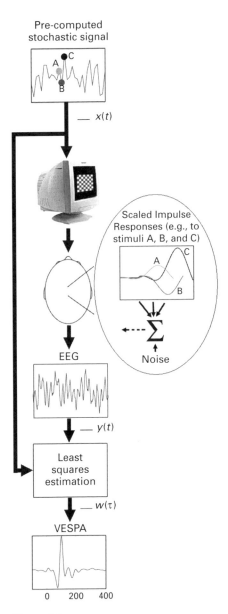

Figure 1.3
Flow diagram of VESPA acquisition. The EEG or MEG is modeled as a sum of overlapping impulse responses scaled by the corresponding stimuli, plus noise. Three such scaled impulse responses are shown, corresponding to stimulus values A, B, and C.

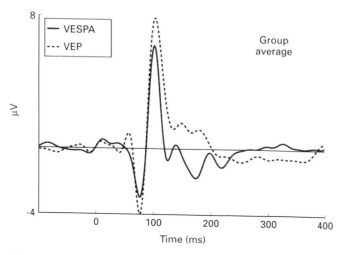

Figure 1.4

VESPA elicited by stochastic modulation of the contrast of a checkerboard stimulus and the standard VEP obtained in response to the same checkerboard pattern reversing in phase every second. Both responses are for data at electrode location Oz and are averaged across a group of 10 subjects, each of whom underwent two 120 s runs for each method.

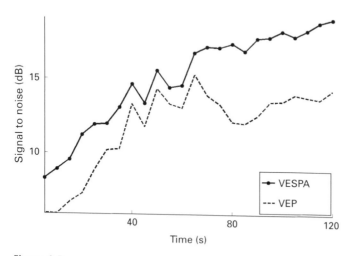

Figure 1.5

Signal-to-noise ratio as a function of acquisition time for the VESPA and VEP elicited by checkerboard stimuli at electrode location Oz. SNRs were calculated for VESPAs and VEPs averaged across two 120 s runs for 12 subjects.

100 ms interval immediately preceding the stimulus and the signal as the mean of the squared values in the interval 35 to 175 ms poststimulus. The VESPA achieves a SNR higher than that obtained using the standard method at every time point and is almost 5 dB higher after 120 s.

Extension to Quadratic Terms

The standard linear VESPA method described above can easily be extended to higher orders. For example, in the case of a quadratic analysis, this is accomplished by including in the least squares estimation not only the first-order values of the modulating signal within the desired window but also all second-order products of these values (for details, see appendix B or Lalor et al. 2008). This allows us to determine how the EEG depends not only on the individual input signal values but also on interactions between inputs at different time lags. For example, the VESPA value at (75, 100) ms indicates the relationship between the EEG or MEG and the interaction between the input stimulus values 75 and 100 ms earlier. Figure 1.6 illustrates the average quadratic VESPA response at electrode location Oz for data gathered from 11 subjects each of whom undertook 10 minutes of testing. To reduce processing time, the estimation was restricted to a 120 ms window starting 20 ms poststimulus. A strong positive

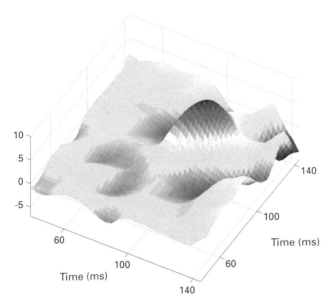

Figure 1.6
Surface plot of the second-order VESPA response at electrode location Oz for data gathered from 11 subjects, each of whom undertook 10 minutes of testing.

relationship can be seen between the EEG and the input stimulus interactions around (100, 100) ms, which is analogous to the positive component around 100 ms in the case of the linear VESPA. Some nonzero VESPA values can be seen off the diagonal, indicating that the second-order VESPA carries information not present in the linear VESPA. Further work will elucidate the relationship between the relative information contained in the linear and the nonlinear VESPA.

Cell Populations Activated by the VESPA and the VEP

The fact that the stimuli used to elicit the VESPA and VEP are so different begs the question: Do they represent activity of the same neuronal populations? Figure 1.7 shows a scalp topography for the VESPA (bottom row) that is quite distinct from that of the VEP (top row). The abiding characteristic of the early VESPA maps is the persistently delimited focus over midline occipital scalp without any evidence for the characteristic early bilateral spread over lateral occipital scalp regions that is consistently seen for the standard VEP (Gomez-Gonzalez et al. 1994; Foxe and Simpson 2002). This pattern suggests that the VESPA may well have a distinct cellular activation pattern from that of the VEP, favoring midline structures such as striate cortex and neighboring retinotopically mapped extrastriate regions as well as regions in the dorsal visual stream, activation of which is known to produce midline scalp topographies. Previous

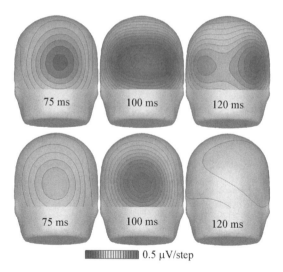

0.5 μV/step

Figure 1.7
Topographic maps indicating the scalp distribution of the VEP (*top row*) and the VESPA (*bottom row*) at 75, 100, and 120 ms. Activity at 100 ms is much more focused over the midline for the VESPA. The bilateral spread evident at 120 ms for the VEP is not manifest in the VESPA. (See plate I.)

studies have shown that the bilateral maps found during the early components of the VEP represent, in large part, activation of structures in the ventral visual stream such as the lateral occipital complex (Doniger et al. 2001; Foxe and Simpson 2002; Murray et al. 2004). Therefore one implication of this major difference is that the parvocellular system, which provides the major input to the ventral stream, may not be effectively activated by the VESPA.

This hypothesis can be considered with regards to the stimulus preferences of magno and parvo cells. Parvo cells with their spectrally opponent nature are know to be less sensitive to luminance contrast than magno cells (Kaplan et al. 1990; Lee et al. 1990). While the high contrast gain of cells in the magnocellular pathway might suggest that they may be more sensitive to the contrast modulations of the VESPA stimulus, their response saturates at fairly low contrasts (10–15 percent; e.g., Baseler and Sutter 1997). Parvocellular neurons meanwhile have lower contrast gain but do not saturate (see Butler et al. 2007). Furthermore it has been suggested that the temporal responses of the parvocellular system are much more linear than those of magnocellular cells (Kaplan and Benardete 2001). Given that the stimulus used to generate the VESPA shown in figure 1.7 spent less than 2 percent of its time below 15 percent contrast (Lalor et al. 2006), and that the analysis method used was strictly linear, it seems reasonable to conclude that this VESPA may actually reflect mostly activity of parvocellular pathways.

How then to explain the dramatic differences in scalp distribution and in particular the fact that, unlike the VEP, there is no lateralization of the P1 component for the VESPA? One good reason is that the VESPA analysis used assumes that the measured EEG is linearly related to the modulation of the simple luminance or contrast feature of the input stimulus. It is likely that this assumption holds truest for the relatively simple cells of early visual areas, particularly those in striate cortex, and less strongly for complex cells in higher order areas such as in parietal or inferotemporal (IT) cortex. Furthermore regions like IT are optimized for object recognition and thus are presumably not well suited to the analysis of stationary objects flickering at 60 Hz.

In order to further investigate the cellular origins of the VESPA, one can exploit the flexibility of the method to alter the characteristics of the stimulus. For example, one could adjust the temporal frequency statistics and/or the range over which the stimulus modulates in order to bias one subsystem over the other. Figure 1.8 shows VESPA responses to stimuli biased toward magnocellular and parvocellular pathways through restriction of the contrast modulation to within ranges of 0 to 10 percent and 32 to 100 percent respectively.

The dramatically different morphologies of these VESPA response strongly suggest that they index activity of distinct subpopulations of cells and is an example of the flexibility of the VESPA method. It is also clear from this figure that the parvocellularly biased VESPA much more closely resembles the standard VESPA, providing further

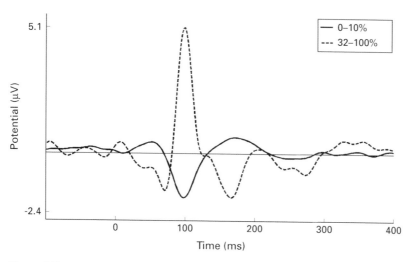

Figure 1.8
Plot of VESPA responses to stimuli whose contrast modulation was restricted to 0 to 10 percent and 32 to 100 percent. The 0 to 10 percent stimulus likely preferentially stimulates the magnocellular pathway, with the 32 to 100 percent stimulus reflecting activity mostly from parvo cells.

evidence that the standard VESPA indexes activity of parvo cells. (See Lalor and Foxe 2008 for more details.)

The ability to obtain responses biased toward one subsystem over the other could be very useful in both research and clinical settings. Aside from studies designed to gain a better insight into the processing mechanisms of the magnocellular and parvocellular pathways in general, each of these subsystems has also been studied in patients with various eye disorders such as retinitis pigmentosa (Alexander et al. 2004, 2005), glaucoma (McKendrick et al. 2007) and strabismic amblyopia (Davis et al. 2006). Furthermore magnocellular pathway function has been reported to be relatively more impaired in neurocognitive disorders such as schizophrenia (Foxe et al. 2005; Butler et al. 2005, 2007; Kim et al. 2005) and dyslexia (Chase and Stein 2003). Studies utilizing the standard VEP have moreover consistently demonstrated that patients with schizophrenia exhibit relatively severe deficits in early visual sensory processing, as indexed by a robust decrement in amplitude of the occipital P1 component (e.g., Foxe et al. 2001, 2005; Butler et al. 2001, 2007; Doniger et al. 2002; Spencer et al. 2003; Schechter et al. 2005; Haenschel et al. 2007). In a first investigation of the VESPA in schizophrenia, the standard VESPA from a group of patients was shown to be virtually identical to that from a group of controls, with the same two groups displaying dramatic differences in the P1 component of their respective VEPs (Lalor et al. 2008).

This finding clearly shows that the information provided by the VESPA and VEP is not identical and that the VESPA may be of great use in clinical investigation, perhaps in conjunction with the standard VEP. A second study involving patients with schizophrenia is underway using the magnocellularly biased VESPA.

Multiple Simultaneous Stimuli

One of the major advantages of the VESPA method is the ability to obtain separate responses to multiple simultaneously presented stimuli. This is accomplished by placing stimuli in distinct regions of the visual field and modulating those stimuli using mutually orthogonal stochastic signals. It is not necessary that the modulating signals have different frequency content. They can in fact have exactly the same statistics; that is, they can simply be different instantiations of the same random process. Two VESPAs acquired from data at electrode location Oz in response to two concurrently presented bilateral stimuli are shown in the left panel of figure 1.9. The responses shown represent the average across a group of ten subjects, each of whom underwent two 120 s runs.

   An obvious application of this ability is to the study of visual spatial attention. Visual attention is largely controlled endogenously but is also affected exogenously through the influence of novel stimuli and events in our visual field. While ERP/VEP studies investigating endogenous attention have been widely reported, these experiments have a serious limitation in that the suddenly onsetting stimuli used to elicit the ERP inevitably have an exogenous, attention-grabbing effect on the subject. Using the VESPA method, it is possible to investigate the effect of endogenous spatial attention on visual processing with excellent temporal resolution and without the use of suddenly onsetting stimuli. Furthermore, unlike with the traditional VEP, it is possible to emulate the more common real-life situation where both relevant and irrelevant information are present in the visual field at the same time. Obtaining VESPAs to attended and unattended stimuli simultaneously affords greater flexibility in the investigation of the mechanisms of enhancement and suppression in attentional deployment. The effect of attention on the VESPA in response to one of two simultaneously presented stimuli is shown in the bottom panel of figure 1.9. See Lalor et al. (2007) for more details of the use of the VESPA for the study of visual spatial attention.

Extensions

The approach outlined for the VESPA in this chapter could also be used to investigate other sensory systems. For example, an auditory analog of the VESPA could be elicited by stochastically modulating the amplitude of an auditory carrier signal. As with the VESPA, this method could afford a great deal of flexibility in the design of complex stimuli, allowing for a thorough analysis of the properties of the sensory system under

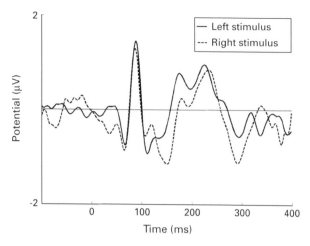

a

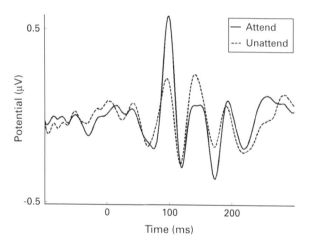

b

Figure 1.9
(a) Two VESPA responses obtained to concurrent, bilaterally presented stimuli. The responses shown represent the average across a group of 10 subjects, each of whom underwent two 120 s runs and are from data at electrode location Oz. (b) The effect of visual spatial attention on one of two simultaneously presented VESPA stimuli. Notice the significant enhancement of the peak around 100 ms in the attended condition. This plot represents the average response at Oz from a group of 15 subjects, each of whom underwent 50 trials of 40 s for both attend and unattend conditions.

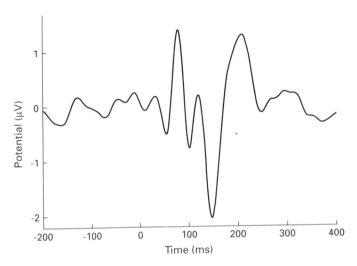

Figure 1.10
Auditory analogue to the VESPA response at electrode location Fz (referenced to the left mastoid) to a 1 kHz audio signal whose intensity was modulated by a stochastic signal with power spread uniformly over the range 0 to 30 Hz. The response shown was obtained from one subject who undertook ten 120 s runs.

investigation. A plot of an auditory analog to the VESPA obtained from one subject using an amplitude modulated 1 kHz auditory tone can be seen in figure 1.10.

The auditory and visual responses shown in this chapter also suggest the utility of the VESPA method in investigation of multisensory integration processes (Foxe and Schroeder 2005). By mutual manipulation of the statistics of the auditory and visual modulation signals one could determine the sensitivity of multisensory processing as a function of the correlation between the temporal variations in the different modalities.

Summary

We have described a method for obtaining a novel robust visual evoked response, known as the VESPA, that can be rapidly and continuously obtained using one or more simultaneously presented, unobtrusive stimuli. It is hoped that the VESPA method will prove to be a useful tool for research into schizophrenia and other areas as well as in clinical practice. The ease with which multiple spread spectrum stimuli can be incorporated into more natural experimental paradigms should render them very useful in studies which require short time monitoring of endogenous visual attention as well as in the design of brain–computer interfaces. Extensions to research on other modalities have been shown, and further extensions proposed.

Appendix A: Estimation of the VESPA

To perform the least squares fit we form the n-dimensional column vector x_t consisting of the sampled points of the precomputed modulating input signal

$$(x(t - t_0), x(t - (t_0 + 1)), \ldots, x(t - (t_0 + n - 1)))^T, \tag{A1}$$

where n is the number of sampled points of the impulse response function, w, that we wish to estimate and t_0 is the estimation window offset. The values for t_0 and n used in this chapter, for example, were −100 ms and 500 ms respectively. The values of x_t are normalized to between 0 and 1 and are then scaled by multiplying by the refresh rate of the monitor and dividing by the sampling rate of the acquisition device. This is to take into account the fact that the input stimulus and the data are both discrete in time and that the sampling rate of each affects the estimated values of the impulse response in a linear fashion. We can then estimate the n-dimensional vector, w, consisting of the sampled points of the response function

$$(w(t_0), w(t_0 + 1), \ldots, w(t_0 + n - 1))^T \tag{A2}$$

by minimizing

$$E = \left\langle \|w^T x_t - y_t\|^2 \right\rangle = w^T \left\langle x_t x_t^T \right\rangle w - 2 w^T \left\langle x_t y_t \right\rangle + \left\langle y_t y_t \right\rangle,$$

where $\langle \bullet \rangle$ indicates an average over t.

Expanding $dE/dw = 0$ gives

$$w = \left\langle x_t x_t^T \right\rangle^{-1} \left\langle x_t y_t \right\rangle. \tag{A3}$$

Here w can be solved for straightforwardly by first constructing the $n \times n$ matrix $x_t x_t^T$ at each time point of our stimulus signal, determining a running sum across all time points and dividing the sum by the number of time points. Second, the n-dimensional vector $x_t y_t$ is calculated, again at each time point and the mean is determined across all time points, again using a running sum. The final step involves a simple matrix inversion and multiplication.

We can further improve the quality of our estimate by adding a regularization term. This serves to increase the bias but reduce the variance of the estimate resulting in a net reduction in estimation error. Adding a term that quadratically penalizes the difference between each two neighboring terms of w we obtain the equation

$$w = \left\langle x_t x_t^T + \lambda M \right\rangle^{-1} \left\langle x_t y_t \right\rangle,$$

where

$$M = \begin{pmatrix} 1 & -1 & & & & \\ -1 & 2 & -1 & & & \\ & -1 & 2 & -1 & & \\ & & \cdots & \cdots & \cdots & \\ & & & -1 & 2 & -1 \\ & & & & -1 & 1 \end{pmatrix}. \tag{A4}$$

An empirically determined value of $\lambda = 4.4 \times 10^{-3}$ results in reduced estimation error without penalizing the heights of actual components.

Appendix B: Extension to Higher Orders

The VESPA analysis can very easily be extended to higher orders. For example, one can expand the VESPA estimation to a quadratic model of how the EEG depends on the input stimulus by replacing (A1) with a vector of $n + n(n + 1)/2$ elements, where n is the window size, containing the n first-order elements as before, and the $n(n + 1)/2$ second-order elements (all products of the form $x(t - t_0 - i)x(t - t_0 - j)$, where $0 \le i \le j \le n$). The quadratic VESPA w of this same dimensionality can be solved using

$$w = \langle x_t x_t^T + \delta I \rangle^{-1} \langle x_t y_t \rangle, \tag{A5}$$

where δ is a different regularization parameter and I is the identity matrix. Using values of 20 and 100 ms for t_0 and n respectively with an empirically determined $\delta = 5 \times 10^{-6}$ gives a good reduction in the estimation error. Incorporating higher than second-order terms proceeds in exactly the same way, albeit with ever larger increments in required computation time.

References

Alexander KR, Rajagopalan AS, Seiple W, Zemon VM, Fishman GA. 2005. Contrast response properties of magnocellular and parvocellular pathways in retinitis pigmentosa assessed by the visual evoked potential. *Investig Ophthalmol Visual Sci* 46:2967–73.

Alexander KR, Barnes CS, Fishman GA, Pokorny J, Smith VC. 2004. Contrast sensitivity deficits in inferred magnocellular and parvocellular pathways in retinitis pigmentosa. *Investig Ophthalmol Visual Sci* 45:4510–19.

Baseler HA, Sutter EE. 1997. M and P Components of the VEP and their visual field distribution. *Vision Res* 37:675–90.

Butler PD, Martinez A, Foxe JJ, Kim D, Zemon V, Silipo G, Mahoney J, Shpaner M, Jalbrzikowski M, Javitt DC. 2007. Subcortical visual dysfunction in schizophrenia drives secondary cortical impairments. *Brain* 130:417–30.

Butler PD, Schechter I, Zemon V, Schwartz SG, Greenstein VC, Gordon J, Schroeder CE, Javitt DC. 2001. Dysfunction of early-stage visual processing in schizophrenia. *Am J Psychiat* 158: 1126–33.

Butler PD, Zemon V, Schechter I, Saperstein AM, Hoptman MJ, Lim KO, Revheim N, Silipo G, Javitt DC. 2005. Early-stage visual processing and cortical amplification deficits in schizophrenia. *Archiv Gen Psychiat* 62:495–504.

Chase C, Stein J. 2003. Visual magnocellular deficits in dyslexia. *Brain* 126:E2.

Coppola R. 1979. A system transfer function for visual evoked potentials. In: Lehmann D, Callaway E, eds. *Human Evoked Potentials: Applications and Problems, NATO III: Human Factors,* vol. 9. New York: Plenum Press, 69–82.

Davis AR, Sloper JJ, Neveu MM, Hogg CR, Morgan MJ, Holder GE. 2006. Differential changes of magnocellular and parvocellular visual function in early- and late-onset strabismic amblyopia. *Investig Ophthalmol Visual Sci* 47:4836–41.

DeAngelis GC, Ohzawa I, Freeman RD. 1993. The spatiotemporal organization of simple cell receptive fields in the cat's striate cortex. II. Linearity of temporal and spatial summation. *J Neurophysiol* 69:1118–35.

deBoer E, Kuyper P. 1968. Triggered correlation. *IEEE Trans Biomed Eng* 15:169–79.

Doniger GM, Foxe JJ, Schroeder CE, Murray MM, Higgins BA, Javitt DC. 2001. Visual perceptual learning in human object recognition areas: a repetition priming study using high-density electrical mapping. *NeuroImage* 13:305–13.

Doniger GM, Foxe JJ, Murray MM, Higgins BA, Javitt DC. 2002. Impaired visual object recognition and dorsal/ventral stream interaction in schizophrenia. *Archiv Gen Psychiat* 59:1011–20.

Foxe JJ, Simpson GV. 2002. Flow of activation from v1 to frontal cortex in humans: a framework for defining "early" visual processing. *Exp Brain Res* 142:139–50.

Foxe JJ, Doniger GM, Javitt DC. 2001. Early visual processing deficits in schizophrenia: impaired P1 generation revealed by high-density electrical mapping. *Neuroreport* 12:3815–20.

Foxe JJ, Murray MM, Javitt DC. 2005. Filling-in in schizophrenia: a high density electrical mapping and source-analysis investigation of illusory contour processing. *Cerebr Cortex* 15:1914–27.

Foxe JJ, Schroeder CE. 2005. The case for feedforward multisensory convergence during early cortical processing. *Neuroreport* 16: 419–23.

Gomez-Gonzalez CM, Clark VP, Fan S, Luck SJ, Hillyard SA. 1994. Sources of attention-sensitive visual event-related potentials. *Brain Topogr* 7:41–51.

Haenschel C, Bittner RA, Haertling F, Rotarska-Jagiela A, Maurer K, Singer W, Linden DEJ. 2007. Impaired early-stage visual processing contributes to working memory dysfunction in adolescents with schizophrenia: a study with event-related potentials and functional magnetic resonance imaging. *Archiv Gen Psychiat* 64:1229–40.

Hung G, Stark L. 1977. The kernel identification method: review of theory, calculation, application, and interpretation. *Math Biosci* 37:135–90.

Jones JP, Palmer LA. 1987. The two-dimensional spatial structure of simple receptive fields in cat striate cortex. *J Neurophysiol* 58:1187–1211.

Kaplan E, Lee BB, Shapley RM. 1990. New views of primate retinal function. In: Osborne N, Chader G, eds. *Progress in Retinal Research*, vol. 9. Oxford: Pergamon Press, 273–336.

Kaplan E, Benardete E. 2001. The dynamics of primate retinal ganglion cells. *Progr Brain Res* 134:17–34.

Kim D, Zemon V, Saperstein A, Butler PD, Javitt, DC. 2005. Dysfunction of early-stage visual processing in schizophrenia: harmonic analysis. *Schizophr Res* 76:55–65.

Lalor EC, Foxe JJ. 2008. Visual evoked spread spectrum analysis (VESPA) responses to stimuli biased towards magnocellular and parvocellular pathways. *Vision Res.* doi:10.1016/j.visres.2008.09.032.

Lalor EC, Kelly SP, Pearlmutter BA, Reilly RB, Foxe JJ. 2007. Isolating endogenous visuo-spatial attentional effects using the novel visual evoked spread spectrum analysis (VESPA) technique. *Eur J Neurosci* 26:3536–42.

Lalor EC, Pearlmutter BA, Reilly RB, McDarby G, Foxe JJ. 2006. The VESPA: a method for the rapid estimation of a visual evoked potential. *NeuroImage* 32:1549–61.

Lalor EC, Yeap S, Reilly RB, Pearlmutter BA, Foxe JJ. 2008. Dissecting the cellular contributions to early visual sensory processing deficits in schizophrenia using the VESPA evoked response. *Schizophr Res* 98:256–64.

Lee BB, Pokorny J, Smith VC, Martin PR, Valberg A. 1990. Luminance and chromatic modulation sensitivity of macaque ganglion cells and human observers. *J Opt Soc Am* A7:2223–36.

Lee YW, Schetzen M. 1965. Measurement of the Wiener kernels of a nonlinear system by cross-correlation. *Int J Control* 2:237–54.

Marmarelis VZ. 2004. *Nonlinear Dynamic Modeling of Physiological Systems*. Piscataway, NJ: IEEE Press.

Marmarelis PZ, Marmarelis VZ. 1978. *Analysis of Physiological Systems: The White Noise Approach*. New York: Plenum Press.

Marmarelis VZ, McCann GD. 1977. A family of quasi-white random signals and its optimal use in biological system identification. Part II: Application to the photoreceptor of calliphora erythrocephala. *Biol Cybern* 27:57–62.

Marmarelis PZ, Naka KI. 1972. White-noise analysis of a neuron chain: an application of the Wiener theory. *Science* 175:1276–78.

McKendrick AM, Sampson GP, Walland MJ, Badcock DR. 2007. Contrast sensitivity changes due to glaucoma and normal aging: low-spatial-frequency losses in both magnocellular and parvocellular pathways. *Investig Ophthalmol Visual Sci* 48:2115–22.

Meister M, Pine J, Baylor DA. 1994. Multi-neuronal signals from the retina: acquisition and analysis. *J Neurosci Meth* 51:95–106.

Murray MM, Foxe DM, Javitt DC, Foxe JJ. 2004. Setting boundaries: brain dynamics of modal and amodal illusory shape completion in humans. *J Neurosci* 24:6898–6903.

Sakai HM, Naka K. 1987. Signal transmission in the catfish retina. V. Sensitivity and circuit. *J Neurophysiol* 58: 1329–50.

Schetzen M. 1981. Nonlinear system modeling based on the Wiener theory. *Proc IEEE* 69:1557–73.

Schechter I, Butler PD, Zemon VM, Revheim N, Saperstein AM, Jalbrzikowski M, Pasternak R, Silipo G, Javitt DC. 2005. Impairments in generation of early-stage transient visual evoked potentials to magno- and parvocellular-selective stimuli in schizophrenia. *Clin Neurophysiol* 116:2204–15.

Spencer KM, Nestor PG, Niznikiewicz MA, Salisbury DF, Shenton ME, McCarley RW. 2003. Abnormal neural synchrony in schizophrenia. *J Neurosci* 23:7407–11.

Wiener N. 1958. *Nonlinear Problems in Random Theory*. Cambridge: MIT Press.

2 Principles of Topographic Analyses for Electrical Neuroimaging

Micah M. Murray, Marzia De Lucia, Denis Brunet, and Christoph M. Michel

This chapter presents both the rationale for as well as the implementation of a set of analyses of surface-recorded event-related potentials (ERPs) that uses the reference-independent spatial (i.e., topographic) information available from high-density electrode montages to render statistical information concerning modulations in response strength, latency, and topography both between and within experimental conditions and/or groups of subjects. We also present new methods of analyses for single-subject and single-trial data sets. These topographic analysis methods allow the experimenter to obtain additional statistically based information and neurophysiologic interpretability beyond what is available from canonical waveform analyses. For each of these analyses we provide the reader with both a conceptual and mathematical description of its implementation, its outcome, and its interpretability. Topographic analysis methods are intuitive and easy-to-use approaches that can remove much of the guesswork often confronting ERP researchers and also assist in identifying the information contained within data sets.

Background

ERPs can be used as a neuroimaging technique capable of providing the experimenter not only with information regarding *when* experimental conditions differ, but also *how* conditions differ in terms of likely underlying neurophysiologic mechanisms. These latter attributes stem from the fact that ERPs comport information beyond simply the time course of brain responses or "components" that correlate with a psychological/psychophysical parameter. They can identify and differentiate modulations in the strength of responses, modulations in the latency of responses, modulations in the underlying sources of responses (vis-à-vis topographic modulations), as well as combinations of these effects. Moreover this information can be parsed as a function of time with sub-millisecond temporal resolution. In this chapter we provide a tutorial for how to extract such information both from the ERP as well as from single-trial/subject EEG with minimal experimenter bias and to test such information statistically.

Researchers, particularly newcomers, using ERPs might find themselves overwhelmed by the quantity of data that can now be routinely acquired. Affordable amplifier systems with anywhere from 64 to 256 channels allow the experimenter to record data at rates from 500 Hz upward. The quantity of data, coupled with the myriad analysis strategies and also the plethora of names of ERP components appearing in the literature (e.g., Luck 2005 for a recent overview), can leave one at a loss for how to best analyze/interpret the data. A prevailing and often recommended approach in ERP research has been for the experimenter to a priori select time periods or components of interest (often based on hypotheses generated from prior studies) as recorded at a chosen subset of electrodes (e.g., Luck 2005; Handy 2005). In a set of published guidelines for conducting ERP research Picton et al. (2000, p. 141) proposed that "the simplest approach is to consider the ERP waveform as a set of waves, to pick the peaks (and troughs) of these waves, and to measure the amplitude and latency at these deflections." Aside from the experimenter bias inherent to this approach, there are several additional weaknesses of analyzing ERP voltage waveforms that render the results arbitrary and of severely limited (neurophysiologic) interpretability. For example, an a priori focus on one or a few components of interest leads to the possibility that other (earlier) time periods and effects are overlooked, such as during periods of low amplitude in a given waveform (e.g., Pourtois et al. 2005, 2008). In the sections below we provide the concrete example of the analysis of visual evoked potentials (VEPs) in response to initial and repeated presentations of common line drawing objects.[1] With this example we show how waveform analyses can (likely) lead to misinterpretation of the results. While we encourage researchers to abandon using canonical waveform analyses, we also provide researchers here with alternative and easy-to-use spatiotemporal analysis methods[2] that can render a far more complete and informative interpretability without any a priori bias regarding the time periods or scalp locations included in the analysis.

When and Why Waveforms Go Awry

The core limitation (and pitfall) of analyzing voltage ERP waveforms is that they are reference-dependent. Although there is a long history of viewpoints concerning the "best" or "most appropriate" reference (e.g., Desmedt et al. 1990; Pascual-Marqui and Lehmann 1993; Dien 1998; see also Michel et al. 2004a for a more recent discussion), it will *always* remain a choice and therefore a source of bias introduced by the experimenter. More important is the fact that this choice will critically impact the (statistical) outcome the experimenter observes when analyzing waveform measurements and by extension the interpretation of the data (e.g., Dien and Santuzzi 2005). This section therefore illustrates precisely these points.

Figure 2.1 displays the results of millisecond-by-millisecond and electrode-wise paired t-tests between VEPs from initial and repeated image presentations, using an α-criterion of $p \leq 0.05$ and a temporal criterion of 15 consecutive time points (see

Guthrie and Buchwald 1991). Each panel depicts the results of these tests as a function of the choice of the reference electrode. Note that the timing and apparent scalp location of statistical differences varies across the panels. In addition to these statistical consequences, the ERP waveform shape will itself change with different reference electrodes (see Murray et al. 2008a, fig. 1). When a frontal electrode (AFz) serves as the reference, differences between conditions are observed over two time windows: roughly 50 to 150 ms and roughly 250 to 400 ms. The earlier effect is diffusely observed across the montage, whereas the later effect is generally constrained to the left-most and posterior-most electrodes. When a vertex (Cz) reference is used, differences are observed over two time windows: roughly 50 to 150 ms and roughly 250 to 500 ms. The earlier effect is constrained to the frontal-most electrodes, whereas the later effect is more diffuse and may perhaps be dissociable into two distinct effects based on which scalp locations are exhibiting modulations. When a posterior (Oz) reference is used, differences are only observed over the roughly 250 to 450 ms period and roughly exclude the posterior quarter of electrodes. Finally, when the common average reference is used, differences are observed over two time windows: roughly 50 to 150 ms and roughly 250 to 500 ms, though the earlier effect is observed at comparatively few electrodes. Depending on which reference electrode noted above is used, the experimenter might or might not conclude that repetition effects begin as early as around 50 ms or instead only at around 250 ms. The experimenter might likewise arrive at different interpretations as to where the effects occur.[3]

Which of the patterns of results shown in figure 2.1 and their subsequent interpretations is correct? While all are equally correct from a statistical perspective, where on the scalp and when in time the responses to initial and repeated object stimulation differ cannot be unequivocally addressed by this analysis. Even if it is customary for a given ERP community or lab to use one reference over another, the above-mentioned analytical and interpretational pitfalls will remain present. That is, the obtained waveform shape and statistical result only apply for that chosen reference. Supposing that all ERP researchers were to reach an agreement on use of a common reference location, there would still be the problem of neurophysiologic interpretability. Put alternatively, which of the sets of results depicted in figure 2.1 accurately represent and describes the underlying neurophysiology?

Therefore the first step for making ERP analyses more informative is to identify a reference-independent measure. For this step we direct the reader to the right-sided portion of figure 2.1 where the voltage topography at 100 ms post-stimulus onset is shown in response to initial image presentations. The projected axis and equator indicate the 0 μV plane (i.e., the reference). As before, several points should be noted by comparing topographies when different reference channels are used. First, changing the reference shifts vertically the position of the 0 μV plane. Second, and far more important, the shape of the topography remains constant even though the grayscale

a. Frontal (AFz) reference

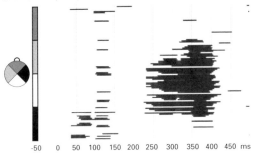

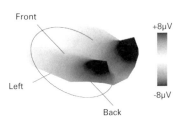

Front

Left

Back

+8µV

-8µV

-50 0 50 100 150 200 250 300 350 400 450 ms

b. Vertex (Cz) reference

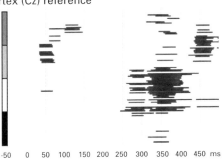

-50 0 50 100 150 200 250 300 350 400 450 ms

c. Posterior (Oz) reference

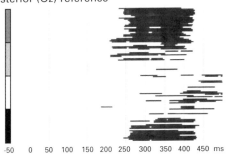

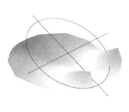

-50 0 50 100 150 200 250 300 350 400 450 ms

d. Average reference

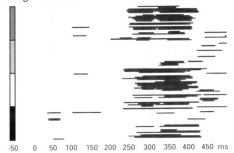

-50 0 50 100 150 200 250 300 350 400 450 ms

value ascribed to a given position changes (see Michel et al. 2004a, fig. 3; Murray et al. 2008a, fig. 1). That is, the configuration of the electric field at the scalp (i.e., the topographic map) is independent of the reference (Lehmann 1987; Geselowitz 1998). In terms of Dietrich Lehmann's example, a mountain range's shape remains constant even if the altitude at which sea level is designated (i.e., the reference elevation) were to change (Lehmann 1987).

As will be shown below, the methods presented in this chapter capitalize on the fact that topographic differences have direct neurophysiologic interpretability and can be quantified and statistically tested. Changes in the topography of the electric field at the scalp can only be caused by changes in the configuration of the underlying intracranial sources (given the exclusion of artifacts eye movements, muscle activity, etc.), though the converse need not be the case (Vaughan 1982; Fender 1987; Lehmann 1987).

A waveform-based measure of topography appears in the so-called current source density (CSD) or Laplacian waveforms[4] (e.g., Vaughan and Arezzo 1988; Nunez et al. 1994; Saron et al. 2001; Murray et al. 2001). Such waveforms are undoubtedly beneficial in that they indeed eliminate the reference-dependent problem inherent to voltage waveforms (as well as contributions of volume conduction within the plane of the scalp) and are a suitable alternative for those researchers more accustomed to handling voltage waveform data. However, CSD waveforms considered in isolation cannot in and of themselves provide information concerning the underlying neurophysiologic mechanism(s) giving rise to a modulation between experimental conditions. As such, interpreting modulations in CSD waveforms is not straightforward, in much the same way that neurophysiologic interpretation of the results in figure 2.1 is not straightforward. Additionally the CSD is not readily calculated at the border of the electrode montage, and the CSD is generally more sensitive to the level of noise in the data. Finally, the experimenter would still be faced with the choice of which CSD waveforms from the electrode montage and which time periods to analyze. Thus, aside from resolving the reference-dependence of voltage waveforms, the gains of CSD-based analyses are not wholly evident, unless the topography of the CSD were to be considered in the same way as what we detail below.

Figure 2.1
Effects of reference electrodes. The left-hand side of the figure depicts statistical tests for each electrode as a function of time. Each panel displays the results when different reference electrodes are used (see inset in panel *a* for the electrode topology). The right-hand side of the figure depicts the voltage topography at 100 ms poststimulus onset from VEPs to initial object presentations. The reader should note that although the grayscale value ascribed to a given location changes with the choice of the reference (indicated by the projected axis and equator), the shape of the topography is independent of the reference.

Why Use the Average Reference

In the discussion above we highlighted the caveats of reference-dependent measurements. However, EEG requires the use of a reference. So which one should be used? We advocate the use of a common average reference (Lehmann and Skrandies 1980) for the following reason: inverse solution methods (i.e., methods to reconstruct the intracranial sources of surface-recorded data) recalculate the data to a common average reference. This is because of the biophysical assumption of quasi-stationarity—namely that the net source activity at each instant in time within the brain sums to zero. Because the reference electrode adds a constant potential value to the value recorded at each electrode and instant in time, a "re-centering" of the data (i.e., a removal of this constant value) is necessary before applying an inverse solution so as to avoid violating the quasi-stationarity assumption mentioned above. Mathematically this is equivalent to calculating the average reference of the surface-recorded EEG (Pascual-Marqui and Lehmann 1993).

When using the average reference, it is therefore important to have adequate sampling of the electric field at the scalp. Discussions of how many electrodes and appropriate interelectrode distances are outside the scope of this chapter and have been treated elsewhere (e.g., Srinivasan et al. 1996; Lantz et al. 2003; Michel et al. 2004a). However, the relatively low cost of EEG equipment makes high-density montages accessible to most laboratories. Another important issue when using the average reference, performing the analyses detailed here, and estimating intracranial sources, is how to cope with artifact-contaminated channels. This applies to both the single-subject and group-averaged data. Values at such channels are typically interpolated (Perrin et al. 1987; see also Michel et al. 2004a for discussion for different methods). Likewise group-averaged data should include normalization to the same electrode configuration/positions before averaging (Picton et al. 2000).

It is worthwhile to mention a common misunderstanding in how the average reference should be computed. Typically the recording reference is discarded, even though the data at this location (provided it is near the brain and not elsewhere on the body surface or even off the body) is nevertheless a valid sampled value of the brain's electric field. As such, it should be included in the electrode montage and data analyses, being ascribed a value of $0\,\mu V$ as a function of time in all the formulae, including in the calculation of the average reference (see table 2.1). Once the data have been recalculated to the average reference, the reference electrode is just another electrode within the montage with a measurement of potential varying as a function of time. However, this procedure is made particularly problematic in several situations. First, if the reference has been placed far away from the brain, then it is probably preferable to exclude it from the montage and calculate the average reference from the remaining electrodes, particularly if the montage includes a relatively small number of electrodes. Second, if the reference itself contains artifacts (eye movements, cardiac activity, etc.), then

Table 2.1

Definitions and formulas

Some general definitions	n is the number of electrodes in the montage, *including the reference.* U_i is the measured potential of the ith electrode, for a given condition U, at a given time point t (also including the reference). V_i is the measured potential of the ith electrode, either from another condition V, or from the same condition U but at a different time point t'.	
Average reference	$$\bar{u} = \frac{1}{n} \cdot \sum_{i=1}^{n} U_i$$ $$u_i = U_i - \bar{u}$$	$\bar{u}$ is the mean value of all U_i's (for a given condition, at a given time point t). u_i is the average-referenced potential of the ith electrode (for a given condition, at a given time point t).
Global field power (GFP)	$$GFP_u = \sqrt{\frac{1}{n} \cdot \sum_{i=1}^{n} u_i^2} = \sigma_u$$	The GFP for a given condition, at a given time point. GFP is equivalent to the standard deviation of the electrode values (at a given time point t).
Global dissimilarity (DISS)	$$DISS_{u,v} = \sqrt{\frac{1}{n} \cdot \sum_{i=1}^{n} \left(\frac{u_i}{GFP_u} - \frac{v_i}{GFP_v} \right)^2}$$ $$DISS_{u,v} = \sqrt{2 \cdot (1 - C_{u,v})}$$	The DISS between two conditions at the same time point, or between two different time points of the same condition. (See below for the definition of C.)
Spatial correlation (C)	$$C_{u,v} = \frac{\sum_{i=1}^{n} u_i \bullet v_i}{\|u\| \cdot \|v\|} = 1 - \frac{DISS_{u,v}^2}{2}$$ $$\|u\| = \sqrt{\sum_{i=1}^{n} u_i^2} \ , \ \|v\| = \sqrt{\sum_{i=1}^{n} v_i^2}$$	Spatial correlation between two conditions at the same time point, or between two different time points of the same condition. (C is equivalent to the Pearson cross-correlation coefficient.)

the same exclusion procedure should be applied. Third, if the recording reference is not one unique electrode on the scalp but instead an average of several electrodes each with fluctuating impedance over time (e.g., linked earlobes), then the reference is actually undefined.

Despite all of these points extolling the average reference, we must emphasize that the analyses presented in this chapter are completely independent of the reference electrode, even the average reference. The results will therefore not change when a different reference is applied.

Global Field Power

We now return to the kinds of neurophysiologic information we wish to extract from the ERP data, beginning with response strength. In the preceding section we detailed

a. Hypothetical data matrices

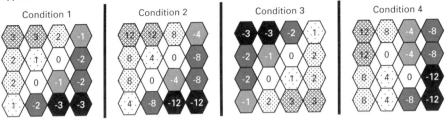

b. Squared values at each electrode and resultant GFP

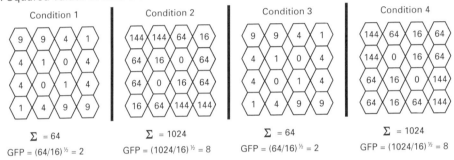

c. GFP-normalized values at each electrode

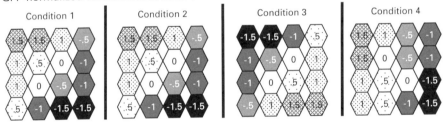

d. Squared difference at each electrode and resultant DISS

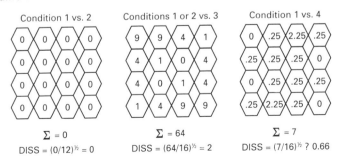

the pitfalls and limitations of analyzing ERP voltage waveforms due to their being dependent on the choice of the reference electrode(s). Global field power (GFP), by contrast, constitutes a single, reference-independent measure of response strength. GFP was first introduced to ERPs by Lehmann and Skrandies (1980) and has since become a commonplace measure among MEG users. Mathematically GFP equals the root mean square (RMS) across the average-referenced electrode values at a given instant in time. In statistical terms GFP is the standard deviation of all electrodes at a given time, with the mean being zero because of the average reference (see table 2.1). In the case of ERPs, the resultant GFP waveform is a measure of potential (µV) as a function of time. GFP can be assessed statistically using approaches common to ERP research (time point by time point, area measures, peak measures, etc.). Note that because GFP is a nonlinear transformation, the GFP of the mean ERP is *not* equivalent to the mean of the GFP across individual subjects. Caution should be exercised when visually inspecting or displaying GFP waveforms.

What GFP tells the researcher is on average how strong a potential (µV) has been recorded across the electrode montage. What GFP does *not* tell the researcher is any information about how this potential is distributed across the electrode montage— namely where large and small potentials were measured. These points are illustrated in figure 2.2, which displays four hypothetical data matrices (i.e., the potential values recorded from 16 electrodes at a given latency). The four conditions differ in the following ways: the values in condition 2 are precisely fourfold those of condition 1 at each electrode, resulting in an identical spatial distribution of values that are simply

Figure 2.2

Measurements of GFP and DISS. The basis for the reference-independent measurement of response strength and topography is shown. Grayscale and stippling values throughout this figure denote polarity, with darker grayscale indicating negative values and denser stipples positive values. (a) Hypothetical data from four different conditions with an array of 16 electrodes. Note that condition 2 is precisely 4 times the value of condition 1 at each electrode and that condition 3 is the inverse of the values of condition 1 (i.e., the value at each electrode has been multiplied by −1). Further condition 4 is a spatial re-arrangement of the values of condition 2, making it differ in both strength and topography from condition 1. (b) The squared value at each electrode, the summed value across electrodes, and the resulting GFP. Note that conditions 1 and 3 have the same GFP, even though their topographies are inverted, and that conditions 2 and 4 have 4 times the GFP of conditions 1 and 3. (c) The GFP-normalized values of the original data displayed in (a). Note that once strength differences are normalized, conditions 1 and 2 have the same topography, whereas the topography of condition 3 is the inversion of conditions 1 and 2 (the extreme case) and the topography of condition 4 is slightly different from that of the other conditions. (d) The squared difference of the values in (c) at each electrode as well as the resulting DISS. Note that DISS ranges from 0 to 2, with the former indicating identical topographies and the latter inverted topographies.

stronger in condition 2. Condition 3 is the mathematical inverse of condition 1 (i.e., the value at each electrode was multiplied by −1). This results in a different spatial distribution (i.e., topography) of the same values. Note that condition 3 is included to illustrate an extreme case that is unlikely under typical experimental conditions. Condition 4, by contrast, represents a more typical observation in that it varies in both strength and topography from condition 1. It is in fact a re-distribution in space of the values used for condition 2. Figure 2.2b displays the squared value of these potentials at each electrode, the sum of these values across electrodes, and the resultant GFP. Note that while conditions 1 and 3 have the same GFP and conditions 2 and 4 have the same GFP, conditions 1 and 3 have a GFP one-fourth that of conditions 2 and 4. As such, it is important to note that the observation of a GFP modulation does not exclude the possibility of a contemporaneous change in the electric field topography. Recall that conditions 1 and 3 are topographic inversions of each other. Nor does it rule out the possibility that topographic modulations would nonetheless yield statistically indistinguishable GFP values. For example, in the case of the VEPs presented above, there is no evidence of a reliable GFP difference between responses to initial and repeated object presentations (figure 2.3a). However, we should add that the observation of a GFP modulation in the absence of a topographic modulation would most parsimoniously be interpreted as a modulation of the number of synchronously activated but statistically indistinguishable generators across experimental conditions (Skrandies 2007). Next we present methods for identifying and quantifying topographic modulations.

Global Dissimilarity

Global dissimilarity (DISS) is an index of configuration differences between two electric fields, independent of their strength. Like GFP, DISS was first introduced to EEG/ERPs by Lehmann and Skrandies (1980). This parameter equals the square root of the mean of the squared differences between the potentials measured at each electrode (vs. the average reference), each of which is first scaled to unitary strength by dividing by the instantaneous GFP (see table 2.1). To provide a clearer sense of the calculation of DISS, consider again the data in figure 2.2. As already mentioned in the section above, conditions 1 and 2 have the same topography but different strengths, whereas conditions 1 and 3 have the same strength but different (inverted) topographies. Finally, conditions 1 and 4 differ in both their strength and topography. Figure 2.2a shows the original data, whereas the data in figure 2.2c have been GFP-normalized. Having thus re-scaled all four conditions in figure 2.2c to have the same GFP, the topographic similarities and differences between conditions becomes readily apparent. As shown in figure 2.2d, DISS can range from 0 to 2, where 0 indicates topographic homogeneity and 2 indicates topographic inversion. It is directly related to the spatial correlation coefficient (Brandeis et al. 1992; see table 2.1).

a. GFP waveforms

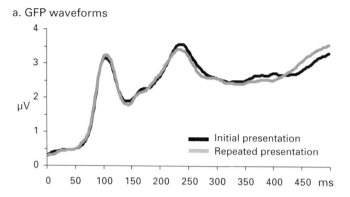

b. Global dissimilarity and TANOVA results

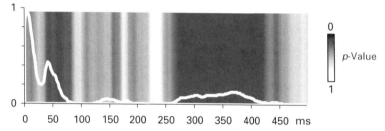

Figure 2.3

Reference-free measures and analyses of VEPs in response to initial and repeated presentations of visual objects. (a) The GFP waveforms. Analysis of these waveforms failed to reveal any statistically reliable differences. (b) The global dissimilarity as a function of time (white trace) superimposed on the results of the TANOVA analysis (grayscale intensity plot). VEPs topographically differed over the roughly 40 to 80 ms and roughly 220 to 470 ms poststimulus periods.

Because DISS is a *single* measure of the distance between two vectors (each of which represents one electric field topography), rather than a separate measure for each condition about which a mean and variance can be calculated, nonparametric statistical tests should be conducted, wherein the dependent measure is the DISS between two maps at a given point in time, *t*. We and others have colloquially referred to this analysis as "topographic ANOVA" or TANOVA (e.g., Murray et al. 2004, 2008a, b; Pourtois et al. 2005; Yoshino et al. 2006; De Santis et al. 2007a, b; Spierer et al. 2007, 2008; Ruz and Nobre 2008; Wylie et al. 2009; see also Kondakor et al. 1995; Sergent et al. 2005), although we would immediately remind the reader that no analysis of variance is being conducted. Instead TANOVA entails a nonparametric randomization test (Manly 1991). To do this for a within-subjects design, an empirical distribution of possible DISS values is determined by (1) re-assigning single-subject maps to different experimental conditions at a within-subject level (i.e., permutations of the data), (2) recalculating the group-average ERPs, and (3) recalculating the resulting DISS value for these "new" group-average ERPs. The number of permutations that can be made with a group-average ERP based on n participants is 2^n, although Manly (1991) suggests that 1,000 to 5,000 permutations is sufficient. The DISS value from the actual group-average ERPs is then compared with the values from the empirical distribution to determine the likelihood that the empirical distribution has a value higher than the DISS from the actual group-average ERPs. This procedure can then be repeated for each time point. Figure 2.3b displays the observed DISS values as well as the TANOVA results that indicate significant topographic differences between initial and repeated object presentations over the roughly 40 to 80 ms and roughly 220 to 470 ms poststimulus periods. For a between-subjects design the analysis is generally identical, except that the permutations are performed by first putting all participants' data into one pool irrespective of experimental condition/group. Then new conditions or groups are randomly drawn and group-average ERPs are calculated for determining the empirical distribution.

Another method for statistically identifying topographic modulations has been proposed by McCarthy and Wood (1985; see also Srebro 1996), after confronting the pitfalls in the interpretation of condition × electrode interactions observed in an ANOVA using voltage waveform data. They rightly pointed out how this analysis cannot differentiate modulations in topography from modulations in amplitude when data are not first scaled. They presented three scaling methods. One involves identifying the instantaneous maximum and minimum for each condition and subtracting the minimum value as well as the difference between the maximum and minimum from each electrode. A second involves scaling by a predefined value (see Hanson and Hillyard 1980), the shortcomings of which are detailed in McCarthy and Wood (1985). The third, which they (and we) favor, involves dividing the value at each electrode by the instantaneous GFP, a procedure that they refer to as vector scaling. Note that this scaling is precisely that involved in calculating global dissimilarity. The methods proposed by McCarthy and Wood (1985) are routinely referred to and often applied/recommended (Picton et al. 2000). As such, it is worthwhile to mention an important caveat to how this method has been applied. McCarthy and Wood's (1985) approach is only valid when the data from the *entire* electrode montage is included in the ANOVA, a practice nowadays seldom performed by most ERP researchers.

At a neurophysiologic level, because electric field changes are indicative of changes in the underlying generator configuration (e.g., Vaughan 1982; Fender 1987; Lehmann 1987), this test provides a statistical means of determining if and when the brain networks activated by the two conditions differ. In this way the reader should note how response strength (GFP) and response topography (DISS) can be measured and analyzed independently and in a completely reference-independent manner without the necessity of a priori selecting time periods or electrodes for analyses. Moreover these two attributes can (and in our view should *always*) be analyzed as a function of time without the necessity of the experimenter a priori choosing time periods or components of interest.

Some considerations in interpreting results of analyses with DISS are worth mentioning. Primary among these is that although a significant effect is unequivocal evidence that the topographies (and by extension configuration of intracranial generators) differ, this analysis does not in and of itself differentiate between several alternative underlying causes. For example, a significant difference may stem from one condition having one single and stable ERP topography during a given time period and the other condition another single and stable ERP topography over the same time period. That is, representing the electric field topography at a given time point by a letter, one condition might read "AAAAAA" and the other "BBBBBB." Alternatively, each condition may be described by either single- or multiple-stable ERP topographies over the same time period (i.e., "AAABBB" vs. "CCCDDD" or "AAAAAA" vs. "BBCCDD"). Topographic differences might likewise stem from a latency shift between conditions ("ABCDEF" vs. "BCDEFG"). Because all of these alternatives could result in highly similar (if not identical) patterns of statistical outcomes, additional analyses have been devised to determine the pattern of topographies both within and between conditions.

Cluster Analysis and Single-Subject "Fitting"

In the analysis of ERPs an important issue parallel to those already outlined above is how to define or select time intervals. This applies both when identifying components and when performing statistical analyses and source estimations. The approach of averaging the measured potentials over a fixed and/or experimenter-defined time interval assumes that the electric field configuration is stable; an assumption that is seldom empirically verified. Our approach derives from the principle of functional microstates, which was first introduced by Dietrich Lehmann (e.g., Lehmann 1987; reviewed in Michel et al. 1999, 2001, 2004a; Murray et al. 2008a). This principle is based on the empirical observation in both continuous EEG and ERPs that the electric field configuration at the scalp does not vary randomly as a function of time but rather exhibits stability for tens to hundreds of milliseconds with brief intervening intervals of topographic instability.

Here we give an overview of the analysis used for identifying the periods of topographic stability within and between experimental conditions. To return to the example in the preceding section, these analyses serve to identify the sequence, duration, explanatory power of the "letters" in the ERP. The overarching procedure in the case of ERPs is the following: A clustering algorithm is applied to the collective group-averaged data across all experimental conditions/groups. This clustering does not account for the latencies of maps, but only for their topographies. It is done as a hypothesis generation step wherein the template maps that best account for the data are identified. The hypotheses generated at the group-average level are then statistically tested by means of a fitting procedure based on the spatial correlation between template maps obtained from the group-average ERPs and the single-subject ERP data (see table 2.1 for formulas). This approach has also been called topographic component recognition (Brandeis et al. 1992; Pegna et al. 1997). Several different dependent measures can be obtained from this fitting procedure, which we discuss below.

Two clustering algorithms have been predominantly used in EEG/ERP research. One is based on k-means clustering (Pascual-Marqui et al. 1995), and the other on hierarchical clustering (Tibshirani et al. 2005). An intuitive way of understanding the main difference between these approaches is that the k-means approach operates independently for each number of clusters, whereas the hierarchical clustering approach operates in a bottom-up manner wherein the number of clusters is initially large and progressively diminishes.

The k-mean clustering algorithm is particularly useful with data containing little variation in its strength (i.e., GFP) or with data that have been normalized. However, it has the disadvantage of varying from one run to the other because of the iterative randomization nature of the algorithm (see Murray et al. 2008a). By contrast, the version of hierarchical clustering that we have developed and that we present here is completely driven by the quantification of global explained variance (GEV; table 2.2). As such, its results will not vary from one run to another with the same data set. Hierarchical clustering takes the instantaneous GFP of the data being clustered into consideration when calculating which clusters to retain and therefore preferentially considers as robust clusters time periods with higher signal quality. Because ERPs typically consist of series of GFP peaks and troughs (similar to those observed in voltage waveforms), hierarchical clustering seems to be well suited for the analysis of ERPs, whereas k-means clustering has advantages in data with less distinct peaks, such as spontaneous EEG. We briefly describe each approach.

k-Means Clustering

First, a concatenated data set is defined using the group-averaged ERPs across all conditions or groups of the experiment. In the example of this tutorial there are two experimental conditions (initial and repeated object presentations) that each contains 275 time points of data (i.e., all 550 time points of data). Second, n data points (where the term "data point" refers to the ERP from all scalp electrodes at a given instant in time) from this concatenated data set (hereafter, template maps) are randomly selected from the concatenated data set. The number of data points can range from 1 to the number of total data points. Third, the spatial correlation (table 2.1) between each of the n template maps and each time point of the concatenated data set is calculated. This gives a spatial correlation value for each template map as a function of time, and for any given time point one of the n template maps yields highest spatial correlation value. As alluded to above, what is empirically observed in ERP data is that a given

Table 2.2
Topographic pattern analysis

Clustering results	$L_{u,t} = SegmentIndex$ T_k $\bar{T}_k = 0,\ |T_k| = 1$ $T_t = T_{L_{u,t}}$	A labeling L, which holds the index of the segment attributed, for condition U, at time point t. T_k is the kth template map (a vector of n dimensions). T_k has a mean of 0, and is normalized.
Global explained variance (GEV) *This can be computed only after a segmentation.	$$GEV = \frac{\sum_{t=1}^{t_{max}} (GFP_u(t) \cdot C_{u,T_t})^2}{\sum_{t=1}^{t_{max}} GFP_u^2(t)}$$	t is a given time point within the data. $GFP_u(t)$ is the GFP of the data for condition U at time point t. T_t is the template map assigned by the segmentation for condition U at time point t. C_{u,T_t} is the spatial correlation between data of condition U at time point t, and the template map T_t assigned to that time point by the segmentation.
	$$GEV = \sum_{k=1}^{q} GEV_k$$	q is the number of segments/template maps.
	$$GEV_k = \frac{\sum_{t=1}^{t_{max}} (GFP_u(t) \cdot C_{u,T_t})^2 \cdot \gamma_{u,k,t}}{\sum_{t=1}^{t_{max}} GFP_u^2(t)}$$	The GEV can also be broken down into its partial contributions GEV_k for each segment k.
	$$\gamma_{u,k,t} = \begin{cases} 1 & \text{if } k = L_{u,t} \\ 0 & \text{if } k \neq L_{u,t} \end{cases}$$	$\gamma_{u,k,t}$ is set to 1 only for time points where data have been labeled as belonging to the kth segment, and 0 otherwise.

Table 2.2 (continued)

Krzanowski–Lai criterion	$W_q = \sum_{r=1}^{q} \frac{1}{2 \cdot n_r} \cdot D_r$	W is the measure of dispersion for q clusters. n_r is the number of maps for cluster r.
	$D_r = \sum_{u,v \in cluster\_r} \|u - v\|^2$	D_r is the sum of pairwise distances between all maps of a given cluster r.
	$KL_q = \frac{d_{q-1} - d_q}{M_{q-1}}$ $d_q = M_q - M_{q+1}$ $M_q = W_q \cdot q^{2/n}$	KL_q is the Krzanowski–Lai criterion for q clusters (formula adapted to compute the normalized curvature of W). Moreover KL_q is set to 0 if $d_{q-1} < 0$ or $d_{q-1} < d_q$ so that only concave shapes of the W curve are considered.

template map will yield the highest spatial correlation for a sustained period of time after which another and different template map will yield the highest spatial correlation, and so on. From these spatial correlation values, the global explained variance (GEV) of these template maps is calculated (table 2.2). GEV gives a metric of how well these n template maps describe the whole data set. Each of the n template maps is then redefined by averaging the maps from all time points when the ith template map yielded the highest spatial correlation versus all other template maps. Spatial correlation for each of these redefined template maps and the resultant GEV are recalculated as above. This procedure of averaging across time points to redefine each template map, recalculating the spatial correlation for each template map, and recalculating the GEV is repeated until the GEV becomes stable. In other words, a point is reached when a given set of n template maps cannot yield a higher GEV for the concatenated data set. Because the selection of the n template maps is random, it is possible that neighboring time points were originally selected, which would result in a low GEV. To ensure that this procedure obtains the highest GEV possible for a given number of n template maps, a new set of n template maps is randomly selected and the entire above procedure is repeated. It is important to note that the number of these random selections is user-dependent and will simply increase computational time as the number of random selections increases. The set of n template maps that yields the highest GEV is retained. Finally, the same steps are conducted for $n + 1$ template maps and iterated until n equals the number of data points comprising the concatenated data set. These steps provide information on how well n, $n + 1$, $n + 2$, . . . , etc. template maps describe the concatenated data set. An important issue for this analysis is the determination of the optimal number of template maps for a given data set. We return to this computation below after first providing an overview of hierarchical clustering.

Hierarchical Clustering

The version of hierarchical clustering that has been devised by our group is a modified agglomerative hierarchical clustering termed AAHC for "atomized and agglomerate hierarchical clustering." It has been specifically designed for the analysis of ERPs so as to counterbalance a side effect of classical hierarchical clustering. Ordinarily two clusters (i.e., groups of data points or, in the case of ERPs, groups of maps) are merged together to proceed from a total of n clusters to $n - 1$ clusters. This leads to the inflation of each cluster's size because they progressively aggregate with each other like snowballs. While this is typically a desired outcome, in the case of ERPs it is potentially a major drawback when short-duration periods of stable topography exist. In terms of classical hierarchical agglomerative clustering, such short-duration periods would eventually be (blindly) disintegrated, and the data would be assigned to other clusters, even if these short-duration periods contribute a high GEV and therefore play a prominent role in the response. In the modified version that is described here, clusters are given priority, in terms of their inclusion as one progresses from n to $n - 1$ clusters, according to their GEV contribution. This way, short-duration periods can be (conditionally) maintained. In other words, this feature is a way of implementing the observation that temporal boundaries between segments tend to be stable across a range of segmentations, such that boarders observed on the kth clustering tend also to be found on the $(k - 1)$th and the $(k + 1)$th clustering. This way the modified AAHC also yields greater temporal stability across numbers of segments.

Given such modification, the AAHC procedure is then the following: as above, the concatenated data set is defined as the group-averaged ERPs across all conditions/groups of the experiment. Initially each data point (i.e., map) is designated as a unique cluster. Upon subsequent iterations the clusters denote groups of data points (maps) whose centroid (i.e., the mathematical average) defines the template map for that cluster. Then the "worst" cluster is identified as the one whose disappearance will "cost" the least to the global quality of the clustering. Here the selection is done by identifying the cluster with the lowest GEV. This "worst" cluster is then atomized, meaning that its constituent maps are "freed" and no longer belong to any cluster. One at a time these "free" maps are independently re-assigned to the surviving clusters by calculating the spatial correlation between each free map and the centroid of each surviving cluster. The "free" map is assigned to that cluster with which it has the highest spatial correlation. The method proceeds recursively by removing one cluster at a time, and stops when only a single final cluster is obtained (even though the latter is useless). Finally, for each level, namely for each set of n clusters, it is possible to back-project the centroid/template maps onto the original data. The backprojection obtains an output whose visualization depicts the sequence of maps as a function of time, experimental condition, and group. An important next step will be to determine the optimal number of template maps (clusters).

Identifying the Optimal Number of Template Maps

Having identified a set of template maps to describe the group-averaged ERPs, the next issue is how many clusters of template maps are optimal. Unfortunately, there is no definitive solution. This is because there is always a trade-off between the facts that the more clusters one identifies the higher the quality of the clustering (vis-à-vis GEV) but the lower the data reduction, and the converse. On one extreme, if the number of clusters is low, then the explained variance will remain low, and the data set will be highly compressed because it will now be represented by a small number of template maps. On the other extreme, if the number of clusters is high, then the explained variance will also be high but the data set will not be compressed. The goal is to determine a middle ground between such extremes. In many previous studies we have used a modified cross-validation criterion to define the optimal number of clusters (Pascual-Marqui et al. 1995). However, this criterion directly depends on the number of electrodes and often fails to find a minimal value when high-density montages are used. Here we present a new method based on the Krzanowski–Lai (*KL*) criterion (Tibshirani et al. 2005; see table 2.2 for formula).

The Krzanowski–Lai criterion works by first computing a quality measure of the AAHC, termed dispersion (*W*). *W* tends toward 0 as the quality of the clustering results increases, in much the same manner that the GEV tends toward 1 as the quality of the clustering improves. The shape of the resulting *W* curve is then analyzed by looking for its *L*-corner, which is the point of highest deceleration where adding one more segment will not greatly increase the quality of the results. The *KL* measure has been slightly adapted to be a relative measure of curvature of the *W* curve (see table 2.2). As a consequence its highest value should, in principle, indicate the optimal clustering. In practice, however, the *KL* will nearly always peak for three clusters due to the very nature of the data we analyze. That is, there is systematically a steep deceleration of the *W* curve when progressing from one and two clusters (which are unsurprisingly "very bad" in terms of their overall quality in accounting for the concatenated data set) to three clusters (which therefore always appears to then be "far better"). Although this peak at three clusters can theoretically be of some interest, we advise considering the subsequent highest peak as the one indicating the optimal number of template maps. Nevertheless, additional peaks may also ultimately be of interest if they lead to statistically significant results.

Temporal Considerations in Clustering

A parallel issue, which is somewhat particular to ERPs, concerns how to incorporate known temporal structure when using a clustering algorithm. As mentioned throughout this chapter, a central feature of ERPs is its topographic stability as a function of time—meaning its components. This notion was particularly advanced by Dietrich Lehmann and the concept of functional microstates, which receives empirical support from countless data sets. This notion carries implications for clustering, particularly when one objective is to reduce a data set to the minimal number of template maps while also taking into consideration the often recursive nature of mental processes as a function of time. We can therefore consider the whole microstate segmentation as involving first a clustering process (covered above) and then the temporal re-processing of the clusters.

A common and reasonable practice is therefore to apply a temporal threshold for the minimal duration of a template map (i.e., a minimal number of consecutive time points that must be clustered together). One basis for this practice is that there is temporal autocorrelation in ERP data sets (e.g., Guthrie and Buchwald 1991 for a consideration of this issue when applied to the analysis of individual waveforms). Another more physiological basis is the observation that neural responses remain stable for brief periods of time (e.g., Rolls and Tovee 1994).

a. Clustering results (AAHC)

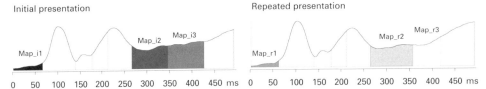

b. Single-subject fitting

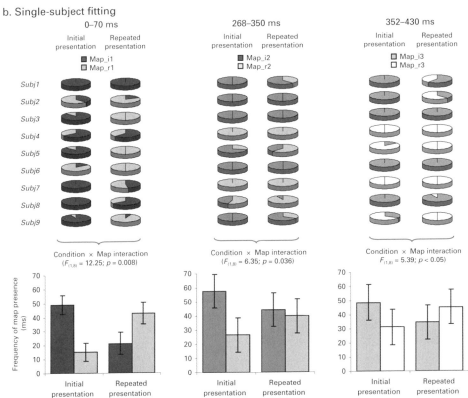

c. Time-resolved fitting

Spatial Correlation-Based Fitting and Its Dependent Measures

The experimenter is now confronted with the question of how to statistically assess the validity of the hypothesis that emerges from the clustering algorithm performed on the group-average data set. The method we present here is based on calculating the spatial correlation between maps and depends neither on the type of clustering nor the specific criterion for optimal segmentation. Here the calculation is between single-subject ERPs and identified template maps (see also the topographic component recognition approach developed by Brandeis et al. 1992). We colloquially refer to this calculation as "fitting." Several different dependent measures from this fitting procedure can be obtained and statistically analyzed. For example, one might identify for each experimental condition, subject (and group) the number of data points where a given template map yields a higher spatial correlation than other template maps. This would give a metric of map duration or the frequency of map presence. Alternatively, one might identify the GEV of a given template map over a specific time period and test whether it is greater for one condition/group over another. Finally, one might also assess the specific latencies and periodicity with which a given template map characterizes the single-subject data. For all of these measures the researcher is typically interested in assessing whether the factor "template map" significantly interacts with either the factor of experimental condition or participant group. A fuller listing of these dependent measures and their interpretability appears elsewhere (Murray et al. 2008a). In addition these dependent measures can in turn be correlated with behavioral measures (e.g., Murray et al. 2006a; Spierer et al. 2007, 2008; Arzy et al. 2007), behavioral/mental states (e.g., Koenig et al. 2002; Katayama et al. 2007), and/or parametric variations in stimulus conditions (e.g., Pegna et al. 1997; Overnay et al. 2005; Thierry et al. 2007).

Figure 2.4 shows the outcome of the AAHC clustering and fitting procedure when applied to the VEPs presented throughout this chapter. Figure 2.4a shows the pattern

Figure 2.4

Topographic pattern analyses applied to VEPs in response to initial and repeated presentations of visual objects. (a) The outcome of the clustering algorithm (AAHC) applied to the group-averaged VEPs. Shaded regions indicate time periods when different template maps were identified across experimental conditions. These included the 0 to 70 ms, 268 to 350 ms, and 352 to 430 ms time periods. (b) The outcome of fitting the template maps identified in the group-averaged VEPs to those of individual subjects. The pie charts show the relative amount of time over the above-mentioned periods when each template map yielded a higher spatial correlation with the single-subject data. The group-average (s.e.m. shown) and ANOVA results are shown in the bar graphs. (c) The time-resolved results of fitting the template maps identified over the 0 to 70 ms, such that the mean probability (s.e.m. shown) of a given subject's data being fitted with map_i1 are displayed for each experimental condition. Note that the probability of being fitted with map_r1 is simply 100 percent minus the values for map_i1 because only two template maps were identified over this time period.

of template maps identified in the group-average ERPs in response to initial and repeated object presentation. To orientate the reader accustomed to visualizing ERPs in terms of peaks and troughs, the pattern is displayed beneath the GFP waveforms and differences between conditions are indicated by different shadings. There is a generally similar sequence of template maps across conditions, with the exception of the initial 0 to 70 ms period of the ERP as well as the period from around 270 to 430 ms when different template maps were identified in each condition. In fact the clustering algorithm identified two subperiods of stable topography over the roughly 270 to 430 ms period. This pattern observed at the level of group-average ERPs is then statistically evaluated using the above-mentioned fitting procedure. That is, each data point from each time period from each of the nine subjects and both experimental conditions was labeled on either template map depending on which resulted in a higher spatial correlation. The correlation can be graphically represented as a pie chart for each subject/condition or as bar graphs displaying the mean across subjects as a function of experimental condition and template map (figure 2.4b). These data can then be statistically analyzed with ANOVA. In the case of initial versus repeated object presentations, what these analyses show is that over the 0 to 70 ms, 268 to 350 ms, and 352 to 430 ms time periods one template map better accounts for responses to initial presentations, whereas another map better accounts for responses to repeated presentations. Fitting can also be conducted as a function of time (figure 2.4c) in order to determine the specific time ranges when a given experimental condition was better accounted for by one template map versus another. In the present example effects reliably began at 36 ms, which is in agreement with what was observed using TANOVA (figure 2.3b). From these analyses the reader should see how topographic analyses can assist a researcher in identifying and differentiating the neurophysiologic bases of effects without necessitating the a priori selection of either a subset of electrodes or a specific window of time.

From Topography to Tomographic Source Estimations

Having conducted a series of analyses of the surface-recorded ERP, the researcher is now well-positioned to guide the selection of time periods for source estimation that can and should be predicated on the identification of periods of stable topography within each experimental condition—namely components. The selection of data to submit to source estimation is a particularly crucial choice. One reason is that if data are averaged as a function of time (either at the group-average or single-subject level), then the experimenter must assure that the topography is stable over the averaged time period. If not, then spurious source estimations can be obtained. The topographic pattern analysis discussed above serves as a method for identifying these stable periods. In addition, after determining time periods for source estimation, the experimenter is confronted with several choices for how to proceed both in terms of which source model to use and which (if any) statistical analysis to perform (reviewed in Michel et al. 2004a). While the topic of source models is beyond the scope of this chapter, we discuss here a few issues regarding their statistical analysis.

First, when using single or multiple dipole localization algorithms, statistical tests can be applied to the dipole moment (i.e., its strength) and/or its location along each Cartesian axis. The researcher can then draw conclusions about possible significant shifts in either the strength and/or location of the dipolar source(s). Even if the single dipole may not adequately or accurately represent the actual sources in case of distributed activation patterns, a statistically significant shift of the "center of gravity" of all sources due to an experimental manipulation can provide indications of a change of the global activity distribution within the brain. Whether this analysis also allows interpretation about the brain areas that have been differently activated will ultimately depend on how accurately the dipole model represents the underlying generators. Such notwithstanding, if the only conclusion from such an analysis was that the underlying source configuration changed, then it would not be evident what would have been gained from the source estimation that could not have been obtained from the topographic analyses above. That is, in this case the source estimation would not provide additional interpretational power or neurophysiologic information.

Second, when using distributed source estimation algorithms (sLORETA [Pascual-Marqui 2002], LAURA [Grave de Peralta Menender et al. 2001, 2004], etc.) statistical analyses can be performed at each node/voxel throughout the volume of the head model in a highly similar manner to what is done with data sets from hemodynamic imaging methods (e.g., positron emission tomography and functional magnetic resonance imaging; PET and fMRI, respectively) that apply statistical parametric mapping (SPM; Friston et al. 2007). Such an approach has several advantages, particularly over displaying the source estimations of the group-averaged data. For one, group-averaged data can be dominated by sources that are identical across experimental conditions such that weak, but nonetheless consistent differences risk being overlooked due to the applied threshold. Second, statistical analyses can serve to minimize spurious or so-called ghost sources that are likely to be inconsistent in their localization across individuals (unless there is a flaw in the algorithm) and therefore unlikely to remain robust after statistical contrasts have been performed. Finally, information from the analysis of distributed source estimations can complement that from the analyses above of the surface-recorded ERP to reveal which brain regions modulate their strength and/or location across experimental conditions (for recent examples of such analyses with ERP data sets, see Murray et al. 2004, 2008b; Lorenzo-Lopez et al. 2008; Spierer et al. 2008; Pourtois et al. 2008; Wirth et al. 2008). The group-average source estimations for initial and repeated object presentations are displayed in figure 2.5

a. Initial presentation

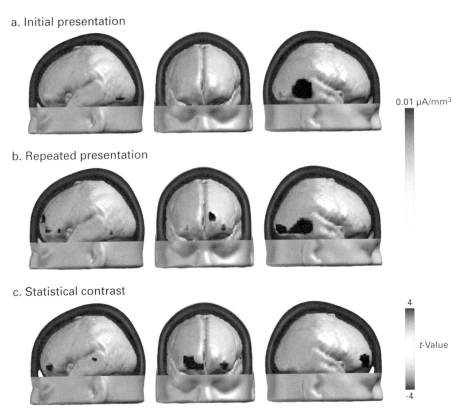

0.01 µA/mm³

b. Repeated presentation

c. Statistical contrast

4

t-Value

-4

Figure 2.5
Source estimations and their statistical analysis over the 36 to 70 ms period. (a–b) The group-average source estimations rendered within the Montreal Neurological Institute's average brain for initial and repeated presentations, respectively. (c) The statistical contrast (paired *t*-test) between conditions with a threshold of $t_{(8)} \geq 4$ ($p \leq 0.004$).

along with their statistical contrast. Although there are prominent occipitotemporal sources over this time period (36–70 ms), the frontal differences were those that were statistically robust (see also Michel et al. 2004b for similar findings with novel and repeated face presentations).

Single-Trial Topographic Analyses

Throughout this chapter we have focused on topographic analyses of ERPs where the overarching strategy is to base statistical analyses on inter-subject variance. While this approach is indeed highly informative, it is equally important to acknowledge the kinds of information that are inevitably lost. Averaging across trials to generate an

ERP is performed on the one hand to isolate those signals that are time-locked and stationary with respect to stimulus (or other event) presentation and on the other hand to reduce contributions of physiological and instrumental noise (which are typically not time-locked to stimulus presentation). However, any signals that are generated by reorganization of the background or pre-stimulus activity as well as any signals that are not time-locked will also be reduced (if not lost altogether) as a result of this averaging procedure. Consequently ERPs represent only part of the information likely contained within an EEG data set. Moreover the fact that each participant contributes one ERP per experimental condition obfuscates the possibilities of examining intra-subject variance and of conducting single-subject analyses. Such information would enhance many neuroscientific domains of investigation, including (but not limited to) brain–computer interface and neuroprosthetics, determining the efficacy of neurorehabilitation strategies and pharmacologic agents, and identifying the neurophysiologic bases of EEG and ERPs.

Most existing methods for the analysis of single-trial and single-subject data are largely based on specific hypotheses regarding the *temporal* features of the EEG signal. These techniques often imply an ad hoc selection either of the single waveforms to be analyzed (as for wavelet decomposition; Quiroga et al. 2003; Jongsma et al. 2006) or of the components (as in independent component analysis; Makeig et al. 2002; Makeig et al. 2004; see also Tang et al. 2006 for another case of blind source separation algorithms). However, such experimenter-based ad hoc selections not only introduce bias, they risk losing out on the added information that high-density electrode montages comport. Consequently, and due to the extremely variable nature of the temporal properties of the EEG signals, practical means for defining general guidelines for single-trial analysis are very limited.

Our approach therefore focuses on the spatial features of the electric field topography without presuming a priori there to be information in a similar manner as it has been established at the level of ERPs. In this novel approach we model the overall electrical response, which includes both event-related and ongoing activity, as a mixture of Gaussians (i.e., as a set of clusters having a Gaussian distribution in an M-dimensional space, where M is the number of the electrodes in the montage; Hastie 2001). Advanced machine learning techniques allow for estimating not only the means of each of the clusters within a set (i.e., the template maps, using the nomenclature above for clustering of ERPs) but also their covariance matrices, which can in turn be used to determine the conditional probability for each time point of the EEG/ERP (i.e., each map) to belong to each of the clusters. Estimation of the mixture of Gaussians parameters can be obtained by maximizing the likelihood of having Q Gaussians by means of the Baum-Welch algorithm (Dempster et al. 1977). The computation is initialized by a k-means algorithm and iteratively improves the estimation of means, covariances and priors of the Q Gaussians until the likelihood reaches a plateau. The estimated parameters can be used to compute the conditional probability that each topography belongs to each of the clusters. For each time point and trial we are provided with Q conditional probabilities that relate the topographies to the clusters. The brain responses can now be conveniently described as an intensity plot in which each time point and trial are labeled in correspondence to the cluster having the highest conditional probability. In addition to this compact ERP representation, the conditional probabilities can be statistically evaluated to identify topographic differences within or between conditions at both single-subject and group levels (e.g., De Lucia et al. 2007). Figure 2.6 displays an example of this analysis applied to single-subject data from an auditory object discrimination experiment (see Murray et al. 2006b for details). A coherent pattern or "structure" is readily apparent both across trials and experimental conditions (i.e. responses to sounds of living and human-made environmental objects). In a manner similar to the fitting applied above, the conditional probability can also be statistically analyzed within and across experimental conditions. One application of these methods is to assess whether data from a given individual or patient deviate from those of a larger population. Further development of this approach also promises to address challenging questions at the level of variability in single-subject responses and to cast light on the contributions of induced and evoked activity to the generation of ERPs (see also chapter 3 of this volume).

Conclusions

This chapter provides the details of the rationale for as well as the implementation of a set of topographic analyses of multichannel surface-recorded ERPs. A key advantage of these methods is their independence of both the reference and also a priori selection of certain electrodes or time points. These measures render statistical information concerning modulations in response strength, latency, and topography both between and within experimental conditions. In these and other ways topographic analysis techniques allow the experimenter to glean additional information and neurophysiologic interpretability beyond what is available from canonical waveform analysis.

   In addition to the progress in analysis tools and data interpretability, multichannel EEG systems have become readily affordable for nearly all clinical and research laboratories. However, a potential risk of this ease of access to the equipment is that it may not be paralleled by researchers fully understanding or appropriately applying these analysis tools. As a result EEG/ERPs as a research field risks becoming divided between those who apply only a minimal level of analysis and those who seek to more fully capitalize on the interpretational power of the technique. One goal of this chapter was to show even to newcomers to the field that information-rich analyses can also be easy to use and interpret.

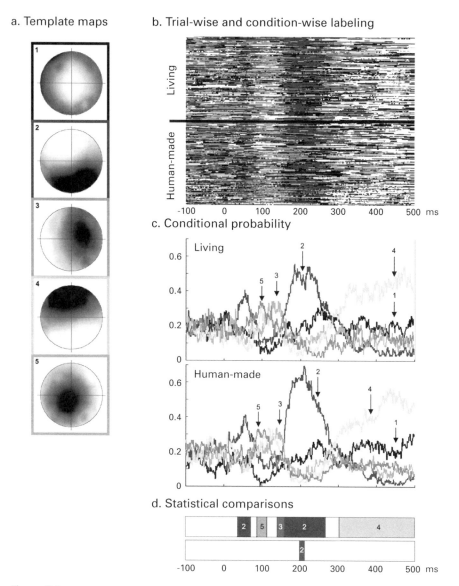

a. Template maps

b. Trial-wise and condition-wise labeling

Living

Human-made

-100   0   100   200   300   400   500 ms

c. Conditional probability

Living

Human-made

d. Statistical comparisons

-100   0   100   200   300   400   500 ms

Figure 2.6

Examples of single-trial and single-subject topographic analyses. (a) The template maps (i.e., centroids of each of the five Gaussians) estimated from the entire dataset (positive voltages in white and negative in black). (b) The labeling of each trial and time point from each experimental condition (i.e., sounds of living and human-made objects). Note the temporal "structure" across trials, and that the given poststimulus periods are predominantly labeled with one or another template map. (c) The mean conditional probability of labeling with each template map as a function of time for each experimental condition. (d) The top portion shows time periods when the conditional probability of one template map was significantly higher than all other template maps regardless of experimental condition; the bottom portion shows time periods when the conditional probability of the same template map significantly differed between experimental conditions. In all analyses a 10 time point (i.e., 10 ms) temporal criterion was applied.

Acknowledgments

Cartool software can be freely downloaded from http://brainmapping.unige.ch/Cartool.htm and is supported by the EEG Brain Mapping Core of the Center for Biomedical Imaging (www.cibm.ch). Financial support has been provided by the Swiss National Science Foundation (grants 3100A0–118419 to MMM, k-33k1_122518/1 to MDL, and 320030–111783 to CMM) and the Leenaards Foundation (2005 Prize for the Promotion of Scientific Research to MMM).

Notes

1. These data are from nine healthy participants who were performing an old–new discrimination task with Snodgrass and Vanderwart (1980) line drawings presented for 500 ms (details can be found in Murray et al. 2004). The precise data we present in this chapter are immaterial to the points we will make. However, we have chosen these data to provide the reader with a concrete example of how topographic analyses and electrical neuroimaging can be applied to typical topics in cognitive neuroscience research, such as repetition priming/suppression.

2. The methods/issues we will describe here appear in several prior works dating back to the 1980s, including the seminal work of Dietrich Lehmann and his scholars (e.g., Lehmann and Skrandies 1980; Lehmann 1987; Brandeis and Lehmann 1986; Skrandies 1990, 1993; Brandeis et al. 1992; Michel et al. 1992, 1999; Koenig and Lehmann 1996), although several others are also noteworthy (Duffy 1982; Fender 1987; Gevins et al. 1987; Michel et al. 2001, 2004; Murray et al. 2008a).

3. We would strongly encourage researchers to refrain from drawing inferences on the localization of EEG/ERP effects unless source estimations are performed. Even then, conclusions should be appropriately tempered to reflect the caveats of the particular source estimation method used.

4. For readers less familiar with CSD derivations, it is perhaps worthwhile to briefly describe what is being calculated that makes them reference-independent. The CSD or Laplacian derivation involves calculating the second spatial derivative across the electrode montage (i.e., the degree of change of the degree of change in the voltage measured at electrode x relative to its neighbors). As such, CSD derivations are intrinsically based on *spatial* gradients in the electric field at the scalp.

References

Arzy S, Mohr C, Michel CM, Blanke O. 2007. Duration and not strength of activation in temporo-parietal cortex positively correlates with schizotypy. *Neuroimage* 35:326–33.

Baillet S, Mosher JC, Leahy RM. 2001. Electromagnetic brain mapping. *IEEE Signal Process* (Nov): 14–30.

Brandeis D, Lehmann D. 1986. Event-related potentials of the brain and cognitive processes: approaches and applications. *Neuropsychologia* 24:151–68.

Brandeis D, Naylor H, Halliday R, Callaway E, Yano L. 1992. Scopolamine effects on visual information processing, attention, and event-related potential map latencies. *Psychophysiology* 29:315–36.

De Lucia M, Michel CM, Clarke S, Murray MM. 2007. Single-subject EEG analysis based on topographic information. *Int J Bioelectromagnet* 9:168–71.

De Santis L, Spierer L, Clarke S, Murray MM. 2007a. Getting in touch: segregated somatosensory "what" and "where" pathways in humans revealed by electrical neuroimaging. *Neuroimage* 37:890–903.

De Santis L, Clarke S, Murray MM. 2007b. Automatic and intrinsic auditory "what" and "where" processing in humans revealed by electrical neuroimaging. *Cerebr Cortex* 17:9–17.

Dempster A, Laird N, Rubin D. 1977. Maximum likelihood from incomplete data via the EM algorithm. *J Roy Stat Soc* B39:1–38.

Desmedt JE, Tomberg C, Noel P, Ozaki I. 1990. Beware of the average reference in brain mapping. *Electroencephalogr Clin Neurophysiol Suppl* 41:22–27.

Dien J. 1998. Issues in the application of the average reference: review, critiques, and recommendations. *Beh Res Meth Instrum Comput* 30:34–43.

Dien J, Santuzzi AM. 2005. Application of repeated measures ANOVA to high-density ERP datasets: a review and tutorial. In: Handy TC, ed. *Event-Related Potentials: A Methods Handbook.* Cambridge: MIT Press, 57–82.

Duffy FH. 1982. Topographic display of evoked potentials: Clinical applications of brain electrical activity mapping (BEAM). *An NY Acad Sci* 388:183–96.

Fender DH. 1987. Source localisation of brain electrical activity. In: Gevins AS, Remond A, eds. *Handbook of Electroencephalography and Clinical Neurophysiology.* Vol. 1: *Methods of Analysis of Brain Electrical and Magnetic Signals.* Amsterdam: Elsevier, 355–99.

Friston KJ, Ashburner JT, Kiebel SJ, Nichols TE, Penny WD. 2007. *Statistical Parametric Mapping: The Analysis of Functional Brain Images.* London: Academic Press.

Geselowitz DB. 1998. The zero of potential. *IEEE Eng Med Biol* 17:128–32.

Gevins AS, Morgan NH, Bressler SL, Cutillo BA, White RM, Illes J, Greer DS, Doyle JC, Zeitlin GM. 1987. Human neuroelectric patterns predict performance accuracy. *Science* 235:580–85.

Grave de Peralta Menendez R, Andino SG, Lantz G, Michel CM, Landis T. 2001. Noninvasive localization of electromagnetic epileptic activity: I. Method descriptions and simulations. *Brain Topogr* 14:131–37.

Grave de Peralta Menendez R, Murray MM, Michel CM, Martuzzi R, Gonzalez Andino SL. 2004. Electrical neuroimaging based on biophysical constraints. *NeuroImage* 21:527–39.

Guthrie D, Buchwald JS. 1991. Significance testing of difference potentials. *Psychophysiology* 28:240–44.

Handy TC. 2005. *Event-Related Potentials: A Methods Handbook*. Cambridge: MIT Press.

Hanson JC, Hillyard SA. 1980. Endogenous brain potentials associated with selective auditory attention. *Electroencephalogr Clin Neurophysiol* 49:277–90.

Hastie T, Tibshirani R, Friedman J. 2001. *The Elements of Statistical Learning*. New York: Springer.

He B, Lian J. 2002. High-resolution spatio-temporal functional neuroimaging of brain activity. *Crit Rev Biomed Eng* 30:283–306.

Jongsma MLA, Eichele T, Van Rijn CMV, Coenen AML, Hugdahl K, Nordby H, Quiroga RQ. 2006. Tracking pattern learning with single-trial event-related potentials. *Clin Neurophysiol* 117:1957–73.

Katayama H, Gianotti LR, Isotani T, Faber PL, Sasada K, Kinoshita T, Lehmann D. 2007. Classes of multichannel EEG microstates in light and deep hypnotic conditions. *Brain Topogr* 20:7–14.

Koenig T, Lehmann D. 1996. Microstates in language-related brain potential maps show noun-verb differences. *Brain Lang* 53:169–82.

Koenig T, Prichep L, Lehmann D, Sosa PV, Braeker E, Kleinlogel H, Isenhart R, John ER. 2002. Millisecond by millisecond, year by year: normative EEG microstates and developmental stages. *Neuroimage* 16:41–48.

Kondakor I, Pascual-Marqui R, Michel CM, Lehmann D. 1995. Event-related potential map differences depend on prestimulus microstates. *J Med Eng Technol* 19:66–69.

Lantz G, Grave de Peralta R, Spinelli L, Seeck M, Michel CM. 2003. Epileptic source localization with high density EEG: how many electrodes are needed? *Clin Neurophysiol* 114:63–69.

Lehmann D. 1987. Principles of spatial analysis. In: Gevins AS, Remond A, eds. *Handbook of Electroencephalography and Clinical Neurophysiology*. Vol. 1: *Methods of Analysis of Brain Electrical and Magnetic Signals*. Amsterdam: Elsevier, 309–54.

Lehmann D, Skrandies W. 1980. Reference-free identification of components of checkerboard-evoked multichannel potential fields. *Electroencephalogr Clin Neurophysiol* 48:609–21.

Lorenzo-Lopez L, Amenedo E, Pascual-Marqui RD, Cadaveira F. 2008. Neural correlates of age-related visual search decline: a combined ERP and sLORETA study. *NeuroImage* 41:511–24. doi: 10.1016/j.neuroimage.2008.02.041.

Luck SJ. 2005. *An Introduction to the Event-Related Potential Technique*. Cambridge: MIT Press.

Makeig S, Westerfield M, Jung TP, Enghoff S, Townsend J, Courchesne E, Sejnowski TJ. 2002. Dynamic brain sources of visual evoked responses. *Science* 295:690–94.

Makeig S, Debener S, Onton J, Delorme A. 2004. Mining even-related brain dynamics. *Trends Cogn Neurosci* 8:204–10.

Manly BF. 1991. *Randomization and Monte Carlo Methods in Biology.* London: Chapman Hall.

McCarthy G, Wood CC. 1985. Scalp distributions of event-related potentials: An ambiguity associated with analysis of variance models. *Electroencephalogr Clin Neurophysiol* 62:203–208.

Michel CM, Henggeler B, Lehmann D. 1992. 42-channel potential map series to visual contrast and stereo stimuli: perceptual and cognitive event-related segments. *Int J Psychophysiol* 12:133–45.

Michel CM, Seeck M, Landis T. 1999. Spatio-temporal dynamics of human cognition. *News Physiol Sci* 14:206–14.

Michel CM, Thut G, Morand S, Khateb A, Pegna AJ, Grave de Peralta R, Gonzalez S, Seeck M, Landis T. 2001. Electric source imaging of human cognitive brain functions. *Brain Res Rev* 36:108–18.

Michel CM, Murray MM, Lantz G, Gonzalez S, Spinelli L, Grave de Peralta R. 2004a. EEG source imaging. *Clin Neurophysiol* 115:2195–2222.

Michel CM, Seeck M, Murray MM. 2004b. The speed of visual cognition. *Suppl Clin Neurophysiol* 57:617–27.

Murray MM, Foxe JJ, Higgins BA, Javitt DC, Schroeder CE. 2001. Visuo-spatial neural response interactions in early cortical processing during a simple reaction time task: a high-density electrical mapping study. *Neuropsychologia* 39:828–44.

Murray MM, Michel CM, Grave de Peralta R, Ortigue S, Brunet D, Andino SG, Schnider A. 2004. Rapid discrimination of visual and multisensory memories revealed by electrical neuroimaging. *Neuroimage* 21:125–35.

Murray MM, Imber ML, Javitt DC, Foxe JJ. 2006a. Boundary completion is automatic and dissociable from shape discrimination. *J Neurosci* 26:12043–54.

Murray MM, Camen C, Gonzalez Andino SL, Bovet P, Clarke S. 2006b. Rapid brain discrimination of sounds of objects. *J Neurosci* 26:1293–1302.

Murray MM, Brunet D, Michel CM. 2008a. Topographic ERP analyses: a step-by-step tutorial review. *Brain Topogr* 20:249–64.

Murray MM, Camen C, Spierer L, Clarke S. 2008b. Plastic representations of environmental sounds revealed by electrical neuroimaging. *Neuroimage* 39:847–56.

Overney LS, Michel CM, Harris IM, Pegna AJ. 2005. Cerebral processes in mental transformations of body parts: recognition prior to rotation. *Brain Res Cogn Brain Res* 25:722–34.

Pascual-Marqui RD, Lehmann D. 1993. Comparison of topographic maps and the reference electrode: comments on two papers by Desmedt and collaborators. *Electroencephalogr Clin Neurophysiol* 88:530–31, 534–36.

Pascual-Marqui RD, Michel CM, Lehmann D. 1995. Segmentation of brain electrical activity into microstates, model estimation and validation. *IEEE Trans Biomed Eng* 42:658–65.

Pascual-Marqui RD. 2002. Standardized low-resolution brain electromagnetic tomography (sLORETA): technical details. *Meth Find Exp Clin Pharmacol* D24:5–12.

Pegna AJ, Khateb A, Spinelli L, Seeck M, Landis T, Michel CM. 1997. Unravelling the cerebral dynamics of mental imagery. *Hum Brain Mapp* 5:410–21.

Perrin F, Pernier J, Bertrand O, Giard MH, Echalier JF. 1987. Mapping of scalp potentials by surface spline interpolation. *Electroencephalogr Clin Neurophysiol* 66:75–81.

Picton TW, Bentin S, Berg P, Donchin E, Hillyard SA, Johnson R Jr, Miller GA, Ritter W, Ruchkin DS, Rugg MD, Taylor MJ. 2000. Guidelines for using human event-related potentials to study cognition: recording standards and publication criteria. *Psychophysiology* 37:127–52.

Pourtois G, Thut G, Grave de Peralta R, Michel CM, Vuilleumier P. 2005. Two electrophysiological stages of spatial orienting toward fearful faces: early temporo-parietal activation preceding gain control in extrastriate visual cortex. *Neuroimage* 26:149–63.

Pourtois G, Delplanque S, Michel CM, Vuilleumier P. 2008. Beyond conventional event-related brain potentials (ERPs): exploring the time course of visual emotion processing using topographic and principal component analyses. *Brain Topogr* 20:265–77.

Quiroga RQ, Garcia H. 2003. Single trial event-related potentials with wavelet de-noising. *Clin Neurophysiol* 114:376–90.

Rolls ET, Tovee MJ. 1994. Processing speed in the cerebral cortex and the neurophysiology of visual masking. *Proc Roy Soc* B257: 9–15.

Ruz M, Nobre AC. 2008. Attention modulates initial stages of visual word processing. *J Cogn Neurosci* 20:1727–36. doi: 10.1162/jocn.2008.20119.

Saron CD, Schroeder CE, Foxe JJ, Vaughan HG Jr. 2001. Visual activation of frontal cortex: segregation from occipital activity. *Cogn Brain Res* 12:75–88.

Sergent C, Baillet S, Dehaene S. 2005. Timing of the brain events underlying access to consciousness during the attentional blink. *Nat Neurosci* 8: 1391–1400.

Skrandies W. 1990. Global field power and topographic similarity. *Brain Topogr* 3:137–41.

Skrandies W. 1993. EEG/EP: new techniques. *Brain Topogr* 5:347–50.

Skrandies W. 2007. The effect of stimulation frequency and retinal stimulus location on visual evoked potential topography. *Brain Topogr* 20:15–20.

Snodgrass JG, Vanderwart M. 1980. A standardized set of 260 pictures: norms for name agreement, image agreement, familiarity, and visual complexity. *J Exp Psychol Hum Learn* 6. 174–215.

Spierer L, Tardif E, Sperdin H, Murray MM, Clarke S. 2007. Learning-induced plasticity in auditory spatial representations revealed by electrical neuroimaging. *J Neurosci* 27:5474–83.

Spierer L, Murray MM, Tardif E, Clarke S. 2008. The path to success in auditory spatial discrimination: electrical neuroimaging responses within the supratemporal plane predict performance outcome. *Neuroimage* 41:493–503. doi: 10.1016/j.neuroimage.2008.02.038.

Srebro R. 1996. A bootstrap method to compare the shapes of two scalp fields. *Electroencephalogr Clin Neurophysiol* 100:25–32.

Srinivasan R, Nunez PL, Tucker DM, Silberstein RB, Cadusch PJ. 1996. Spatial sampling and filtering of EEG with spline Laplacians to estimate cortical potentials. *Brain Topogr* 8:355–66.

Tang AC, Sutherland MT, Wang Y. 2006. Contrasting single-trial ERPs between experimental manipulations: improving differentiability by blind source separation. *Neuroimage* 29:335–46.

Thierry G, Martin CD, Downing P, Pegna AJ. 2007. Controlling for interstimulus perceptual variance abolishes N170 face selectivity. *Nat Neurosci* 10:505–11.

Tibshirani R, Walther G, Botstein D, Brown P. 2005. Cluster validation by prediction strength. *J Comput Graphical Stat* 14:511–28.

Vaughan HG Jr. 1982. The neural origins of human event-related potentials. *An NY Acad Sci* 388:125–38.

Vaughan HG Jr, Arezzo JC. 1988. The Neural basis of event-related potentials. In: Picton TW, ed. *Human Event-Related Potentials: EEG Handbook* (rev. ser.), vol. 3. New York: Elsevier, 45–96.

Wirth M, Horn H, Koenig T, Razafimandimby A, Stein M, Mueller T, Federspiel A, Meier B, Dierks T, Strik W. 2008. The early context effect reflects activity in the temporo-prefrontal semantic system: Evidence from electrical neuroimaging of abstract and concrete word reading. *Neuroimage* 42:423–36. doi: 10.1016/j.neuroimage.2008.03.045.

Wylie GR, Murray MM, Javitt DC, Foxe JJ. 2009. Distinct neurophysiological mechanisms mediate mixing costs and switch costs. *J Cogn Neurosci* 21:105–18. doi:10.1162/jocn.2009.21009.

Yoshino A, Kawamoto M, Yoshida T, Kobayashi N, Shigemura J, Takahashi Y, Nomura S. 2006. Activation time course of responses to illusory contours and salient region: a high-density electrical mapping comparison. *Brain Res* 1071:137–44.

3   Noninvasive Estimation of Local Field Potentials: Methods and Applications

Rolando Grave de Peralta Menendez, Micah M. Murray, Gregor Thut,
Theodor Landis, and Sara L. Gonzalez Andino

Improving our understanding of brain function requires both the ability to localize the regions underlying a particular function and also to track the time course of brain activity within these localized regions. To understand functions of the intact and healthy brain, it is further essential to achieve these goals using noninvasive measurements. Advances in brain imaging techniques, in particular, functional magnetic resonance imaging (fMRI), have improved our ability to localize functional brain networks. Parallel improvements are likewise being achieved in solving the electromagnetic inverse problem. The inverse problem refers to the determination of the generators of scalp-recorded electroencephalographic (EEG) and magnetoencephalographic (MEG) data, both of which have sub-millisecond temporal information. The successful solution of the inverse problem therefore promises both the ability to localize distributed brain function and track it in real time.

However, the success of inverse solutions is hampered by the fact that different generator configurations can produce the same measured field at the scalp. Consequently researchers must rely on independent a priori information to select the more likely of possible generator configurations. Variations in the kinds of a priori information applied has led to different types of inverse solutions (Scherg 1994; van Oosterom 1991; Vrba and Robinson 2001).

We have recently shown (Grave de Peralta Menendez et al. 2000; Grave de Peralta Menendez et al. 2004; Thut et al. 2001) that biophysically derived a priori information exists that allows the inverse problem to be reformulated in terms of a restricted source model. This source model then makes it possible to estimate local field potentials (LFP) in depth from scalp-recorded voltage data. A physically driven regularization strategy is used that achieves uniqueness in the solution of the inverse problem by incorporating as a priori information the physical laws predicting the decay of the strength of potentials and fields with the distance to their generation site. In this approach to solve the inverse problem, termed ELECTRA, both the regularization strategy and the source model emulate the behavior of the actual generators of recordable brain activity. Empirical results of the analysis of event-related potential data in conjunction with

the noninvasive estimation of LFPs based on biophysical constraints have been published previously (Gonzalez Andino et al. 2008; Gonzalez Andino et al. 2007; Gonzalez
Andino et al. 2005b; Gonzalez Andino et al. 2005c; Grave de Peralta Menendez et al.
2000; Grave de Peralta Menendez et al. 2004; Morand et al. 2000; Thut et al. 2001).
These studies demonstrate that such estimations represent a useful tool for the study
of brain function in healthy subjects. The first goal of this chapter is to summarize
the basic theory, implementation, and theoretical advantages of the noninvasive
estimation of LFPs through the ELECTRA source model.

It is becoming increasingly evident that a fuller understanding of brain function
will depend on our ability to examine single events within individual subjects or
patients. One level of the importance of single-trial events can readily be gleaned from
a consideration of learning and decision-making phenomena. Similarly single-trial
information is of critical importance for the field of neuroprosthetics (Muller-Putz
et al. 2006; Nicolelis 2001) aimed at helping severely disabled or locked-in patients.
One shortcoming of event-related potential data is that it forcibly diminishes the
impact of inter-trial variation and information in brain processes through its assumption of homogeneity across trials. A second shortcoming is that averaging in event-
related potentials is an incomplete representation of ongoing brain activity. In other
words, activity that is asynchronous with stimulus delivery or response execution will
tend to be averaged out across trials. In particular, this includes oscillatory brain activity that is often not phase locked with stimulus delivery or response execution. The
second goal of this chapter is therefore to demonstrate that intracranial LFPs can
indeed be accurately estimated from single trials of scalp-recorded data. Indeed application of ELECTRA to issues in neuroprosthetics is beginning to show some promising
results (Grave de Peralta Menendez and Gonzalez Andino 2008; Grave de Peralta
Menendez et al. 2003; Grave de Peralta Menendez et al. 2005)

Single-trial analysis is a serious challenge for all neuroimaging techniques since the
signal of interest is buried within the background electrical or magnetic signals. Here
we illustrate how electrical neuroimaging can be combined with specific statistical
techniques to extract relevant neurophysiological information from multiple repetitions of single trials. In particular, we describe an approach to construct individual
images of brain areas that significantly differ between two or more experimental conditions. This method is based on computing selected features of the estimated LFPs
over all single trials and then performing nonparametric statistical tests to assess the
significance of the differences at each pixel over trials. Such procedures can be applied
to the analysis of features in either the temporal or the spectral domains. These procedures are illustrated here in the analysis of the differences between self-paced left
and right finger movements in a healthy subject.

The chapter starts by giving the basic theory underlying LFP estimation from scalp-
recorded EEG data followed by some practical issues related to the implementation of
this approach. Among the practical issues we discuss are how to build a simple realistic

head model and the way to select the regularization parameter needed to deal with the noise inherent to the data. This theoretical section is followed by the description of the statistical techniques employed to build individual images from single trials that reflect differences between experimental conditions in the temporal or spectral domain. Examples of applications of these procedures are then given with a brief discussion about the neurophysiological meaning of the results. We conclude with a discussion of the advantages of using this single-trial approach to confer statistical reliability to electrical neuroimaging.

Computing Local Field Potentials: Theoretical and Practical Issues

Theoretical Aspects of LFP Computation
The formal relationship between intra-cerebral currents and scalp-measured fields can be derived from Maxwell equations that describe the propagation of electromagnetic fields within arbitrary volume conductor models, that is,

$$\nabla \circ \mathbf{E} = \frac{\rho}{\varepsilon}, \tag{1'}$$

$$\nabla \times \mathbf{E} = -\frac{\partial \mathbf{B}}{\partial t}, \tag{2'}$$

$$\nabla \circ \mathbf{B} = 0, \tag{3'}$$

$$\nabla \times \mathbf{B} = \mu \left(\mathbf{J} + \frac{\varepsilon \partial \mathbf{E}}{\partial t} \right), \tag{4'}$$

where $\mathbf{E}$ and $\mathbf{B}$ are the electric and magnetic fields, $\mathbf{J}$ is the total current density vector, ε and μ stand for physical properties of the media, and ρ is a (charge or current) density.

Equations (2') and (4') indicate that time varying electric and magnetic fields are interrelated. However, since the range of frequencies (Plonsey and Heppner 1967) associated with electromagnetic fields in vivo-media is usually less than 1,000 Hz, it is possible to neglect the contribution of the temporal terms. This is referred to as the quasi-static approach and implies that the capacitive and inductive effects produced by the temporal variations of the electric field $\mathbf{E}$ and the magnetic field $\mathbf{B}$ (see equations 2' and 4') are irrelevant. The practical consequence of the quasi-static approach is that electric and magnetic fields recorded at the scalp are instantaneously reflecting the underlying neural processes and thus, electromagnetic processes taking place in the past are irrelevant for the present measurements. No evidence against this approximation has been reported so far.

This quasi-stationary assumption allows for the separate modeling of the electromagnetic fields; that is, the electric field is not dependent on temporal variations of the magnetic field, and vice versa:

$$\nabla \circ \mathbf{E} = \frac{\rho}{\varepsilon}, \tag{1}$$

$$\nabla \times \mathbf{E} = 0 \Leftrightarrow \mathbf{E} = -\nabla \mathbf{V}, \tag{2}$$

$$\nabla \circ \mathbf{B} = 0 \Leftrightarrow \mathbf{B} = \nabla \times A, \tag{3}$$

$$\nabla \times \mathbf{B} = \mu \mathbf{J} \Rightarrow \nabla \circ \mathbf{J} = 0. \tag{4}$$

The total current emerging in biological tissue is usually split into two terms: a primary and neurophysiologically driven current ($\mathbf{J}_p$), and the volume or secondary current ($\sigma \mathbf{E}$; i.e., $\mathbf{J} = \mathbf{J}_p + \sigma \mathbf{E}$). From equation (4) there derives that the divergence of the total current ($\mathbf{J}$) is zero, which when combined with previous decomposition, and equation (2) yields Poisson's equation for the electric potential field:

$$\nabla \circ (\sigma \nabla V) = \nabla \circ J_p. \tag{5}$$

This equation establishes that the actual generators of potential V are determined by the divergence of the primary current.

Scarce information is available to build or estimate the conductivity tensor σ. While we had pinned all our hopes on diffusion tensor imaging, it actually seems that the required detailed information will hardly come from that source. For that reason we will assume in the following that the conductivity is piecewise constant. In that case the conductivity σ is not affected by the divergence operator, and the differential operator reduces to the Laplacian (see equation 11 below) of the intracranial fields used to define the sources and the sinks and also called the current source density (CSD).

Denoting by Q the head volume and using the Green function Ψ associated to the solution of (5), we can rewrite (5) as a (first-kind) Fredholm linear integral equation:

$$V(s) = -\int_Q \nabla \circ J_p(r) \psi(s, r) dr. \tag{6}$$

Designating the (vector) lead field by $L(s, r) = \nabla_r \Psi(s, r)$ and noting that the primary current source distribution is confined to a volume Q containing the brain, after the application of some Green identities, we obtain the standard formulation of the neuroelectromagnetic inverse problem

$$V(s) = \int_Q L(s, r) \circ J_p(r) dr \tag{7}$$

denoting the relationship between the data measured at the external point, $V(s)$, and the superposition of the contribution of the unknown current source density distribution J_p at locations r inside the brain (Fuchs et al. 1999; Grave de Peralta Menendez et al. 2004; Greenblatt 1993; M. Hämäläinen 1993; Sarvas 1987).

Several (theoretical) source models have been used to solve equation (7) and thus to describe the sources of the electromagnetic activity of the brain, for example, dipoles, monopoles, and current density vector. Without entering into a formal discussion about the plausibility of these mathematical models, it is important to note that none of these theoretical source models actually exists within the brain nor is any physically measurable. Instead real measurements are the result of quantifiable potentials at different "measurable" levels. At the microscopic (neuron) level, this potential is the extracellular potential. At the macroscopic (region) level, this potential is the local field potential (LFP). Through volume conduction the effect of these potentials arrives at the scalp where they are measured as the electroencephalogram (EEG). It is then natural to question whether potentials inside the brain can be related to and thus computed from potentials measured at the scalp.

A positive answer to this question can be given if we notice that macroscopic primary sources, namely the generators of the EEG, are dominated by microscopic secondary (volume) currents or in Plonsey words (Plonsey 1982): "the fields measured do not even arise from J_p—the current source density vector field—but rather from secondary sources only. These secondary sources in turn depend on both the electrical field and the interfaces, and hence are related to divergence of J_p and the geometry." This kind of source corresponds to a potential distribution inside the brain.

A definitive theoretical argument can be obtained if we note that the current density vector field can be decomposed as the sum of a solenoidal vector field plus an irrotational vector field plus the gradient of a harmonic function. That is,

$$J_p = J_s + J_i + J_h = \nabla \times A + \nabla \phi + \nabla \Omega, \tag{8}$$

where $J_h = \nabla \Omega$ with Ω harmonic in the brain region, $J_s = \nabla \times A$ and $J_i = \nabla \phi$ fulfill $\nabla \circ J_s \equiv \nabla x J_i \equiv \nabla^2 \Omega \equiv 0$. Here zero denotes the neutral for the addition of functions of each space.

Substitution of decomposition (8) in equation (6) yields

$$V(s) = -\int_Q \nabla \circ J_s(r) \psi(s, r) dQ - \int_Q \nabla \circ J_i(r) \psi(s, r) dQ - \int_Q \nabla^2 \Omega(r) \psi(s, r) dQ. \tag{9}$$

Based on vector identities, it follows that only the second integral, corresponding to the irrotational current, contributes to the measured potentials (EEG). In mathematical parlance, it means that the current density vector generating the EEG fulfills

$$\nabla x J_p = 0 \Leftrightarrow J_p = \nabla \varphi, \tag{10}$$

where φ is a potential field within the brain. Importantly this result depends only on the quasi-static approximation and the existence of the Green function, not on the assumption of piecewise conductivity. It is due to the fact that the potential V (EEG) is generated by the divergence of the primary sources. And thus divergenceless sources do not contribute to the EEG. It does not mean that the sources inside the head are necessarily irrotational but that, since only the irrotational part contributes to the EEG, it is useless to look for more complex sources.

Under the assumption of piecewise constant conductivity σ, substitution of (10) into Poisson's equation (5) shows that φ has the same sources and sinks as the EEG potential V, that is,

$$\sigma\nabla \circ (\nabla V) = \nabla \circ (\nabla\varphi) \Leftrightarrow \sigma\nabla^2 V = \nabla^2\varphi. \tag{11}$$

Note that plotting the modulus of the estimated primary current obtained by solving (7), which we would note has thus far been the common procedure used to depict inverse solutions results, does not reflect the actual generators. Instead the actual generators are determined by the sources and the sinks obtained from the Laplacian of potential field φ or $\nabla \circ J_p$ (the divergence of the primary current density vector).

The irrotational source model corresponds to the solution of the following equation:

$$V(s) = -\int_Q \nabla\varphi(r') \circ \nabla\psi(s,r')dQ = \int_Q \nabla \circ J_p(r')\psi(s,r')dQ \tag{12}$$

with respect to one of the following magnitudes: (1) the estimation of an irrotational current density vector $J_p = \nabla\varphi$ with the vector lead field $L = \nabla\psi$; (2) the estimation of a scalar field, the current source density (CSD), $\nabla \circ J_p = I$ with the scalar lead field ψ; or (3) the estimation of a scalar field, the potential distribution φ in Q with a transformed scalar lead field $\nabla\psi \circ \nabla$.

The third alternative relating the potential distribution inside the brain with the potential distribution on the scalp (EEG) can be written as

$$V(s) = \int_Q L(s,r') \circ \nabla\varphi(r')dQ. \tag{13}$$

In real conditions, neither the measurements nor the lead field functions are known for arbitrary surface/brain locations but rather only at restricted discrete sites. Thus it is reasonable to introduce a discrete formalism where the integral equation in (13) is approximated by a discrete sum, which leads to the following underdetermined system of linear equations:

$$\mathbf{v} = \mathbf{Lf}. \tag{14}$$

Vectors $\mathbf{v}$ and $\mathbf{f}$ and matrix $\mathbf{L}$ represent the discretization of the continuous functions, that is, $\mathbf{v}_k = V(s_k)$ for k = 1 to numbers of sensors and $\mathbf{f}_m = \phi(r_m)$ for m = 1 to number of solution points; here $\mathbf{L}_{km} = w_{km} L(s_k, r_m) \circ \nabla$ and w_{km} are the quadrature weights.

Unfortunately, the restriction of the source model is not enough to ensure a unique solution to equations (13) and (14). For this reason additional information (independent of the measured data) should be included in the solution. In principle, any mathematical method proposed for the solution of ill-posed problems can be considered. For reviews, see (Menke 1989; Tikhonov and Arsenin 1977). While there is a wide range of solutions, we would like to caution the reader about the selection of a method based on figures of merit obtained from the localization of single sources, such as the zero dipole localization or location bias. We have previously demonstrated that these measures are neither necessary nor sufficient for assessing the performance of inverse solutions (Grave de Peralta Menendez and Gonzalez Andino 2000; Grave de Peralta-Menendez and Gonzalez-Andino 1998).

Since our goal of additional information is to better imitate the behavior of real sources in the head, we prefer to use additional information derived from biophysical laws. Therefore we copy the spatial structure of the well-known potential field generated by a dipolar source that is irrotational at all points except at the location of the dipole; that is,

$$\phi(r) = M \cdot \frac{r - r'}{|r - r'|^3} = \frac{|M|\cos\theta}{|r - r'|^2}, \tag{15}$$

expressing that the potential field at a given point r depends on the activity at another brain site r' according to a square inverse law. While this law relates one solution point with all the others, in our current implementation (see the next section) we use only neighborhoods with no more than 26 points. This range is enough to compute the local autoregressive average (LAURA) regularization operator (Grave de Peralta Menendez et al. 2001; Grave de Peralta Menendez et al. 2004). We would note that this is not the same exponent that we use for vector fields where we consider a cubic inverse distance instead.

In summary, the main advantages of the irrotational source model are as follows:

1. Reduction of the number of unknowns. Since we need to estimate only a scalar field instead of a vector field, the number of unknowns is reduced threefold. Given that the ratio between the number of unknowns and the number of sensors is a measure of uncertainty, we can say that the inverse problem with irrotational sources (13) is better determined than the unrestricted (arbitrary current density vector) estimation problem (7). In practice, this results in images with rather detailed patterns (see Grave de Peralta Menendez et al. 2000 for examples of visual evoked potentials).

2. Use of a scalar magnitude facilitating the inclusion of additional a priori information from other modalities of brain images (e.g., fMRI, PET, and SPECT) and reducing the computational load. In addition postprocessing of the single time series associated to each solution point might be easier than the analysis of three time series of the current density vector model.

3. Unquestionable constraints. The existence of sources with an irrotational part is a condition necessary and sufficient for the existence of EEG. Put simply, EEG recorded at the scalp surface is due to, and only due to, the irrotational part of the sources. This constraint is independent of the data.

4. Experimentally verifiable model. Although defined up to a sign change, the potential distribution produced by this source model can be directly compared with intracranial

potentials and measures (spectrum energy, etc.) derived from them. Related to this point, these estimated LFPs could also be compared with similar measurements from other species.

At this point we would like to warn the reader about some typical misunderstandings about ELECTRA source model. First, we would like to emphasize that the irrotational model does not imply that the primary source is $J_p = \sigma\mathbf{E}$. Second, ELECTRA does not correspond to the estimation of the irrotational part of the total current $\mathbf{J}$. Instead ELECTRA assumes that the primary current is, by its very origin, mainly composed by irrotational sources. Then the total current can be approximated by the sum of two irrotational components $\mathbf{J} = \sigma\mathbf{E}_m + \sigma\mathbf{E}$, where $\mathbf{E}_m$ is the electric field (different from $\mathbf{E}$!) produced by the electromotive force of the neurons, namely the primary sources. We would note that the experimental and theoretical evidences available so far support this selection. Anyway, this model can be hardly questioned with EEG measurements, since we will never know if the real brain sources contain more than the irrotational part, not at least with EEG. There is, however, a clear criticism to all the source models (irrotational or not) presented so far. All these models somehow disregard the differences between the microscopic and the macroscopic Maxwell's equations, that is, ignore the possible polarization and magnetization effects. As reported in Poulton et al. (1999), already in 1892 Lord Rayleigh showed that in general, multipolar rather than simply dipolar effects needed to be taken into account to fully describe the process of transition between the microscopic and the macroscopic viewpoints.

A final theoretical point to discuss is whether magnetic measurements (MEG) might contain more information about the invisible sources of the EEG. While the general electromagnetic formulation cannot exclude the existence of rotational sources (rotor or curl different from zero), the conclusions of Plonsey about the sources of the bioelectric and biomagnetic fields seems to be conclusive: "Even if the divergence and curl of the primary source were independent (and hence were both needed to define the primary source), because the secondary sources all arise from the divergence of the primary source, the magnetic field reflects the same source component as the electric field" (Plonsey 1982). Then, as seems to be the case, the inverse solution computed from magnetic measurements will hardly provide more information about the brain sources.

Practical Issues of LFP Computation

To compute local field potentials (LFP), that is, to compute one solution of equation (14) we need a set of data measurements $\mathbf{v}$ and the matrix $\mathbf{L}$. Methods to compute the vector lead field matrix associated with the current density vector J_p are widely used and well known. For this reason we propose here a simple alternative to compute

L as the product of the vector lead field matrix associated to J_p (as in equation 7) and a discrete version of the gradient operator.

One simple alternative to compute the vector lead field matrix is the symmetric spherical head model with anatomical constraints (SYSMAC) method (Grave de Peralta Menendez et al. 2006). Based on the transformation of the MRI into a sphere, it shares the simplicity of the spherical model computations and the detailed description of the geometry (scalp, brain, etc.) of boundary element methods.

The main characteristic of SYSMAC is that anatomical landmarks (Inion, Nasion, and Vertex) are selected at the central plane separating both hemispheres (interhemispheric fissure or brain symmetry plane). This information is used as a hard constraint for the computation of the center of the best-fitting sphere. Note that the fitting is only applied to a subset of points of the smooth part of the MRI, that is, scalp points with a positive projection on the direction orthogonal to the nasion-inion line and pointing toward the vertex. Once the center is correctly located at the symmetry plane of the MRI, two orthogonal rotations are enough to make the nasion–inion line of both systems parallel. An additional orthogonal rotation will make parallel the pre-auricular lines. On this way SYSMAC guarantees that the symmetry plane of both systems (i.e. the MRI image and the electrode configuration) perfectly coincides, thereby avoiding that the solution change from one hemisphere to the other as might happen with the SMAC method (Michel et al. 2004). Errors in the alignment of the theoretical (spherical) model and the MRI (figure 3.1) results in asymmetric lead field matrices and biased source reconstructions.

To obtain matrix **L,** hereafter termed the (scalar) lead field matrix, of equation (14), we (right) multiply the vector lead field matrix obtained from SYSMAC by the matrix associated to the discrete version of the gradient operator.

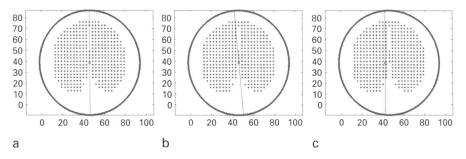

a   b   c

Figure 3.1

Alignment between spherical model and MRI. (a) Correct: plane of symmetry of both models coincides. (b–c) Incorrect symmetry plane of both systems not aligned because of incorrect position of the center (c) or lack of parallelism (b).

Regularization

The general solution of equation (14) can be obtained as the solution of the following variational problem (Grave de Peralta-Menendez and Gonzalez-Andino 1998; Menke 1989):

$$\min (\mathbf{Lf} - \mathbf{v})^t \, \mathbf{W}_v (\mathbf{Lf} - \mathbf{v}) + \lambda^2 \, (\mathbf{f} - \mathbf{f}_p)^t \, \mathbf{W}_f (\mathbf{f} - \mathbf{f}_p), \tag{16}$$

where $\mathbf{W}_v$ and $\mathbf{W}_f$ are symmetric (semi) positive definite matrices representing the (pseudo) metrics associated with the measurement space and the source space, respectively. Vector $\mathbf{f}_p$ denotes any available a priori value of the unknown, for example, from other varieties of brain functional images. The regularization parameter is denoted by λ. Independently of the rank of $\mathbf{L}$, the solution to (16) is unique if and only if the null spaces of $\mathbf{W}_f$ and $\mathbf{L}^t\mathbf{W}_v\mathbf{L}$ intersect trivially, that is, $\mathrm{Ker}(\mathbf{W}_f) \cap \mathrm{Ker}(\mathbf{L}^t\mathbf{W}_v\mathbf{L}) = \{0\}$. In this case the estimated solution vector $\mathbf{f}$ can be obtained making the change of variable $f = f_p + \mathbf{h}$ and solving the resulting problem for $\mathbf{h}$, that is,

$$\mathbf{f} = \mathbf{f}_p + [\mathbf{L}^t\mathbf{W}_v\mathbf{L} + \lambda^2\mathbf{W}_f \,]^{-1}\mathbf{L}^t\mathbf{W}_v [\mathbf{v} - \mathbf{Lf}_p] = \mathbf{f}_p + \mathbf{G}[\mathbf{v} - \mathbf{Lf}_p]. \tag{17}$$

If and only if matrices $\mathbf{W}_f$ and $\mathbf{W}_v$ are positive definite, equation (17) is equivalent to

$$\mathbf{f} = \mathbf{f}_p + \mathbf{W}_f^{-1}\mathbf{L}^t [\mathbf{LW}_f^{-1}\mathbf{L}^t + \lambda^2\mathbf{W}_v^{-1}]^{-1} [\mathbf{v} - \mathbf{Lf}_p] = \mathbf{f}_p + \mathbf{G}[\mathbf{v} - \mathbf{Lf}_p]. \tag{18}$$

The latter equation might be used when the same head model is used with several electrode configurations. Storing the inverse of the metric $\mathbf{W}_f$ and $\mathbf{W}_v$, we can repeatedly use equation (18) that only requires the inversion of a matrix of size equal to the number of sensors.

   The definition of the metric matrices and the a priori vector $\mathbf{f}_p$ vary according to the data available. For example, when dealing with average event-related potentials or another EEG window we could define $\mathbf{W}_v$ as the inverse of the covariance matrix. If we use all the single trials of one experiment, we can build a covariance matrix for each time point. In the following we will assume that we have no information about matrix $\mathbf{W}_v$ and vector $\mathbf{f}_p$. That is, we will use $\mathbf{W}_v$ = identity and $\mathbf{f}_p = 0$.

   To compute the metric of the source space, consider the auxiliary matrix A associated to the autoregressive averages with coefficients according to the square inverse law (equation 15):

$$A_{ii} = \frac{N}{N_i} \sum_{k \subset V_i} d_{ki}^{-2}, \quad A_{ik} = -d_{ki}^{-2}, \tag{19}$$

where V_i denotes the vicinity of each solution point, defined as the hexahedron centered at the point and comprising at most $N = 26$ neighbors. N_k is the number of neighbors of point k and d_{ki} stands for the Euclidean distance from point k to point i.

Then we can define the metric of the source space as

$$\mathbf{W}_f = A^t A. \tag{20}$$

For the computation of the regularization parameter we use the generalized cross validation method as described in (Davies 1992); that is, we look for the value of λ that minimizes the following expression:

$$\frac{\frac{1}{N}\|\{\mathbf{I} - R(\lambda)\}\,\mathbf{v}\|^2}{\left[\frac{1}{N}\mathrm{Trace}[\mathbf{I} - R(\lambda)]\right]^2}, \tag{21}$$

where $\mathbf{R}(\lambda)$ is the influence matrix, also called the data resolution matrix (Menke 1989), defined as the product of the lead field matrix and the inverse matrix. That is, $\mathbf{R}(\lambda) = \mathbf{L}\mathbf{G}(\lambda)$ and $\mathbf{G}(\lambda)$ is the inverse defined by equations (17) or (18) for a particular value of λ.

In summary, the computation of LFPs comprises the following steps:

1. Compute the scalar lead field matrix as the product of the vector lead field matrix times the gradient operator matrix. Consider a central difference formula for the evaluation of the numerical gradient.
2. Compute the metric of the source space as described in equations (19) and (20). Select the metric on the data space according the information available as well as the a priori source estimation $\mathbf{f}_p$.
3. Compute the inverse defined by equation (17) or (18) using a regularization parameter obtained by minimizing equation (21). To tune the regularization parameter, consider maps with lower to medium signal-to-noise ratios.
4. To obtain local field potentials, apply the inverse matrix $\mathbf{G}$ to your data.

Statistical Analysis on Single Trials

There are two possibilities to statistically compare single trials from multiple experimental conditions within individual subjects. Either we apply the statistical analysis to the recorded data, with inverse solutions being applied thereafter, or we apply the analysis directly to the inverse solution results. While results from both approaches might considerably differ, there are a certain number of advantages in selecting the second variant. Statistical analysis of scalp maps will result in series of potential maps that when submitted to source localization cannot get rid of the limitations of these methods, that is, ghost and lost sources. Contrarily, the direct statistical comparison of intracranially estimated traces (or features derived from them) can overcome some of these limitations exhibiting results less contaminated by spurious sources and balanced cortical and subcortical activity.

In what follows we describe the experimental paradigm used to record the EEG data and then next two sections explain in more detail the alternatives used to perform statistical analysis over LFPs estimated from single trials in the temporal and spectral domains.

Experimental Paradigm

Subject   A healthy right-handed subject (male, 30 years) completed a self-paced finger-tapping task. The subject was instructed to press at his own rhythm the left mouse button, alternating between the index and middle fingers of a given hand while fixating a white cross at the middle of the computer screen. The interval between successive movements was rather stable at intervals of roughly 500 ms (536 ± 48 ms). The subject was explicitly asked to avoid counting or trying to estimate time to produce rhythm. Two sessions were performed with each hand.

ERP Recording and Analysis   Continuous EEG was acquired with a Geodesics Netamps system (Electrical Geodesics, Inc., USA) from 111 scalp electrodes (impedances <50 kΩ; vertex reference; 1,000 Hz digitization; bandpass filtered 0.1–200 Hz). Head position was stabilized with a head and chin rest. Offline processing of the scalp data consisted uniquely in the identification of artifact-contaminated channels (four) and their interpolation using a simple nearest neighbor's algorithm. Since digitized electrode positions were not available, standard spherical positions provided by Electrical Geodesic, Inc. were used. These positions were projected onto the scalp of the segmented MNI brain.

Given the pace of the subjects movements (~500 ms), the continuous EEG was epoched into periods extending 400 ms premovement to 200 ms postmovement. We restricted here the analysis to the 400 ms period preceding the movement. A total of 680 trials from tapping with the left hand and 634 trials from tapping with the right hand were used. Neither visual nor automatic artifact rejection was applied, and all trials were kept for subsequent analysis.

The precomputed inverse solution (ELECTRA) was then applied to each single trial. Each ELECTRA provided estimates of the 3D distribution of LFP within 4,024 nodes homogeneously distributed within the inner compartment of a realistic head model derived from the Montreal Neurological Institute average brain used by the Human Brain Mapping Consortium. The pixels were restricted to the gray matter of this inner compartment and formed a $6 \times 6 \times 6$ mm regular grid.

Analysis in the Temporal Domain
To evaluate when and where in the brain significant differences are present between two experimental conditions, we can apply a Wilcoxon rank sum test to the ensemble

of LFPs obtained for each single subject at each brain voxel as a function of time. This test can be considered a nonparametric equivalent of the unpaired *t*-test, which assessed whether two independent samples come from the same population. Note that depending on the type of null-hypothesis we would like to test the Wilcoxon test could be replaced by other nonparametric alternatives.

Because the test is applied to every single voxel and every time frame, we have to consider the problem of multiple tests and appropriately adjust our significance criteria. We combine two types of adjustment. In the spatial domain we propose the use of a Bonferroni-type adjustment that considers as the number of tests the actual number of independent samples, that is, the number of electrodes (Grave de Peralta Menendez et al. 2004; Murray et al. 2004) rather than the actual number of pixels in the solution space. In the case of the temporal domain, we propose applying a 20 ms temporal criterion (see Guthrie and Buchwald 1991). As a final step, and to facilitate comparison with more conventional strategies, we apply the ELECTRA source model to the event-related potential data. Although in this chapter we compare two experimental conditions related to the execution of a lateralized motor response, we refer the interested reader to our previous study where we applied this analysis procedure to the examination of auditory-somatosensory multisensory interactions (Gonzalez Andino et al. 2005a).

In summary, the analytic procedure we described can be itemized as follows:

1. Estimate for each single trial the LFP for each brain voxel using ELECTRA. For each experimental condition this step results in a data matrix of

Number of single trials (NS) × Number of voxels (NP) × Time frames (NT).

2. Apply the nonparametric Wilcoxon rank sum test to compare conditions across voxels and time frames. The dependent variable to be compared is LFP amplitude across all single trials. Thus there are NP × NT tests.

3. Adjust the *p*-values for multiple comparisons. First adjust the values for the spatial domain, using the number of independent measurements (i.e., electrodes) and then for the temporal domain using a criterion based on estimations of autocorrelation (e.g., Guthrie and Buchwald 1991).

Results in the Temporal Domain

Significant differentiation between finger tapping with each hand was evident over several contiguous periods prior to, during, and after movement execution. Results are illustrated in figure 3.2 where the significant *p*-values for each pixel (linearly ordered) are plotted as a function of time

Differentiation between right- and left-handed finger tapping seems to be blocky rather than contiguous. Compact periods of significant differences are followed by small periods of no differences between conditions. This aspect is better seen after plotting the obtained *p*-values for a few illustrative brain voxels as in figure 3.3.

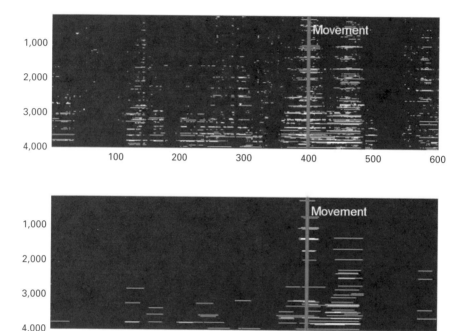

Figure 3.2
Statistical differences between left-handed and right-handed finger tapping in the temporal domain ($p < 0.05$ adjusted both in the spatial and temporal domains). The vertical axis depicts pixels within the head model, and the horizontal axis time relative to movement onset at 400 ms (gray line).

Spatial Distribution of Results in the Temporal Domain

Figure 3.4 displays the spatial distribution of the significant differences between left-hand and right-hand finger tapping obtained above (figure 3.2) as a function of time. The horizontal axis depicts the 400 ms period preceding the execution of the motor response occurring within the frame labeled 380–400. The pictures is constructed by selecting periods when the same pixels remained differentially activated for over 20 ms and computing for each of these periods the mean over time of the p-value. At the initial period (labeled 1–36) significant differential responses were obtained within the parietal lobe. One cluster was centered in the superior parietal lobe (BA 7), and a second in the right and left precuneus (BA 5). During the 300 to 250 ms period before movement onset (labeled 120–150), differential responses remained in very similar areas to those during the preceding period, with the exception that activation along the medial surface of the left hemisphere extended toward the middle cingulate gyrus.

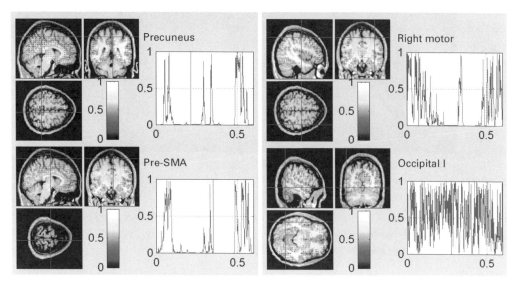

Figure 3.3

Temporally adjusted p-values for some motor and nonmotor areas. The voxels are indicated by the intersection of the blue crosses at the left of each panel. The temporal evolution of the p-value after temporal adjustment is depicted on the right. The horizontal axis depicts the time in seconds with key pressing occurring at 0.4 s. (See plate II.)

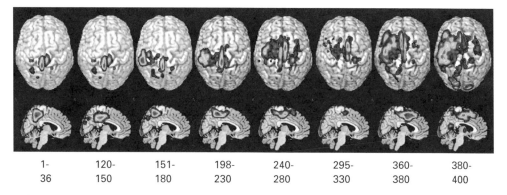

| 1-36 | 120-150 | 151-180 | 198-230 | 240-280 | 295-330 | 360-380 | 380-400 |

Figure 3.4

Spatiotemporal sequence of brain voxels that statistically differ ($p < 0.05$, adjusted) between left and right self-paced finger tapping. The picture is constructed by selecting periods when the same pixels remained differentially activated over time and computing for each of these periods the mean over time of the $(1 - p)$-value. (See plate III.)

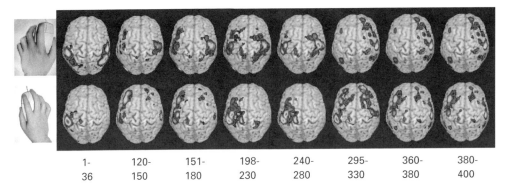

| 1-36 | 120-150 | 151-180 | 198-230 | 240-280 | 295-330 | 360-380 | 380-400 |

Figure 3.5
Electrical neuroimaging (ELECTRA inverse solution) results for the analysis procedure based on ERPs obtained for left-hand (*top plot*) and right-hand finger tapping (*bottom*). The temporal periods presented are identical to those in figure 3.4. (See plate IV.)

The following periods are marked by a shift of the differences toward motor and premotor areas that mainly cover the right hemisphere. Cluster centers are located at the right premotor cortex (BA 6), right inferior parietal gyrus (BA 40, BA 2), the right precentral gyrus (BA 4), the right parietal superior gyrus (BA 7), and the precuneus. The next period comprising 200 to 170 ms before the key press is characterized by an increase of differences at the level of the medial wall involving the SMA/cingulate area. Differences are more widespread for the period that just precedes the movement (labeled 360–380 and 380–400). An overall tendency for a right hemispheric lateralization of differences at the level of motor and parietal cortices is observed for most of the analyzed periods.

Figure 3.5 depicts the results obtained using the averaged ERP at the scalp as the basis for the inverse solution, rather than single trial data. Results are show for both left-hand and right-hand movements for the same periods shown in figure 3.4. In general, for both movements, the ipsilateral and the contralateral, we see that differences between the different periods are smaller than in figure 3.4. Similar areas around the motor and premotor cortex yield differential activity at several stages preceding the movement. However, while movements of the dominant right hand activate nearly exclusively the contralateral left motor cortex, both left and right cortices are activated when the tapping is done with the nondominant left hand. It is also noticeable that activations along the medial wall of the hemisphere are not clearly identified.

Analysis in the Spectral Domain

The goal of the analysis here is to both provide information within individual subjects on oscillatory activity that consistently differ between experimental conditions and also to localize their neural origin. The most convenient approach to obtain spectral information with minimal assumptions is the use of time–frequency representations (Gonzalez Andino et al. 2005b). For the sake of computational simplicity we describe here the test and results employing conventional spectral analysis.

The power spectral density (PSD) was computed for all voxels and single trials during the selected analysis window of 400 ms before motor response, using a multitaper method. The spectral analysis covered the frequency range from 0 to 250 Hz. To evaluate oscillations that consistently differed between left-hand and right-hand finger tapping, we again used a Wilcoxon rank sum test. The multiple test adjustment followed the same procedure as that used for analyses in the temporal domain.

Results in the Spectral Domain

Left and right finger tapping produced statistically significant differences at several frequencies. These results are illustrated in figure 3.6. Significant differences were observed mainly in the high gamma band and extended over a broad band of high-frequency oscillations to encompass frequencies up to 230 Hz. Significant differences

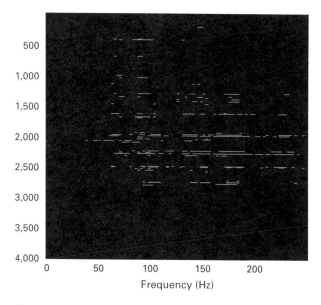

Figure 3.6
Statistical differences between left-handed and right-handed finger tapping in the spectral domain. The vertical axis indicates voxels in the solution space, and the horizontal axis frequencies in Hz. Significant differences after correction for multiple tests are shown (adjusted p-values <0.05 in gray and adjusted p-values <0.01 in white).

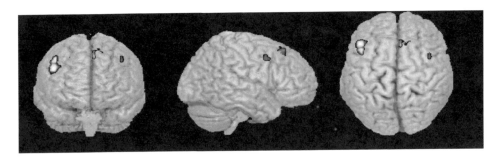

Figure 3.7
3D rendering of brain voxels showing significant differences ($p < 0.01$) in neural oscillations
between left-hand and right-hand self-paced finger tapping.

at the 0.01 level where spatially localized and confined to a few brain voxels that
differed over a broad range of high or even very high-frequency oscillations.

Spatial Distribution of Results in the Spectral Domain
Figure 3.7 depicts a 3D rendering of brain voxels showing significant differences at
the $p < 0.01$ significance level between left-hand and right-hand finger tapping. Results
provide a summary of the 60 to 230 Hz interval, since there is no described division
in the literature for such an elevated range of frequencies. Voxels are restricted to
bilateral premotor areas and the SMA.

Discussion

We have described a methodological approach that combines noninvasive LFP estimation on single trials with statistical procedures to reveal consistent differences between
experimental conditions at the individual subject/patient level. This strategy is illustrated here in the analysis of voluntary finger tapping with the left and right hands,
which yielded some findings that deserve brief discussion.

Differences in response amplitudes between finger movements of the right and left
hands were mainly lateralized to motor areas of the right hemisphere. This lateralization seems to reflect the fact that while dominant hand movements basically activated
contralateral motor areas, nondominant hand movements do also activated ipsilateral
motor areas (Kollias et al. 2001; Tanji 2001; Volkmann et al. 1998). We would note
that similarly bilateral activation was obtained for source estimations based on the
surface ERPs (figure 3.5).

The earliest differential activity was observed within parietal areas and progressed
over time to premotor areas and then to more frontal motor areas. This progression
is consistent with some studies in humans and animals that assign a fundamental role

to parietal areas when finger movements are coordinated with respect to some spatial reference (Binkofski et al. 1999; Snyder et al. 2000). There is consensus that the human parietal cortex is concerned with the representation of visual space and the mediation of attention within this spatial representation (e.g., Marshall and Fink 2001). Parietal cortex seems to be the first stage where motor intention is reflected (Andersen et al. 1997). Lesions to the parietal cortex have been shown to leave patients unaware of their intention to move (Sirigu et al. 2004), and the same patients lack the readiness potential (Libet et al. 1982) commonly associated with the subject's awareness to move. The readiness potential has a maximum approximately 350 ms prior to movement onset, which coincides with the temporal period when we found a differentiation within the parietal cortex.

Concerning the results in the spectral domain it is interesting that oscillatory activity differences were confined to frequencies far above the classical definition of gamma band (30–80 Hz) considered relevant in electrophysiological studies. Similarly interesting is that effects were not observed in either the alpha or beta bands, both of which have conventionally been used in EEG-based neuroprosthetic control (Wolpaw and McFarland 2004). The present results coincide with a more extended EEG analysis over twelve healthy subjects performing a visuomotor reaction time task (Grave de Peralta Menendez et al. 2006). In this study a different measure of statistical differences was used to asess oscillations differing between left- and right-hand movements. It was consistently observed that differences between hand responses were marked by neural oscillations above 30 Hz and extending up to 220 Hz. A likely reason to explain why such high-frequency oscillations are seldom reported is the fact that human electrophysiology often systematically dismisses oscillations above 80 Hz. This is likely due to the relatively low amplitude of oscillations with frequencies above around 30 Hz, which are further obscured by lower frequency activity of higher amplitude. Nevertheless, recent studies on rats and cats report a correlation between neural oscillations above 100 Hz and extending up to 200 Hz with attentive exploration and visual processing (Chrobak and Buzsaki 1996; Grenier et al. 2001; Siegel and Konig 2003). Intracerebral recordings in monkeys show that 600 Hz oscillations are modulated by somatosensory stimulation (Baker et al. 2003) and that this modulation reflects the timing of cortical spike bursts. Differential oscillatory activity between left and right finger tapping was spatially localized to premotor cortical areas and the SMA. Such focal somatotopic organization coincides well with reports using intracranial recordings in patients that show that high-frequency oscillations in the gamma or even high gamma band are more somatotopically specific and spatially restricted than oscillations in the alpha/beta bands.

The single-trial analysis procedures described in this chapter lead to results that are consistent with available neurophysiological data as previously observed for the case of auditory-somatosensory multisensory data (Gonzalez Andino et al. 2005d).

Interestingly the delineation of the motor areas is better observed in the single-trial analysis than in the averaged ERP. This finding, which might be surprising since the single-trial responses have a worse signal-to-noise ratio than the ERP, is nonetheless quite reasonable considering the known limitations of linear inverse solutions (Grave de Peralta and Gonzalez Andino 1998). The analysis procedure applied here relies on the statistical comparison between two experimental conditions. Such analysis facilitates the detection of deep activity differing systematically between both. This is well exemplified here for the SMA/cingulate activation that dominates the single-trial maps for certain time periods and is not observable in the inverse solutions based on the averaged ERP most likely due to the strong dominance of the activation in nearby motor cortex. Similarly ghost sources common to both conditions tend to disappear. Interestingly these features are exclusive to the type of processing proposed here, namely statistical comparison of the results of the inverse solution. If the statistical comparison is directly done on the recorded EEG data and the localization procedure is applied to the statistically different EEG maps, then the limitations of the inverse solutions will certainly manifest and the resultant image will lack statistical significance.

The approach demonstrated here for analyzing single trials based on contrast between two or more experimental conditions is not exempt from the need to record multiple repetitions of a given task. What it does avoid is the need for averaging the multiple repetitions, a process that will eliminate or smooth out events not tightly time-locked to a given stimulus/response. This aspect is particularly important for understanding the role of oscillatory activity in brain processing and associating it to their neural origins, since no available neuroimaging technique currently exists for this purpose. Results obtained in the spectral domain in this study are highly encouraging in this direction.

Conclusion

This chapter describes the theoretical basis of the noninvasive estimation of LFPs from scalp-recorded data and their application to the computation of single subject images of statistical value reflecting differences in the spectral/temporal domain between experimental conditions. The first step is to convert the scalp data into estimates of intracranial LFPs by means of ELECTRA, an electrical neuroimaging method that relies on biophysical constraints to single out a solution to the bioelectromagnetic inverse problem. The proposed method compares experimental conditions over the single repetitions at all gray matter voxels using a nonparametric statistical test. This can be performed either with the amplitudes of the estimated LFPs or the strength of the neural oscillations. The method then provides information about the brain areas that differ between both experimental conditions for the particular selected feature (i.e., amplitudes over time or spectral power). Performance of the method is illustrated through the comparison of self-paced rhythmic tapping with the left and right hands, and the results are contrasted with those obtained in the more common analyses using the averaged responses (the ERPs). The analysis performed on the LFP amplitudes from unfiltered single-trial data is shown to differ from the instantaneous localization obtained from the averaged responses, with the former providing a richer distribution of motor areas and clarifying their temporal sequence of activation. Specifically a stable differentiation between the laterality of the movements is first observed within parietal areas and primary motor, followed slightly later by premotor cortex and the SMA. This temporal sequence is in solid agreement with results of electrophysiological recordings in primates.

Acknowledgments

Swiss National Foundation Grant 3152A0-100745, the IM2.MI on Brain Machines Interfaces, and the European Projects MAIA and BACS supported this work.

References

Andersen RA, Snyder LH, Bradley DC, Xing J. 1997. Multimodal representation of space in the posterior parietal cortex and its use in planning movements. *An Rev Neurosci* 20:303–30.

Baker SN, Curio G, Lemon RN. 2003. EEG oscillations at 600 Hz are macroscopic markers for cortical spike bursts. *J Physiol (Lond)* 550:529–34.

Binkofski F, Buccino G, Posse S, Seitz RJ, Rizzolatti G, Freund H. 1999. A fronto-parietal circuit for object manipulation in man: evidence from an fMRI-study. *Eur J Neurosci* 11:3276–86.

Chrobak JJ, Buzsaki G. 1996. High-frequency oscillations in the output networks of the hippocampal-entorhinal axis of the freely behaving rat. *J Neurosci* 16:3056–66.

Davies AR. 1992. Optimality in regularization. NATO Advanced Research Workshop, Brussels, 393–410.

Fuchs M, Wagner M, Köhler T, Wischmann H. 1999. Linear and nonlinear current density reconstructions. *J Clin Neurophysiol* 13:267–95.

Gonzalez Andino S, Murray MM, Foxe J, Menendez R. 2005a. How single-trial electrical neuroimaging contributes to multisensory research. *Exp Brain Res* 166:298–304.

Gonzalez Andino SL, Grave de Peralta Menendez R, Khateb A, Landis T, Pegna AJ. 2008. Electrophysiological correlates of affective blindsight. *Neuroimage,* forthcoming.

Gonzalez Andino SL, Grave de Peralta Menendez R, Khateb A, Pegna AJ, Thut G, Landis T. 2007. A glimpse into your vision. *Hum Brain Mapp* 28:614–24.

Gonzalez Andino SL, Michel CM, Thut G, Landis T, Grave de Peralta Menendez R. 2005b. Prediction of response speed by anticipatory high-frequency (gamma band) oscillations in the human brain. *Hum Brain Mapp* 24:50–8.

Gonzalez Andino SL, Murray MM, Foxe J, Grave de Peralta Menendez R. 2005c. How single-trial electrical neuroimaging contributes to multisensory research. *Exp Brain Res* 166:298–304.

Gonzalez Andino SL, Murray MM, Foxe J, Grave de Peralta Menendez R. 2005d. How single-trial electrical neuroimaging contributes to multisensory research. *Exp Brain Res* 166:46.

Grave de Peralta Menendez R, Gonzalez Andino S, Lantz G, Michel CM, Landis T. 2001. Noninvasive localization of electromagnetic epileptic activity. I. Method descriptions and simulations. *Brain Topogr* 14:131–7.

Grave de Peralta Menendez R, Gonzalez Andino SL. 2000. Discussing the capabilities of Laplacian minimization. Brain Topogr 13:97–104.

Grave de Peralta Menendez R, Gonzalez Andino SL. 2008. Non-invasive estimates of local field potentials for brain-computer interfaces: theoretical derivation and comparisons with direct intracarnial recordings. In: Bozovic V, ed. *Medical Robotics*. Vienna: I-Tec Education and Publishing, 103–16.

Grave de Peralta Menendez R, Gonzalez Andino SL, Michel CM, Millan J, Pun T. 2003. Direct non-invasive brain computer interfaces. 9th Int Conf Functional Mapping of the Human Brain.

Grave de Peralta Menendez R, Gonzalez Andino SL, Morand S, Michel CM, Landis T. 2000. Imaging the electrical activity of the brain: ELECTRA. *Hum Brain Mapp* 9:1–12.

Grave de Peralta Menendez R, Gonzalez Andino SL, Perez L, Ferrez P, Millan J. 2005. Non-invasive estimation of local field potentials for neuroprosthesis control. *Cogn Process* 6:59–64.

Grave de Peralta Menendez R, Morier P, Picard F, Landis T, Gonzalez Andino SL. 2006. Simple techniques for EEG source imaging. Int J Bioelectromagnet 8:v/1–8.

Grave de Peralta Menendez R, Murray MM, Michel CM, Martuzzi R, Gonzalez Andino SL. 2004. Electrical neuroimaging based on biophysical constraints. *NeuroImage* 21:527–39.

Grave de Peralta Menendez R, Gonzalez-Andino SL. 1998. A critical analysis of linear inverse solutions to the neuroelectromagnetic inverse problem. *IEEE Trans Biomed Eng* 45:440–8.

Greenblatt RE. 1993. Probabilistic reconstruction of multiple sources in the bioelectromagnetic inverse problem. *Inv Probl* 9:271–84.

Grenier F, Timofeev I, Steriade M. 2001. Focal synchronization of ripples (80–200 Hz) in neocortex and their neuronal correlates. *J Neurophysiol* 86:1884–98.

Hämäläinen M, Ilmoniemi RH, Knuutila J, Lounasmaa OV. 1993. Magnetoencephalography: theory, instrumentation, and applications to noninvasive studies of the working human brain. *Rev Mod Phys* 65:413–97.

Kollias SS, Alkadhi H, Jaermann T, Crelier G, Hepp-Reymond MC. 2001. Identification of multiple nonprimary motor cortical areas with simple movements. *Brain Res Brain Res Rev* 36:185–95.

Libet B, Wright EW Jr, Gleason CA. 1982. Readiness-potentials preceding unrestricted "spontaneous" vs. pre-planned voluntary acts. *Electroencephalogr Clin Neurophysiol* 54:322–35.

Menke W. 1989. *Geophysical Data Analysis: Discrete Inverse Theory,* rev ed. New York: Academic Press.

Michel CM, Murray MM, Lantz G, Gonzalez S, Spinelli L, Grave de Peralta R. 2004. EEG source imaging. *Clin Neurophysiol* 115:2195–222.

Morand S, Thut G, Grave de Peralta R, Clarke S, Khateb A, Landis T, Michel CM. 2000. Electrophysiological evidence for fast visual processing through the human koniocellular pathway when stimuli move. *Cereb Cortex* 10:817–25.

Muller-Putz GR, Scherer R, Pfurtscheller G, Rupp R. 2006. Brain-computer interfaces for control of neuroprostheses: from synchronous to asynchronous mode of operation. *Biomed Tech (Berl)* 51:57–63.

Nicolelis MA. 2001. Actions from thoughts. *Nature* 409:403–7.

Plonsey R. 1982. The nature of sources of bioelectric and biomagnetic fields. *Biophys J* 39:309–12.

Plonsey R, Heppner DB. 1967. Considerations of quasi-stationarity in electrophysiological systems. *Bull Math Biophys* 29:657–64.

Poulton CG, Botten LC, McPhedran RC, Movchan AB. 1999. Source-neutral Green's functions for periodic problems in electrostatics, and their equivalents in electromagnetism. *Proc R Soc (Lond)* A455:1107–23.

Sarvas J. 1987. Basic mathematical and electromagnetic concepts of the biomagnetic inverse problem. *Phys Med Biol* 32:11–22.

Scherg M. 1994. From EEG source localization to source imaging. *Acta Neurol Scand* 152(suppl):29–30.

Siegel M, Konig P. 2003. A functional gamma-band defined by stimulus-dependent synchronization in area 18 of awake behaving cats. J Neurosci 23:4251–60.

Sirigu A, Daprati E, Ciancia S, Giraux P, Nighoghossian N, Posada A, Haggard P. 2004. Altered awareness of voluntary action after damage to the parietal cortex. *Nat Neurosci* 7:80–4.

Snyder LH, Batista AP, Andersen RA. 2000. Intention-related activity in the posterior parietal cortex: a review: *Vision Res* 40:1433–41.

Tanji J. 2001. Sequential organization of multiple movements: involvement of cortical motor areas. *An Rev Neurosci* 24:631–51.

Thut G, Blanke O, Gonzalez S, Grave de Peralta R, Michel CM. 2001. Spatial distribution and strength of early visual EPs in humans: effects of motor significance of the stimulus and attention. *NeuroImage* 13:1267.

Tikhonov AN, Arsenin VY. 1977. *Solutions of Ill-posed Problems*. New York: Wiley.

van Oosterom A. 1991. History and evolution of methods for solving the inverse problem. *J Clin Neurophysiol* 8:371–80.

Volkmann J, Schnitzler A, Witte OW, Freund HJ. 1998. Handedness and asymmetry of hand representation in human motor cortex. *J Neurophysiol* 79:2149–54.

Vrba J, Robinson SE. 2001. Signal processing in magnetoencephalography. *Methods* 25:249–71.

Wolpaw JR, McFarland DJ. 2004. Control of a two-dimensional movement signal by a noninvasive brain-computer interface in humans. *Proc Natl Acad Sci USA* 101:17849–54.

4   A Practical Guide to Beamformer Source Reconstruction for EEG

Jessica J. Green and John J. McDonald

Electrophysiological measures, such as electoencephalography (EEG) and magnetoencephalography (MEG), have been used widely in cognitive neuroscience to examine human brain function noninvasively. Compared to hemodynamic techniques for examining brain function, like functional magnetic resonance imaging (fMRI) and positron emission tomography (PET), EEG provides a relatively low-cost means of exploring the neural basis of human cognition. The principal advantage of EEG/MEG over hemodynamic-based neuroimaging is the improvement in temporal precision: EEG and MEG provide information about neural activities on the order of milliseconds, whereas fMRI provides information about neural activity on the order of seconds to minutes. However, the advantage in temporal precision is coupled with a disadvantage in spatial precision: For EEG and MEG, there is simply no one-to-one relationship between the electromagnetic fields observed at the scalp and the underlying neural sources (i.e., the inverse problem). Consequently there is always a degree of uncertainty involved in localizing the neuroanatomical sources of EEG/MEG data. Fortunately new analytical techniques have been developed to estimate the neural sources of EEG/MEG so that researchers can investigate patterns of human brain activity in both space and time.

Traditionally the neural sources of electrical fields observed at the scalp have been modeled as being generated by a small number of equivalent current dipoles. These dipoles are positioned at the "best-fitting" locations using algorithms that attempt to maximize the amount of variance in the signal that is explained by a particular number of dipoles. The problem inherent in this method is that the number of dipolar sources must be determined in advance. Thus the resultant models of neural activity can be highly dependent on user input (see Luck 2005 for additional discussion). For example, in the case of a frontocentrally distributed ERP component, a user may decide to model the data with either one dipole or two laterally constrained dipoles depending on specific hypotheses, known physiology, and various other factors. A one-dipole model might account for the fronto-central ERP with a source in the vicinity of the anterior cingulate cortex (e.g., error-related negativity; van Veen and Carter 2002), whereas a laterally constrained two-dipole model might account for the same ERP with bilateral sources in the vicinity of auditory cortices (e.g., mismatch negativity; Scherg, Vajsar, and Picton 1989). Both models would fit the data reasonably well, but they would point to very different underlying neural sources. In some cases it may be relatively straightforward to determine the most likely number of discrete neural sources contributing to an ERP component (e.g., sensory-evoked ERP components), but in most situations the number of neural sources contributing to an ERP is not entirely clear. Although there are many ways to facilitate decisions about the number of active dipolar sources (i.e., independent component analysis, Makeig et al. 1996; principal component analysis, Dien and Frishkoff 2005) and to constrain models based on anatomical and functional information from other methodologies (Grent-'t-Jong and Woldorff 2007; Hopfinger, Khoe, and Song 2005), in recent years source modeling techniques that do not require any a priori assumptions about the number of active sources contributing to the scalp recorded activity have become increasingly popular.

One source analysis technique that is becoming more widely used is the beamformer spatial filter. The beamformer provides independent estimates of source activities at multiple locations throughout the brain, resulting in a three-dimensional image of brain function. The beamformer method has been in use for a handful of years now for MEG source estimation (Herdman and Cheyne, chapter 5 in this volume; see also Hillebrand et al. 2005 for a review), but it has been implemented for EEG in freely or commercially available software packages only recently. Although the beamformer technique avoids the problem inherent in traditional dipole modeling of specifying the number of sources in advance, it is not without assumptions and limitations. At present the literature on beamforming consists primarily of technical papers, which makes it difficult for many new users to gain a conceptual and practical understanding of the method. Therefore what follows is a relatively nonmathematical introduction to the beamforming method as applied to EEG, along with examples and discussion of some practical considerations.

What Is a Beamformer?

The beamformer is a signal-processing technique developed originally for radar and sonar applications to discriminate between signals arriving from a location of interest and signals arriving from other locations. For EEG data the beamformer is a set of weights that are used to spatially filter the scalp-recorded data to yield an estimate of the source power for a specific location in the brain. These weights are calculated to pick up signals that originate from a specific location while simultaneously minimizing signals that originate from other locations. This way the beamformer is a spatial filter that allows signals from one location to pass unfiltered while filtering out (although not completely) signals from other locations. A separate beamformer is constructed for each location in the brain independently, resulting in a three-dimensional estimate of source power throughout the brain.

In practice, the first step is to establish locations at which the beamformer spatial filter will be applied to estimate source activity. A beamformer can be applied to a specific region of interest to determine activity at just that location, but it is more common to apply separate beamformers to evenly spaced points in a three-dimensional grid throughout the entire source space. Once the three-dimensional grid of points has been established, the next step is to create a forward model that determines how a source at each point would contribute to the signals measured on the scalp. The forward model of a dipole source at one location in the grid is often referred to as the lead field matrix, with a separate lead field matrix calculated for each source location in the three-dimensional grid.

The goal of beamforming is to determine the strength of the dipolar source at each point, but dipolar sources also vary in their location and orientation. Because only the location of the dipole is fixed, the beamformer algorithm also needs to determine the orientation of the dipole. A nonlinear beamformer implemented for MEG—called synthetic aperture magnetometry (SAM; Robinson and Vrba 1999)—uses an iterative procedure to optimize the dipole orientation over the time window of interest and fixes it at that orientation for the beamformer calculations. In this case the lead field matrix is an $N \times 1$ vector (where N is the number of electrodes or MEG sensors) that contains only the contributions of a dipolar source of the optimized orientation to the measured signals at the scalp. Alternatively, linear beamformers (also called vector beamformers) that have been developed for EEG data often make use of regional sources rather than individual dipoles. The regional source consists of three dipoles with orthogonal orientations to account for activity in the x, y, and z planes. In this case the lead field matrix contains the forward solution for each of the three source orientations, resulting in an $N \times 3$ matrix with a row for each electrode location and a column from each dipole orientation. In essence, separate estimates of source power are calculated for all dipole orientations and are summed together to create a single source power estimate for that source location (Sekihara et al. 2001; van Drongelen et al. 1996; Van Veen et al. 1997).

In simplest terms, the estimate of source power is the result of applying the beamformer weights (i.e., the spatial filter) to the scalp recorded data. Mathematically the spatial filter is a function of the lead field matrix and the data covariance matrix, and an estimate of neural power can be computed from these two values alone (see van Drongelen et al. 1996 for a good mathematical explanation). The data covariance matrix is usually calculated from the single trial EEG epochs. Because of this, the beamformer can estimate source power based on both the evoked activities (i.e., averaged ERPs) and the induced activities that are typically eliminated through averaging. Typically the scalp recorded EEG is first transformed into the time–frequency domain prior to beamformer analysis. For time–frequency data the beamformer calculations are the same but the input is slightly different. Rather than using the raw single-trial EEG epochs, the epochs are first transformed into the time–frequency domain. Then the power for a particular frequency in a time interval of interest is used to calculate the cross-spectral density matrix, the time–frequency equivalent of the data covariance matrix

Cancellation of Correlated Source Activities

The most-cited drawback of the beamformer source estimation is an inability to localize correlated source activities. The main assumption of the beamformer calculations is that the activity at the source location of interest is not linearly correlated with activity at any other source location. The spatial filter is designed to minimize output variance by canceling the correlated portion of activity for the source of interest (Van Veen et al. 1997). If the activities of two sources are perfectly correlated with one another the beamformer source power estimate will be near zero. Such high correlations occur when there is little or no variability across trials in the timing of responses in two or more brain regions. Unfortunately, this is often the case during evoked sensory responses. For example, in the auditory modality sensory signals are transmitted to both left and right auditory cortices simultaneously, which results in almost perfectly correlated activities in the two hemispheres. Use of a traditional beamformer algorithm will not show these sources in the source reconstruction (Van Veen et al. 1997). Correlated activities can be observed not only in homologous regions of the left and right brain hemispheres but also in brain regions working in concert to control higher level cognitive processes such as attention or working memory.

Currently there are two main ways of dealing with the problem of correlated source activities. The first way involves simply using a longer time interval for imaging. The problem with beamforming lies with source activities being correlated in time, so it may be that over a longer period of time the correlation between the activities is reduced to the point where both sources can be localized. Simulation studies have suggested that accurate source power estimates can be obtained as long as the source activities are correlated for less than approximately 40 percent of the time interval used in calculations (Hadjipapas et al. 2005). However, in some situations the use of longer time intervals is not desirable and may not solve the problem of correlated sources. For example, the steady-state evoked potential would be correlated throughout the recording interval (Herdman et al. 2003).

The second way of dealing with correlated sources involves accounting for correlated activities in the beamformer calculations explicitly. This can be done quite easily when the locations of potentially correlated sources are known in advance, such as when sensory stimulation leads to simultaneous activation of homologous sensory regions of the two brain hemispheres. Several strategies have been developed to enable beamformer localization of correlated activities at homologous locations in the two hemispheres. One strategy is to compute beamformers using only the sensors over one hemisphere at a time so that highly correlated activity picked up over the other hemisphere is not part of the beamformer calculations (Herdman et al. 2003; see also chapter 5 of this volume). This strategy is feasible only when different sensors pick up the correlated source activities; it is not generally advisable for EEG because the electrical fields associated with neural source activity can be picked up over large portions of the scalp. A second strategy that works for both MEG and EEG is to include the homologous location in the opposite brain hemisphere in the forward model. For example, a bilateral beamformer has been implemented in the BESA software package. The bilateral beamformer is simply the extension of the traditional linear beamformer algorithm that accounts for correlated activities in homologous regions of the two hemispheres. In the typical beamformer calculations the forward model (lead field matrix) is calculated for a regional source (three orthogonally oriented dipoles) located at one of the three-dimensional grid locations. This lead field matrix has the dimensions $N \times 3$, with one row for each electrode location and a column for each dipole orientation. The bilateral beamformer simply includes a second regional source in the forward model—a source at the homologous location in the opposite hemisphere. The lead field matrix then becomes an $N \times 6$ matrix, with a column for each dipole orientation for each source location. Other researchers have further developed this idea into methods that will allow imaging of correlated sources in any location by adding locations to the forward model (Brookes et al. 2007). However, this is computationally intensive and has not yet been implemented in any software packages.

To demonstrate the performance of both the traditional and the bilateral beamformer algorithms under conditions involving correlated sources of activity, we created simulated data with either perfectly correlated source activities (i.e., 100 percent) or highly correlated source activities (i.e., 85 percent). Three-hundred trials of simulated EEG were created for 64-scalp electrodes using a three-shell spherical head model. For the three simulations, two sources were placed bilaterally in auditory cortex, bilaterally in anterior cingulate cortex, or in the frontal and parietal cortices of the right hemisphere. We then used either the traditional beamformer of the bilateral beamformer to localize the activities. Figure 4.1 shows single horizontal slices from the beamformer scans plotted in three dimensions, where the x and y axes map the coordinates of the grid points for that head slice and the z axis corresponds to the beamformer source power. Distinct peaks in the graphs correspond to well-defined centroids of estimated source activities.

Figure 4.1a through 4.1c shows source power estimates using a traditional beamformer to localize correlated source activities in homologous regions of the two cortical

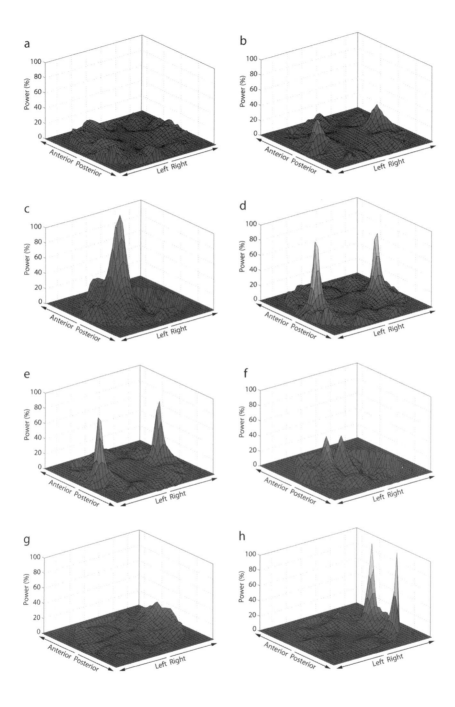

hemispheres. Not surprisingly, the beamformer failed to localize perfectly correlated activities near the lateral surfaces of the temporal lobes (figure 4.1a). However, the beamformer did locate the sources correctly when the correlation of these source activities was reduced to 85 percent (figure 4.1b). That is, the two main peaks in the graph coincided with the locations of the dipolar sources in the temporal lobes. This indicates that in practice the beamformer has difficulties only with sources that are very highly correlated. As long as there is some variability in the timing of activities across trials the beamformer is able to tease apart the sources. The performance of the beamformer in the presence of temporally correlated activities will also vary somewhat depending on the locations of the sources. Correlated sources that are close together will lead to different results than correlated sources that are in distant brain regions (Van Veen et al. 1997). In contrast to the dramatic reduction in source power for correlated activities in lateral temporal lobe (figure 4.1a), when perfectly correlated sources were located in homologous regions of cortex on the medial surface (i.e., anterior cingulate cortex), the source activities were merged into one high-amplitude source in between the two simulated sources (figure 4.1c).

Figure 4.1d through 4.1f shows source power estimates of the same simulated data used in figure 4.1a through 4.1c obtained using a bilateral beamformer. Because the correlated sources in lateral temporal cortex are in homologous regions of the two hemispheres, the bilateral beamformer produces the same output when the sources are perfectly (figure 4.1d) or very highly (figure 4.1e) correlated. When the correlated sources are located bilaterally on the medial surface, the bilateral beamformer separates them into two distinct sources on either side of the midline (figure 4.1f).

At first glance it might seem like the inclusion of the homologue source in the lead field matrix could spuriously produce bilateral sources in the beamformer output. Fortunately, if there truly is a source in only one hemisphere, the beamformer output

Figure 4.1
Effect of correlations between sources on beamformer source reconstruction. The traditional beamformer fails to localize 100 percent correlated sources that are distantly located, as in bilateral auditory activity (a) but is still be able to pick up some activity when the correlation between source activities is lowered to 85 percent (b). When 100 percent correlated activities are closely located, as in bilateral medial frontal activity, the source activities merge together into a single source in between the two actual sources (c). Using the bilateral beamformer, which accounts for correlated activity in the homologue region of the opposite hemisphere, both 100 percent correlated (d) and 85 percent correlated (e) activities in auditory cortex are localizable. With the bilateral beamformer the bilateral activity in medial frontal cortex is separated into two distinct sources (f). When correlated activities occur in the same hemisphere the traditional and bilateral beamformers behave the same way, with 100 percent correlated activity resulting in a reduction in amplitude and smearing of the source locations (g), while 85 percent correlated sources are discriminable (h).

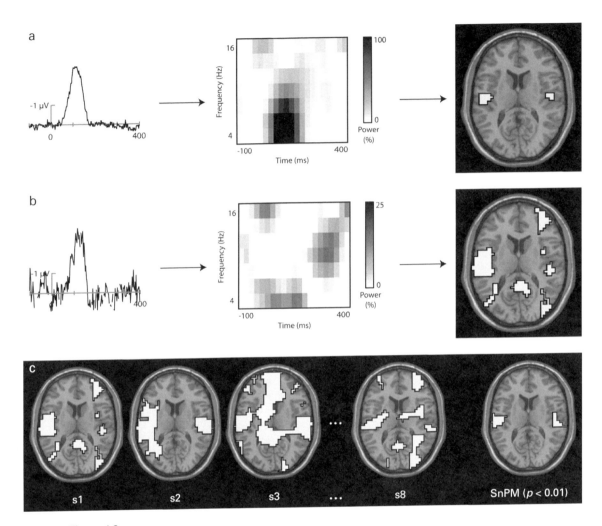

Figure 4.2
Effect of noise on beamformer source reconstruction. (a) The average ERP, time–frequency plot, and beamformer output for a pair of bilateral sources in auditory cortex for data with a high signal-to-noise ratio. (b) The same signal with increased background noise. Information about the activity of interest is difficult to extract from the background noise, resulting in lower power in the time–frequency domain and spurious sources in the beamformer output. (c) Nonparametric statistics performed across a group of participants' separate sources of activity from noise that varies randomly across participants.

will accurately reflect this. The inclusion of an additional source location in the lead field matrix simply eliminates the cancellation of correlated activities between those source locations that occurs in the standard beamformer implementation. When correlated activities occur in the same hemisphere the traditional and bilateral beamformers behave the same way, with 100 percent correlated activity resulting in a reduction in amplitude and smearing of the source locations (figure 4.1g), while 85 percent correlated sources are discriminable (figure 4.1h).

Practical Considerations

Noise

Noisy EEG data (i.e., low signal-to-noise ratio) is a problem for all EEG source analysis methods, including the beamformer. The raw beamformer estimate represents the combined neural activity of sources and noise. Increased noise from background EEG or external interference can increase the spatial spread of activity making it difficult to tease apart sources that are close together and can potentially mask sources whereby the signal of interest is indistinguishable from the background noise. Noise in the EEG can also introduce spurious sources of activity. Thus the raw source power has to be normalized by an estimate of the noise activity.

For the analysis of individual participants' data, the impact of noise on beamformer source estimates can be reduced by accounting for background noise in the beamformer calculations explicitly. Most beamformer algorithms use estimates of background activity, either from a prestimulus baseline period or a control condition, to normalize the source power output for the signal of interest. Unfortunately, data from individual participants are often quite noisy, even after the beamformer output is normalized with an estimate of the noise. As can be seen in figure 4.2, with very low noise the signal of interest shows up strongly in the time–frequency plot, and the beamformer output shows tightly focused sources (figure 4.2a). However, when noise is added to the same signal, power in the time–frequency plot is greatly reduced, and the beamformer output shows spurious "sources" that do not correspond to the location of the signal (figure 4.2b).

If the spurious noise sources in the beamformer output are randomly distributed for each individual participant, statistical analysis can help tease apart the actual and spurious sources. To demonstrate the effects of statistical analysis on moderately noisy data, we created eight simulated data sets by slightly varying (i.e., less than 1 cm in each of the x, y, and z planes) the locations of a bilateral pair of sources in the superior temporal lobes (figure 4.2c). For each individual data set (akin to an individual participant), the beamformer source power estimate includes not only the activity of the actual sources but also the activity of spurious noise sources. However, the results of a nonparametric statistical analysis of the eight data sets more accurately reflect the actual source locations in superior temporal cortices.

Active and Control Conditions

In most implementations of the beamformer the estimated source power is output relative to a prestimulus baseline or a control condition. As mentioned in the previous section, the beamformer calculations for the condition of interest estimate the neural activity of the combined signal and noise in the data. Calculations are performed on this baseline or control condition to serve as an estimate of the noise distribution in the data. For the output source power to accurately reflect the signal of interest, the noise estimate needs to be representative of the noise present in the condition of interest.

Even before data are recorded, a decision should be made about whether one would like to examine the activity in a single condition or the difference between two conditions. If the goal of the study is to estimate the neural sources of an individual ERP component (e.g., the visual P1 or the auditory N1) or a change in oscillatory activity in a single condition (e.g., gamma activity in response to a stimulus), a prestimulus baseline would be used. If the goal of the study is to examine the difference in neural activity between two tasks (e.g., differences in neural activity between focused and divided attention), then one of the tasks is designated the control task and source power estimates are provided relative to the activity in the control condition. When only a single condition is of interest, it is important that the baseline period be chosen carefully so that noise estimate is representative of the noise present in the signal of interest. This may simply mean ensuring that there is a long enough prestimulus interval that the baseline will not be contaminated by activity from responses to other stimuli or other cognitive events.

When the comparison of two active conditions is of interest there are two further considerations that should be taken into account. First, the number of trials in the two conditions should be approximately the same, as the number of trials will change the signal-to-noise ratio of the data. If the signal quality is different between the two active conditions being compared, then the output source power will reflect not only changes in neural activity related to the process of interest but also differences in noise levels. This could potentially introduce spurious noise related sources into the source reconstruction. Prior to conducting an experiment where beamforming is the ultimate goal, consideration of the number of trials in the conditions to be compared should be made. As with ERPs the number of trials is unlikely to be identical as some trials will be rejected due to artifacts like blinks and eye movements. However, large differences in the number of trials should be avoided. For example, if the comparison of interest is between activities preceding correct and incorrect responses but incorrect responses only account for 20 percent of the trials, then some adjustment should to be made, possibly by randomly selecting only 20 percent of the correct responses. In most software packages the analysis will proceed regardless of the number of trials. Thus it is up to the researcher to ensure that they have as close to the same number of trials in each condition as possible.

Second, the baseline activity should be approximately equal in both conditions. For example, a researcher may wish to compare the alpha-band activity in low- and high-load working memory conditions that occur in different blocks of an experiment. Baseline alpha oscillations may be very different in the high-load blocks where more cognitive effort is required. The degree and timing of alpha modulation observed in response to the stimulus display may very well be dependent on the background levels of alpha, making it difficult to determine if differences observed between the conditions are due to the experimental manipulation, differences in the overall level of alpha-band activity, or an interaction between the two. Thus, prior to any comparisons between conditions, the time–frequency analysis should be performed on each individual condition and the baseline levels of activity between the conditions should be assessed. If there are no differences in baseline activities, then the direct comparison of the conditions is valid. However, as with the number of trials, the analysis will proceed regardless of whether this comparison is appropriate, placing the onus once again on the researcher to fully explore the data.

Number of Trials

The number of trials necessary for the beamformer calculations will depend on a number of factors, such as the number of channels from which EEG is recorded and how the data are used for estimation of the covariance matrix. Because the beamformer calculation requires inversion of the covariance matrix, the number of data points must be larger than the number of electrodes (Van Veen et al. 1997). Satisfying this requirement will ensure that the covariance matrix is nonsingular (i.e., can be inverted). A good rule of thumb is to have at least three times the number of data points as there are electrodes. This would mean at least 300 data points for a 100-channel recording.

Given a data set recorded from 100 channels at a sampling rate of 500 Hz, it is possible to localize activity of interest—say an event-related response peaking 100 ms after the onset of an auditory stimulus—using three different strategies to estimate the covariance matrix: (1) one sample point of EEG data for each trial, (2) consecutive sample points from the averaged ERP waveforms, or (3) a small number of consecutive sample points around latency of interest for each trial (van Drongelen et al. 1996; Van Veen et al. 1997). For many experimental paradigms it is not possible, or practical, to obtain hundreds of trials in each condition for each participant. If a single sample point is used for each trial, then for a 100-channel recording at least 300 trials would be necessary. For many experimental paradigms it is not possible, or practical, to obtain this many trials for each subject. Using the averaged ERP, which would eliminate the need for many trials, to obtain 300 data points would require 600 ms of data. However, it is assumed that each data sample used to estimate the covariance matrix represents activity in the same brain locations (Van Veen et al. 1997). In most situations a time interval of this length is unlikely to satisfy the assumption that each data sample represents the same underlying activity. A more practical solution may be to use five consecutive data samples around the peak of activity (i.e., 145–155 ms), which would require only 60 trials. Thus how many trials you need will depend on how you estimate the covariance matrix.

Number of EEG Channels

In theory, the beamformer measures signals from within a spatial passband and attenuates signals from outside the spatial passband. In practice, however, the number of signals outside the spatial passband (i.e., at different locations) that can be filtered out depends on the number of electrodes from which data are recorded. The number of interfering sources that can be filtered out is approximately one-third of the number of electrodes ($N/3 - 1$, where N is the number of electrodes; Van Veen et al. 1997). If data are recorded from 32 electrodes, the maximum number of interfering sources that can be completely filtered out is approximately 9, whereas if data are recorded from 64 or 128 channels, that number increases to approximately 20 or 42 respectively.

Improvement in beamformer localization has been demonstrated when the number of channels increases from 20 to 32 to 64 channels (van Drongelen et al. 1996). It has also been demonstrated that the spatial resolution of dipole source localization improves as the number of electrodes increases, up to approximately 100 electrodes, at which point no further improvement is observed (Gevins 1990; Slotnick 2005). This limit appears to hold true for beamformer source reconstruction as well. We simulated EEG with 64, 128, and 256 electrodes for a single source of activity in parietal cortex. The results of the beamformer source reconstruction can be seen in figure 4.3. For each electrode montage, the beamformer output was centered on the location of the

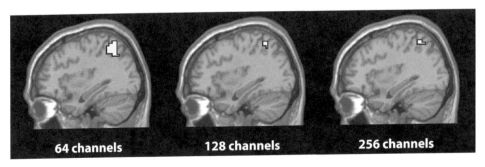

Figure 4.3
Beamformer localization of the same simulated source activity using 64, 128, or 256 electrodes. The peak location of activity is the same for all three channel montages, but with only 64 channels there is greater spatial spread of activity to surrounding regions. No improvement is observed by increasing the number of channels from 128 to 256.

dipole source. However, differences in the spatial extent of the activity were observed across the three electrode montages. Increasing the number of electrodes from 64 to 128 produced a decrease in the amount of spread of the activity. In other words, with 128 channels the beamformer's estimate of the source location was more tightly focused. No such change was observed when the number of EEG channels was increased from 128 to 256. In addition the increase in number of channels also requires an increase in the number of data points needed to calculate the spatial filter (see the previous section). Thus using more than 128 channels will require more data and is unlikely to improve the ability of the beamformer to estimate source activity.

Choice of Head Model

The electric fields produced by neural activity do not pass unimpeded through the skull and scalp. The scalp distribution of the recorded EEG therefore has some degree of spatial smearing that depends on how the skull and scalp conduct electricity. Because we cannot directly determine the volume conduction properties of each individual subjects' brain, scalp, and skull, a model is required to estimate how the electrical fields are conducted through these tissues to the recording electrodes. This head model is used to estimate the lead field matrix, making the choice of models very important. Errors in the head model will result in mislocalization of source activities, usually on the order of about one centimeter (Leahy et al. 1998).

Many different head models have been used for source localization, ranging from relatively simple to complex. The simplest model is a spherical model with one or more layers, or shells, to approximate the conductivity of different layers (e.g., three-shell for brain, skull, and scalp). In addition to being computationally simple, the spherical head model does not require any expensive anatomical scans. This is both an advantage (less expensive) and a disadvantage. The disadvantage is that the inaccuracies in modeling the human head can lead to inaccuracies in source estimations. The use of more complicated head models based on MRI (in general, called realistic head models) will likely provide a more accurate estimate of neural sources (Van Veen et al. 1997). Realistic head models are available for standard heads, but they can also be created for individual subjects using information about their own anatomy. Despite the greater accuracy in modeling the human head, some inaccuracies are unavoidable. For example, the conductivities of various types of tissues that are entered into the forward model are estimates, and they are assumed to be consistent throughout a tissue type. Thus even individual head models will contain some degree of error (Hallez et al. 2007).

In many cases standard realistic head models may be sufficient. Many researchers do not have easy access to MRI equipment or the funds available to obtain a structural MRI for every subject that they can obtain EEG data from. Reasonable estimates of activity can be produced with the beamformer using a standard head model, but it is important for interpretation to remember that individual differences in brain shape and head conductivity have not been accounted for. However, if one wishes to talk more generally about activity in broader brain regions, then the small amount of spatial smear introduced by differences between subjects would be less problematic.

To demonstrate how the choice of head model can affect beamformer source estimations, we applied beamformers to simulated EEG using either the same head model that was used to create the simulated data or a different head model than the one used to create the simulated data. We simulated 64 channels of EEG using a single dipole placed in a three-shell spherical head model, and then we performed three beamformer reconstructions using three different head models: a three-shell spherical model, a four-shell ellipsoidal model, and a realistic head model based on an average brain. The simulated source location and the peaks of the beamformer output for the three head models are displayed in figure 4.4. When the correct head model was used for beamformer calculation, very little localization error occurred (some deviations from the simulated source occur due to random noise in the simulated EEG). When incorrect head models were used for beamformer computations, the localization error increased. For this simulation the realistic head model produced the greatest mislocalization, with the peak of activity located slightly anterior, superior, and more medial than the simulated source location.

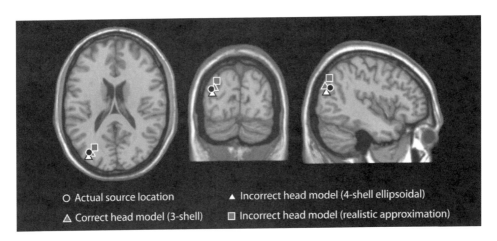

Figure 4.4
Effects of errors in head model on localization accuracy. Raw EEG was simulated for a single source location using a three-shell spherical head model. Using a three-shell head model for the calculation of the forward model, the beamformer localizes the source activity to the correct location. The use of an incorrect head model for calculation of the forward model leads to errors in localization.

Time–Frequency Parameters

Many implementations of the beamformer involve the analysis of data in the time–frequency domain to enable the examination of activities within specific frequency bands. The downside of this increased frequency specificity is the loss of some of the temporal resolution for which EEG is renowned. The main problem is that power cannot be determined for a single point in either the time or frequency domain; instead the estimation of power for a given latency and frequency always includes information from neighboring time points and frequencies. Inherent in time–frequency analysis is a trade-off between the time specificity and the frequency specificity that one can achieve. Increasing temporal resolution (i.e., decreased blurring of temporal information) results in decreased frequency resolution (i.e., increased blurring of frequency information). Conversely, increased frequency resolution results in decreased temporal resolution. The amount of blurring in each of the time and frequency domains is determined by the parameters of the time–frequency transformation that is performed.

The amount of temporal blurring can be an important issue in the interpretation of the beamformer output, particularly if one wants to examine changes in the locus of neural activity over time. The beamformer calculations operate on the covariance matrix calculated across trials for a single point in time. For raw EEG epochs the time interval for the beamformer output can be a single sample point, maintaining the temporal resolution of the EEG. However, for time–frequency data the time point that is used for beamformer calculations will include information from neighboring time points as well. Depending on the frequency of interest and the method of time–frequency transformation, the amount of temporal blurring can be a few milliseconds or a few hundred milliseconds.

Specification of the Three-dimensional Grid

Although the user does not have to determine the number of sources in advance as in traditional dipole source modeling, the beamformer still requires the specification of a three-dimensional grid of possible source locations. The grid spacing (and resulting total number of grid points) will not only have effects on the time required to perform the beamformer computations but will also have implications for the results. There is a trade-off between the ability to resolve sources that are close together and the possibility of introducing spurious sources. With widely spaced grid points (e.g., $10 \times 10 \times 10$ mm) the likelihood of observing spurious beamformer activities where there are no sources is relatively lower because there are fewer chances to find false positive results. Conversely, the likelihood of missing source activities that fall between grid points is relatively high. The opposite is the case with closely spaced grid points (e.g., $2 \times 2 \times 2$ mm): the likelihood of finding spurious beamformer activities is relatively high, whereas the likelihood of missing source activities that fall between grid points is relatively low (Gross et al. 2001; Van Veen et al. 1997).

Ultimately the choice of grid dimensions that are used will depend on many factors, such as the goals of the study and the hypotheses that are made. If the goal is to examine and display the source reconstructions for individual subjects, or if the analysis is more exploratory in nature and only a general idea about possible source locations is of interest, then a larger distance between grid points may be preferable to reduce the possibility of false positives. If the goal is to use statistics to determine which locations show significant activity across a group of subjects then a more closely spaced grid may be preferable. Assuming that any spurious sources are not likely to be at the same grid locations for all subjects, statistical analysis will eliminate false positive sources and only sources of activity that are similar across subjects will emerge, making the increased false positive rate for narrower grids less problematic.

Further Analyses

Because of the variability between subjects, it may be helpful to subject the individual participants' beamformer data to a statistical analysis in order to determine which estimated source locations are statistically significant across the group of participants. Statistical tests are performed for each voxel independently and depending on the grid size chosen for the beamformer calculations the number of voxels can be very large (more than 10,000). Thus methods of statistical analysis need to be chosen carefully to minimize statistical errors and false positives. Fortunately there are a number of statistical analysis methods that have been developed for both fMRI and MEG beamformer analyses that can be used for EEG beamformer analysis as well. The most commonly used statistical analyses are nonparametric procedures that do not assume that the data are normally distributed. For example, random permutation tests can be used, which permute the data a large number of times and recalculate the statistics, creating a distribution of statistical values to which the statistical value calculated from the real data can be compared to (e.g. Singh, Barnes, and Hillebrand 2003).

It is common in functional neuroimaging to display voxel-based statistical results rather than the raw data. The same statistical mapping can be employed for the beamformer technique as well (figure 4.5). This is typically referred to as statistical parametric mapping (SPM) if parametric statistics are used or statistical nonparametric mapping (SnPM) if nonparametric statistics are used. In these types of statistical maps the image displayed represents the degree to which activity in that location was statistically significant across participants. It is important in the interpretation of these results that increases and decreases in the color scale of the image do not necessarily reflect the magnitude of the raw source power. A weak source of activity that was at a highly consistent location across subjects can be statistically significant, while a very strong source that has more intersubject variability in location may not be. For example, the SnPMs in figure 4.5 show significant source activity in occipital, parietal, and frontal brain regions, and the color variation reflects different *p*-values.

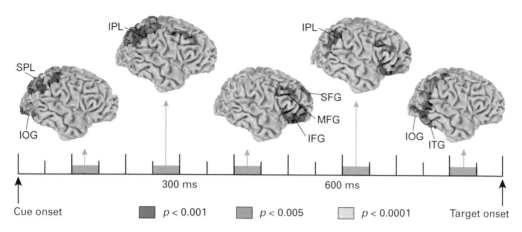

Figure 4.5
Statistical nonparametric mapping of EEG beamformer output. Shown are SnPMs of theta-band activity for five time intervals during the cue-target interval of a spatial cueing task. Only the statistically significant ($p < 0.005$) activity is displayed. Adapted from Green and McDonald (2008). (See plate V.)

As with fMRI data, anatomical regions of interest (ROIs) can be defined and any statistical comparisons can be restricted to those locations. In addition, although the beamformer outputs a single image for the time window and frequency of interest, multiple analyses can be performed so that images are obtained for multiple time points throughout an interval of interest. Thus the time course of activity in a single voxel or in a ROI can be obtained to look at changes in source power over time (figure 4.6). However, there are two important considerations when interpreting the time course of neural activity based on sequential beamformer images. First, unlike dipole modeling, which shows the time course of activity of a static source, for each beamformer image a new spatial filter is created based on the covariance matrix for the data at that time point. In other words, the beamformer activity in one time range is not dependent on the beamformer activity in another time range. Second, depending on the parameters of the time–frequency analysis performed, there will be some degree of temporal blurring of activity. If precise, millisecond level, timing information is desired, then the beamformer analysis can be combined with other techniques. For example, the locations identified with the beamformer analysis could be used to constrain a dipole model, as has been done with fMRI to obtain temporal information (e.g., Grent-'t-Jong and Woldorff 2007; Hopfinger et al. 2005).

The three-dimensional images obtained with the beamformer analysis look strikingly similar to the types of images obtained with hemodynamic imaging techniques (i.e., fMRI and PET) that it is tempting to interpret the results as a true picture of

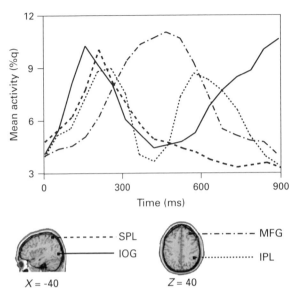

Figure 4.6
Region of interest and time-course analysis of beamformer output displayed in figure 4.5. ROIs were defined from the centroids of statistically significant activity shown in figure 4.5, and then the amplitude of the average signal in 18 consecutive 50 ms time windows was calculated. Adapted from Green and McDonald (2008).

electrical brain activity. However, the beamformer analysis still provides only an estimate of neural activity based on recordings made outside the head. As with any source analysis technique for EEG or MEG, the true sources of neural activity are unknown.

Final Remarks

The main advantage of using electrophysiological techniques remains the ability to obtain information about the timing of neural activity. Like other source analysis techniques, the beamformer method is an attempt to provide information about the neural generators of the EEG. The beamformer method has three main advantages. First, the beamformer method does not require the a priori determination of the number of possible sources. Second, the beamformer is able to localize both the evoked and induced activities and focus source localization on a specific frequency band. Finally, the beamformer provides a spatially filtered estimate of brain activity for each location independently rather than trying to solve the inverse problem by fitting a model to the measured data. Although the true sources of the EEG are unknown and the beamformer can only provide an estimate of brain activity, similar localization results obtained from electrical and hemodynamic neuroimaging methods can provide converging evidence for the role of a particular brain area in a particular cognitive process.

References

Brookes MJ, Stevenson CM, Barnes GR, Hillebrand A, Simpson MIG, Francis ST, Morris PG. 2007. Beamformer reconstruction of correlated sources using a modified source model. *NeuroImage* 34:1454–65.

Dien J, Frishkoff GA. 2005. Principal components analysis of ERP data. In: Handy TC, ed. *Event-Related Potentials: A Methods Handbook*. Cambridge: MIT Press, 189–207.

Gevins AS. 1990. Dynamic patterns in multiple lead data. In: Rohrbaugh JW, Parasuraman R, Johson R Jr, eds. *Event-related Brain Potentials: Basic Issues and Applications*. New York: Oxford University Press, 44–56.

Green JJ, McDonald JJ. 2008. Electrical neuroimaging reveals timing of attentional control activity in human brain. *PLoS Biol* 6:e81.

Grent-'t-Jong T, Woldorff MG. 2007. Timing and sequence of brain activity in top-down control of visuo-spatial attention. *PLoS Biol* 5:e12.

Gross J, Kujala J, Hamalainen M, Timmermann L, Schnitzler A, Salmelin R. 2001. Dynamic imaging of coherent sources: studying neural interactions in the human brain. *Proc Natl Acad Sci USA* 98:694–9.

Hadjipapas A, Hillebrand A, Holliday IE, Singh KD, Barnes GR. 2005. Assessing interactions of linear and nonlinear neuronal sources using MEG beamformers: a proof of concept. *Clin Neurophysiol* 116:1300–13.

Hallez H, Vanrumste B, Grech R, Muscat J, De Clercq W, et al. 2007. Review on solving the forward problem in EEG source analysis. *J NeuroEng Rehab* 4:46.

Herdman AT, Wollbrink A, Chau W, Ishii R, Ross B, Pantev C. 2003. Determination of activation areas in the human auditory cortex by means of synthetic aperture magnetometry. *NeuroImage* 20:995–1005.

Hillebrand A, Singh KD, Holliday IE, Furlong PL, Barnes GR. 2005. A new approach to neuroimaging with magnetoencephalography. *Hum Brain Mapp* 25:199–211.

Hopfinger JB, Khoe W, Song A. 2005. Combining electrophysiology with structural and functional neuroimaging: ERPs, PET, MRI, and fMRI. In: Handy TC, ed. *Event-Related Potentials: A Methods Handbook*. Cambridge: MIT Press, 345–79.

Leahy RM, Mosher JC, Spencer ME, Huang MX, Lewine JD. 1998. A study of dipole localization accuracy for MEG and EEG using a human skull phantom. *Electroencephalogr Clin Neurophysiol* 107:159–73.

Luck SJ. 2005. *An Introduction to the Event-related Potential Technique*. Cambridge: MIT Press.

Makeig S, Bell AJ, Jung T, Sejnowski TJ. 1996. Independent component analysis of electroencephalographic data. In: Touretzky D, Mozer M, Hasselmo M, eds. *Advances in Neural Information Processing Systems 8*. Cambridge: MIT Press, 145–51.

Robinson SE, Vrba J. 1999. Functional neuroimaging by synthetic aperture magnetometry (SAM). In: Yoshimoto T, Kotani M, Kuriki S, Karibe H, Nakasato N, eds. *Recent Advances in Biomagnetism*. Sendai: Tohoku University Press, 302–5.

Scherg M, Vajsar J, Picton TW. 1989. A source analysis of the late human auditory evoked potentials. *J Cogn Neurosci* 1:336–55.

Sekihara K, Nagarajan S, Poeppel D, Miyashita Y. 2001. Reconstructing spatio-temporal activities of neural sources from magnetoencephalographic data using a vector beamformer. *IEEE Trans Biomed Eng* 48:760–71.

Slotnick SD. 2005. Source localization of ERP generators. In: Handy TC, ed., *Event-Related Potentials: A Methods Handbook*. Cambridge: MIT Press, 149–66.

Singh KD, Barnes GR, Hillebrand A. 2003. Group imaging of task-related changes in cortical synchronisation using nonparametric permutation testing. *NeuroImage* 19:1589–1601.

Van Drongelen W, Yuchtman M, Van Veen BD, van Huffelen AC. 1996. A spatial filtering technique to detect and localize multiple sources in the brain. *Brain Topogr* 9:39–49.

van Veen V, Carter CS. 2002. The timing of action-monitoring processes in the anterior cingulate cortex. *J Cogn Neurosci* 14:593–602.

Van Veen BD, van Drongelen W, Yuchtman M, Suzuki A. 1997. Localization of brain electrical activity via linearly constrained minimum variance spatial filtering. *IEEE Trans Biomed Eng* 44:867–80.

5 A Practical Guide for MEG and Beamforming

Anthony T. Herdman and Douglas Cheyne

This chapter presents techniques for recording and analyzing magnetoencephalography (MEG) data and new approaches to MEG source localization based on beamforming. We present general guidelines for end users of MEG and provide a basic introduction to neurophysiology underlying MEG signals and their measurement including participant factors, data collection, and data analyses, with a particular focus on beamforming. More detailed descriptions of the neurophysiology, physics, and mathematics underlying MEG and its analyses can be found in a number of articles, chapters, and books (Baillet, Mosher, and Leahy 2001; Hamalainen et al. 1993; Hillebrand et al. 2005; Lu and Kaufman 2003; Sekihara and Nagarajan 2008).

What Is MEG?

Magnetoencephalography (MEG) is the recording of magnetic fields over the human head (figure 5.1). It is noninvasive and provides complementary information to other neuroimaging methods, such as electroencephalography (EEG), functional magnetic resonance imaging (fMRI), positron emission tomography (PET), and near-infrared spectroscopy (NIRS). Recorded magnetic fields contain changes in magnetic flux that are externally generated from electromagnetic devices (exogenous) and internally generated from the body (endogenous; e.g., muscle and brain). Because magnetic field strength diminishes approximately with the square of the distance from the source, most fields measured over the surface of the head that are internally generated come from the electromagnetic activity within the brain. In 1968 David Cohen used a magnetic detector to record one of the first tracings of the magnetic alpha rhythm outside the human head (Cohen 1968). Although only one sensor was used, Cohen demonstrated the viability of noninvasively recording MEG. Technological advances since have allowed MEG manufacturers and researchers to build systems that can record magnetic fields over the whole head. Modern MEG systems house up to 300 sensors covering an array of positions over the head. Unlike Cohen's initial single sensor measurements, scientists and clinicians can now

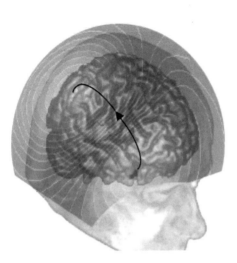

Figure 5.1
Topography of an auditory event-related field (an N1m) represented on a helmet's surface overlaying a participant's head. A green arrowed line depicts the directions of the outgoing (blue) and ingoing (red) magnetic fields. An active auditory source, estimated with an event-related beamformer technique, is projected to the cortical surface lying along the Sylvian fissure. (See plate VI.)

simultaneously record from the excitable neural tissue over spatially disparate brain regions.

Neural Basis of the MEG Signal

Electrical current flowing in a wire creates a circular magnetic field perpendicular to the flow of current in accordance with the right-hand rule: the fingers of the right-hand point in the direction of magnetic field if the thumb points in direction of the induced current (figure 5.2). For currents flowing over very short distances in space, such as those generated by neurons in the brain, the flowing currents can be modeled as small individual current elements or "dipoles."

A conventional description of neuronal information transmission is that neurons receive excitatory or inhibitory synaptic input primarily at the distal portions of their dendritic tree. This input is sent via passive (electronic) conduction to the soma for integration; each dendritic process thus creates a small intracellular current element (figure 5.3). Because the cortical neurons have their main dendritic arbors organized in a parallel manner, the magnetic field resulting from synchronous dendritic post-synaptic potentials (PSPs) will summate to produce a global magnetic signal that can be detected outside the head. When measured from a distance outside of the head, the small individual dipoles can be represented by their total sum. This is often referred

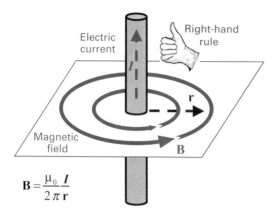

Figure 5.2
Electrical current (*I*) flowing in a wire induces a magnetic field (**B**) perpendicular the wire with a magnitude that diminishes with increasing distance (**r**) from the current source, given by the equation below. The magnetic fields follow the "right-hand" rule in that the thumb points in the direction of the current and the magnetic fields rap around in the direction of the fingers.

to as the "equivalent current dipole (ECD)" model. It should be noted that action potentials traveling along the axons, although substantially greater in local field potential than PSPs, do not contribute significantly to the MEG signal because of the nature of axonal conduction. For an action potential a wave of depolarization is immediately followed by a wave of repolarization that propagates down the axon. Magnetic fields created by these adjacent polarizations are opposing and result in minimal magnetic fields measured at a distance. By this account MEG mainly measures the intracellular PSPs traveling along the dendrites of approximately 10,000 to 100,000 synchronously active pyramidal neurons (Hamalainen et al. 1993).

The equivalent current dipole, or ECD, is a commonly used model for brain source activity. The ECD modeling is based on the assumption that activation of a specific cortical region involves populations of functionally interconnected neurons (macro-columns) within a relatively small area. Because the currents generated by these neural populations are flowing inside the head, which is roughly spherical in shape, the generators of the brain's magnetic field can be mathematically modeled as dipoles in a sphere (figure 5.4). Although ECD modeling can provide a reasonable representation of neural activation of this kind, neural activity might be more like a sheet of distributed dipoles. Thus dipole models might not be appropriate representations of the data in some instances. Moreover overlapping fields from spatially close and simultaneously active neural populations create different magnetic field distributions compared to nonoverlapping fields from single dipoles (e.g., current dipoles simultaneously active in the auditory and somatosensory cortices). Thus, while visualizing MEG

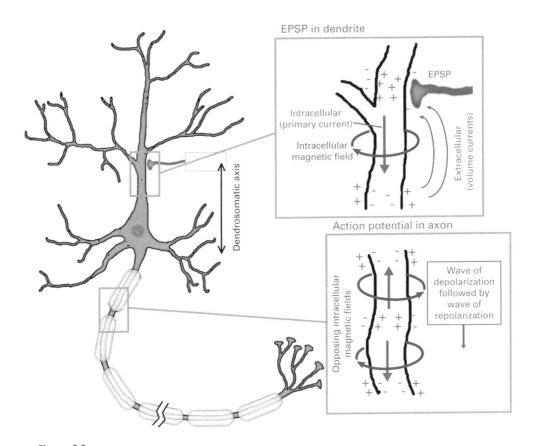

Figure 5.3
Neurophysiological events underlying the generation of the MEG signal. Excitatory postsynaptic potentials (EPSPs) in the apical dendrites of a pyramidal neuron create intracellular current flow (blue arrowed line) toward the soma. This current will create a magnetic field (red arrowed line) perpendicular to the dendrosomatic axis, similar to current flowing in a wire (see figure 5.1), that is recordable in far-field MEG measurements. Action potentials in the axon also create larger intracellular current flow along the length of the axon and perpendicular magnetic fields. However, depolarization and repolarization of the axonal membrane create opposing magnetic fields that are in close proximity to each other (represented as a quadrapole); therefore action potentials result in minimal far-field MEG signals. (See plate VII.)

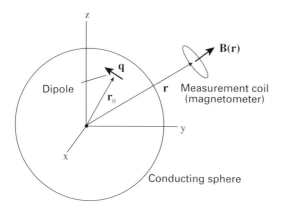

$$\mathbf{B}(\mathbf{r}) = \frac{\mu_0}{4\pi} \frac{\mathbf{q} \times (\mathbf{r} - \mathbf{r}_0)}{|\mathbf{r} - \mathbf{r}_0|^3}$$

Figure 5.4
Relationship between the current in a dipole and the magnetic field measured at the magnetometer. If the current strength of the dipole ($\mathbf{q}$) in Ampere-meters is known, the magnetic field strength at a distance ($\mathbf{r}$) can be computed in units of Tesla, given by the constant $\mu_0 = 4\pi \times 10^{-7}$ Tesla-Amperes/meter.

topography can be useful, interpretation of the underlying MEG generators is difficult with multiple simultaneously active neural populations. Other means are needed to estimate the neural activity underlying MEG.

In order to evaluate MEG, we need to first record the data, then analyze the data, and finally visualize the results. There are many approaches and several systems used to record and analyze MEG data, which will not be covered in detail in this chapter. We summarize general principles with examples in order to provide the appropriate information necessary for a reader to conduct or interpret MEG studies.

Recording Devices
There are a number of different designs of modern MEG systems currently in use, most of which consist of a hundred or more sensor channels for simultaneously recording magnetic fields over the scalp. These systems differ primarily in their sensor design as will be briefly described here. Generally, MEG is recorded from sensors that consist of a loop of wire connected to a highly sensitive flux-to-voltage converter known as a superconducting quantum interference device (SQUID) submerged in liquid helium to maintain superconductivity within a large cryogenic container (dewar). Magnetic flux ($\mathbf{B}$) within the loop of wire will induce a current in the wire,

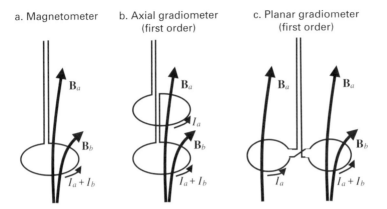

Figure 5.5
Depiction of magnetic sensors, a magnetometer (a), a first-order axial gradiometer (b), and a first-order planar gradiometer (c). Fields from distant sources ($\mathbf{B}_a$) and local sources ($\mathbf{B}_b$) induce currents (I_a and I_b) in the coil closest to the sources (in this example the lower and right coil). For the first-order axial gradiometer the distant-source field ($\mathbf{B}_a$) induces current in both upper and lower coils that are opposing within the circuit and thus result in little to no induced current. A local-source field induces larger current ($\mathbf{B}_b$) in the lower than upper coil and thus results in measurable local field changes. This occurs similarly for planar gradiometers, but the differential in a plane orthogonal to the axial gradiometer's differential plane.

following the right-hand rule (figure 5.5a). This current is coupled into the SQUID device, which in turn is connected to a nonsuperconducting (room temperature) electronic circuit outside the dewar. These superconductive components provide the MEG system with the necessary sensitivity to measure the minute magnetic fields emanating from the brain, but they also measure the larger magnetic field disturbances surrounding the instrument. These disturbances can be minimized by placing the MEG system in a magnetically shielded room (MSR) and by configuring the coils in slightly different ways. For example, the loops of wire forming the pick-up coil can be configured as *magnetometers* (figure 5.5a) or *gradiometers* (figure 5.5b–c). A magnetometer is configured as a single loop with reference to no other sensor. A gradiometer has at least two wire loops in which current flow between them will be additive in a destructive manner. The upper loop in a first-order axial gradiometer will cancel the same field ($\mathbf{B}_a$) entering the lower loop. In this configuration the magnetic fields that have similar strengths between two distances from the source and are equal to or greater than the distances between the upper and lower gradiometer loops will be effectively recorded as a null change in magnetic field. Thus large environmental magnetic fields such as those generated from movement of the device in the earth's magnetic field, or moving metal objects in the surroundings (i.e., "far" sources), will be seen as spatially uniform magnetic fields and will be substantially reduced by gradiometer configurations. Magnetic fields generated by brain sources that are relatively closer to the coils ("near" sources) will still be measured due to the higher spatial rate of change (gradient) of their magnetic fields. As can be seen, different gradiometer configurations can be used to attenuate unwanted long-range fields. Modern biomagnetometer systems use magnetometer configurations as well as "planar" and "axial" gradiometer configurations. A main difference between planar and axial gradiometers is that the recorded spatial field distributions for a simple dipole look substantially different. A system with planar gradiometers has coils oriented in a figure-eight pattern over the scalp surface and thus records the gradient or rate of change of ingoing and outgoing magnetic field in one direction across the scalp surface. This type of gradiometer therefore requires two coils oriented in orthogonal directions for each measurement location, and detects maxima from sensors directly over the source where the change in direction of the magnetic field is greatest. A system with axial gradiometers has coils oriented along a common axis with one coil closest to the head surface. This type of gradiometer will actually detect a null from sensors directly over the source, and maxima and minima from sensors surrounding the source (figure 5.1), which again follows the right-hand rule, and only requires one sensor for each recording location over the head.

Because the dewar (i.e., MEG helmet) is a fixed shape, the human head can be situated in many different locations within it. Typically small insulated coils are placed at landmarks on the head and energized in order to determine the location of the head within the dewar. In many existing designs the coils generate magnetic fields that interfere with the brain's magnetic fields and are energized only at the beginning and end of each recording block to identify their location within the dewar and thus determining how much head movement occurs. Large head movements can be problematic for interpreting results because brain regions generating the MEG will be in different locations and orientations and will therefore be picked up by different sensors from the beginning to the end of the recording block. Head movements are generally acceptable if they are less than 5 to 10 mm, but with proper care to stabilize the head, the movements can be kept to a few millimeters for short duration recordings. Most MEG manufacturers have now developed procedures to continuously activate these coils and thus monitor head movements throughout the recording procedure and potentially remove trials with large movements or compensate for them later.

Practical Considerations

Participant Factors

Because MEG is one of the more noninvasive neuroimaging techniques, most individuals can be scanned. MEG is particularly useful in scanning individuals who would be uncooperative with electrodes (EEG) being placed on the scalp or who are sensitive to noisy and confined environments (fMRI). However, participant factors need to be

considered, such as magnetic artifacts (magnetic impurities), body position, head position in the dewar, head movement, vigilance, and comfort.

Artifacts   One of the most important participant factors for MEG scanning is the
presence of unwanted exogenous (external to body) and endogenous (internal to
body) artifacts. Typically participants are first placed in the MEG to assess if his/her
noise level exceeds a general threshold (e.g., consistent deflections of the recorded
magnetic fields greater than 2 pT). If so, then the search for the sources of the artifacts
commences. Paramagnetic or ferromagnetic materials that might be contained in
jewelry, clothing (underwire bras, zippers), even facial makeup (mascara, face glitter),
and so forth, can cause large artifacts that obscure the brain signal. Therefore such
items should be removed from the MSR before recording MEG. Other paramagnetic
materials that can't be removed from the participant (dental work, surgical pins, etc.;
see figure 5.8a) or implanted devices such as pacemakers will also create large amounts
of unwanted magnetic signal (i.e., noise), unless specialized shielding can be created
as in the case for cochlear implants (Pantev et al. 2006). Artifacts from dental work
and facial makeup may be made worse if the participant was recently scanned in an
MRI device because such materials can become slightly magnetized. For this reason,
if structural MRI scans are obtained in participants for the purpose of MEG source
localization, MEG recordings should be done first.

   Artifacts from magnetically noisy materials will generally produce very large but
very low frequency signals in the data and can usually be easily recognized by having
the subject blink or move, and in some cases these artifacts may be largely removed
after data collection by high-pass filtering the data. However, even in magnetically
uncontaminated subjects, eye movements, eye blinks, and muscle activity will create
additional unwanted endogenous magnetic noise (see figure 5.8c). Such artifacts are
substantially larger than the magnetic brain signal and thus must be dealt with in
order to visualize the embedded neurophysiological signal. Some post hoc artifact
correction methods are discussed later.

Body Position   Most MEG systems allow the dewars to be rotated in order to record
from participants in an upright (dewar perpendicular to floor) or supine (dewar parallel
to floor) position. This is highly beneficial and critical for clinical assessments where
clients/patients are not able to sit upright on their own, are more comfortable lying
down, or need more support of their neck and head. A supine position will help reduce
unwanted head movements but it poses some problems for certain tasks. If participants are required to manually press buttons, the button box is usually at their sides
and out of view. For participants who might have difficulty in remembering the
response-to-button mapping or loose track of the button box they will have difficulty
in pressing the correct button. A solution to this is to allow them to hold the response

pad in front of their chest, but that may cause muscle artifacts from neck muscles in order to maintain such a position. A better solution is to use graspable button response devices (held in the palm of the hand) with a button for the index and a button for the thumb. These can be placed at the participant's sides and do not require recheck-ing of where the finger is relative to the buttons. The seated or upright position is not wrought with this dilemma but can be difficult for participants to minimize head movement, particularly those participants that benefit from supporting their head and neck, such as young children.

Head Position   The head position in the helmet-shaped dewar is important to the task at hand. Research has shown that the head position in the dewar can significantly affect the recorded MEG (Marinkovic et al. 2004). The dewar is a rigid structure, with the helmet area designed to be slightly larger than the average adult head size and doesn't mold to each participants head shape. Thus studies investigating responses from the posterior brain would benefit from asking participants to rest their heads on the back part of the dewar. This will result in larger signals because the MEG sensors are closer to the neural generators (remember the magnetic field recorded at the sensor is inversely proportional to the squared distance from the current source; figure 5.4). Additionally researchers investigating frontal lobe activity should ask participants to place their heads closer to the anterior part of the dewar. This is an even more impor-tant issue for recording from a paediatric population because the average distance between the neural sources and physical sensors is generally larger for children than adults depending on age, noting that head circumference is already close to 90 percent of adult size by 6 or 7 years of age (Nellhaus 1968). In some instances the sensors can be closer to the neural generators in one region of the head for participants with smaller heads. For example, sensors may be closer to the visual cortex if participant's heads are resting on the back of the dewar. However, this means that frontal sensors are farther from the frontal cortex. In these cases researchers must make a decision on which neural generators they wish to optimally measure when recording from partici-pants with small craniums, such as from young (<6 years old) children.

Head Movement   MEG helmets cannot be rigidly fixed to the participant's head; thus sensor-to-head mapping can shift if the head moves during measurement. A partici-pant's head movement should be limited while scanning in order to obtain good spatial localizations of the MEG signals. Spatial smearing of the fields will arise if the partici-pant moves his/her head during the scan thereby increasing the spatial uncertainty for source localization. Head movements during recordings that are larger than 10 mm in any Cartesian plane are generally not considered to be acceptable for further evalua-tion, and most laboratories use a conservative threshold of 5 mm or even less. Care should be taken to acclimatize children to the MEG environment in order to reduce their fidgeting. A possible solution is positioning them in a supine position, where children are as compliant as seated adults in moving their heads less than 5 mm. Recording in the supine position makes it easier for participants to maintain head position because their necks and heads are supported by the bed and dewar and in some systems allows for the use of a specially designed headrest (or "spoon") that can be inserted directly into the helmet. Some laboratories exclusively record from adults and children in the supine position. A difficulty with the supine position, however, is the ability for participants to stay awake and vigilant throughout the recording session. Again, the neural generators in the frontal cortices will be farther from the sensors and thus frontal activity could be reduced in these recordings if the head is not raised from the back of the dewar surface (Marinkovic et al. 2004). Another approach to limiting head movement is to support the head in the dewar using an adjustable air-filled bladder or nonmagnetic foam padding when in a seated position, or a special spoon-shaped headrest molded to the back of the head for supine recordings. This works well for most participants although some can find confining support systems uncomfortable, particularly with special populations. For long duration recordings in particular, care must be taken to avoid any pressure points on the scalp, regardless of which system is used to immobilize the head. Finally, the presentation of visual stimuli is, in principle, more difficult for supine recordings even though most MEG manufacturers have provided solutions to this problem by using mirrored projection systems.

Vigilance and Compliance   A participant's vigilance and task compliance are other important factors and have issues specific to MEG. One issue is that participants being recorded in the supine position often become drowsy and swiftly fall asleep if the participant isn't engaged in a task. This can pose problems to the researcher if this is not an intended outcome, albeit this is beneficial for sleep studies. Cortical brain responses and rhythms are significantly affected by changes in a participant's vigilance. Increases in alpha rhythms over time can be clearly observed in the posterior sensors when participants start to become drowsy. Researchers should closely monitor the online waveforms, note when participants become drowsy, and reinstruct them on the task. Noticeable delays or absences in button presses (if it is a reaction time experiment) are other pieces of evidence that are useful for evaluating a participant's vigilance. A camera is often used to monitor the participant. If the participant looks to be drowsy a quick chat usually will get him/her back on task and can make all the difference in the data quality. Safety issues should always be considered and some participants that are uncomfortable in closed spaces should be counseled before entering the MEG. A possible solution to recording from such individuals is to leave the MEG room door slightly ajar (copper metal touching if possible), but note that the MEG data will be noisier than usual. One of the most efficient ways to obtain good data (i.e., a large signal-to-noise ratio) is to make sure a participant is comfortable, vigilant, and compliant.

Stimulation

Most stimulation procedures used in EEG and fMRI studies can be used in MEG studies. Common procedures include those for recording MEG to auditory, visual, somatosensory stimulation, as well as to motor execution. A technical issue with using these techniques in the MSR is to minimize the possibility of recording stimulus artifacts in the MEG. Most MEG facilities have the stimulus delivery equipment (e.g., the auditory earphone transducers, LCD projector, and electrical/mechanical stimulator) outside the MSR with connectors (plastic tubing for auditory stimulation, mirrors reflecting light from LCD project onto a back-projected screen or ceiling, air bladders attached to the skin) fed through the MSR wall to the participant/patient.

Recordings

Compared to study design and data analysis, recording MEG has become a fairly easy procedure, thanks to the many researchers and engineers who developed the modern MEG systems. Sufficient training is still required to understand and become familiar with recording procedures and how to collect high-quality data. Most MEG systems have up to 300 sensor coils that are interspaced to cover most of the head surface. The spatial resolution at the sensor level depends on the density of the sensor array. The temporal resolution of MEG is only limited by the sampling rate, which in most systems ranges from 10 to 5,000 Hz, with a sample digitized every 100 to 0.2 ms respectively.

Acquisition systems allow researchers to also record trigger inputs from stimulus presentation devices. These triggers should be calibrated to the exact timing of when the stimulus is impinging on a participant's sensory apparatus (retina, cochlea, etc.). The timing of stimuli should be verified by using, for example, photodiodes, sound-level meters, and an oscilloscope.

MEG can be recorded as a continuous data stream or epoched with respect to trigger events. These events could include, but not limited to, onsets/offsets of sensory stimuli such as auditory, visual, or somatosensory, and to the onsets/offsets of motor events, such as finger or eye movements. Although in some circumstances it might be necessary to record epoched MEG data for online assessment of event-related fields, certain analysis procedures benefit from having continuous data, such as some time–frequency analyses (e.g., phase coherence) that require long-duration signals to obtain accurate estimates of narrowband response amplitudes and phases. Furthermore in some situations the MEG recorded between blocks (rest periods) can be used to assess the resting-state brain activity.

Signal Analysis

Unlike behavioral studies using reaction time, MEG involves recording far more trials in order to get a valid estimate of the signal. To design high-quality experiments, the researcher should determine the number of trials needed for signal analysis procedures to yield a stable estimate of the MEG signal of interest. A major goal of signal analysis; therefore, is to maximize the signal-to-noise ratio (SNR). For the most part the signal is the brain activity of interest and the noise is all other magnetic activity. In typical situations and paradigms, neuromagnetic fields (i.e., our signal of interest) are substantially smaller, approximately 30 to 600 femtoTesla (1 femtoTesla = 1×10^{-15} Tesla), than the environmental background noise-source fields that can be in the range of microTesla (1 microTesla = 1×10^{-3} Tesla) or larger. Most of the environmental noise-source fields are attenuated by using magnetic shielding in the walls of the MEG room and/or by using gradiometers, as discussed above. However, residual environmental noise plus ongoing brain activity and other biologically generated "noise" remains, and procedures need to be performed to decrease the noise so that neuromagnetic fields can be analyzed and measured. By increasing the SNR, the researcher increases the study's power of finding significant effects in the dependent variables under investigation. Several review articles and books provide excellent resources for in-depth coverage of signal analyses of EEG/MEG, which we recommend for the reader (Hamalainen et al. 1993; Niedermeyer and Lopes da Silva 2005; Picton, Lins, and Scherg 1995). We briefly outline some approaches in this section.

Data Inspection and Epoching   One of the first steps to signal analysis is to inspect the data. Exceedingly large deflections might indicate artifacts and will thus need to be dealt with in order to increase the SNR. This first step also provides insight into the general amount of noise in the data and helps provide a level of confidence and extra evidence for including or excluding a data set in further analyses. A common next step after data inspection is to place markers in the data that represent specific events, such as onsets of stimuli or motor responses. This step is needed if the events were not automatically marked during the MEG recording from triggers sent out by a stimulus presentation device or additional stimulus event criteria need to be marked. For example, a conditional criterion of a response or no response to a target stimulus might need to be marked as a correctly identified or missed event respectively. Many other types of criteria can be developed based on behavioral responses in order to identify trial types (e.g., hits, correct rejections, misses, and false alarms). These stimulus events are later used to epoch the data and to calculate event-related fields (ERFs), the magnetic counterparts to event-related potentials (ERPs) in EEG.

Additionally, if required by the task, it is important to inspect the behavioral responses that occur during the recording session to get an estimate of the participant's performance. A useful assessment is to plot the reaction times and accuracy as a function of the trial number. This will show if participant's task performance was consistent or variable over a recording session. For example, participant A might have reasonable variability in reaction times and a high level of accuracy throughout the session, whereas participant B might have highly variable reaction times and low accuracy. This could indicate that participant B is not remaining compliant and vigilant throughout the task. Participant B's behavioral results might indicate that the attention and vigilance waxes and wanes from one trial to the next over the session. Thus the MEG from participant A would be expected to be a more valid measure of the dependent variable than for participant B; unless the participants are expected to perform differently and it is the performance difference that the researcher wishes to capture with the MEG. Generally, researchers develop the tasks in an attempt to maintain consistent performance across trials. Performance inspection is therefore another valuable tool and can be used to get a better understanding of the validity of the recorded MEG data.

Filtering   A commonly used procedure to increase the SNR by reducing the noise in the data is filtering. Filtering allows the user to pass the wanted signal energy within defined frequencies while attenuating unwanted signals in other frequencies. This works well if the wanted and unwanted signals have sufficiently disparate spectral energies (as determined by the sampling frequency and filter windowing properties). Unfortunately, most sensory and cognitive cortical responses have main spectral energies within the same frequencies (below 20 Hz) as the unwanted eye movement related artifacts, and therefore they are difficult to separate by filtering. However, filtering can help attenuate other magnetic noise outside the main frequencies of interest. Several types of filtering procedures have been developed and discussion of them exceeds this chapter's scope, but we will describe general procedures and an example of filtering MEG. Generally, for computational efficiency, filtering is performed on the averaged signal or event-related fields (ERFs; see "averaging" below). Nevertheless, some situations require that the filtering be done on the single-trial data, such as in time–frequency analyses. Filtering can be done in the frequency or time domain.

The first step in frequency–domain filtering is to calculate the spectral energies of the recorded waveform using a fast Fourier transforms (FFT). The second step is to construct filter weights for each frequency bin in the FFT. These weights are based on the user-defined filter parameters, for example, a 20 Hz low-pass filter would have all weights for frequencies at and below 20 Hz equal to one and weights for all other frequencies equal to zero. Each frequency bin from the FFT is then multiplied by these weights to yield the filtered spectral response, which is used to reconstruct the filtered waveform by applying an inverse Fourier transform.

Windowing needs to be applied to waveforms that do not continue temporally to infinity. There are several windowing functions that can be applied and all will produce some distortion of the waveform, typically at the beginning and end. It is therefore important to shift the time interval of interest into the middle of the windowed interval or filtering distortions of the responses could occur.

There are two main types of time–domain filters, infinite impulse response (IIR) and finite impulse response (FIR). The FIR filters are generally more useful for MEG analyses because they can be designed to cause no phase distortion of a narrowband signal, which is extremely important for phase-coherence analyses. However, FIR filters come at a computational cost and require long duration intervals. They also require that the previous and future time points be known, and therefore FIR filters are not used for online digital filtering. For FIR filters the weighting coefficients are determined for pre- and post-time points, and the filtered time point is the sum of the weighted pre- and post-time points. The filter weights are dependent on the windowing function used and user-defined filter parameters. IIR filters are generally used for short-duration (1–2 s long) epoched data, and again, the weights are dependent on user-defined parameters and the windowing function. Figure 5.6 shows the results of IIR filtering of auditory ERFs in response to a 40 Hz amplitude-modulated tone using a 100 Hz low-pass (black line), a 20 Hz low-pass (red line), and a 30 to 50 Hz bandpass (blue line) filter. Auditory transients (P1m–N1m–P2m) and a 40 Hz auditory steady-state response (ASSR) are visible in this single-participant's waveform from a sensor over the right temporal-parietal scalp region. Filtering can help separate the transients (in red) and ASSR (in blue) in order to assess their underlying components separately. In addition some of the high-frequency (>50 Hz) noise is attenuated.

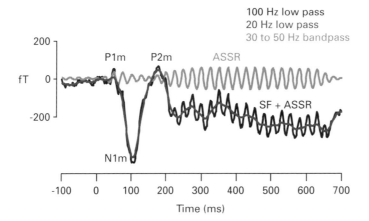

Figure 5.6
Filtering of an auditory event-related field to a 40 Hz amplitude-modulate tone. The ERF filtered with a 100 Hz low-pass filter (black line) shows a typical P1m–N1m–P2m transient followed by a sustained field (SF) with an overriding 40 Hz auditory steady-state response (ASSR). Filtering the ERF with a 20 Hz low-pass filter (red line) removes the 40 Hz ASSR and high-frequency noise, but the transient and sustained fields remain. Filtering the ERF with a 30 to 50 Hz band-pass filter removes the transient and sustained fields, while the 40 Hz ASSR remains. This demonstrates how filtering can be used to separate responses of interests and to remove noise. (See plate VIII.)

Averaging   Averaging of single-participant MEG data can be combined with filtering in order to better resolve wanted signals that are phase locked with respect to an event, referred to as event-related fields (ERFs). For simplicity we refer to phase-locked responses relative to the event onset as *evoked* or *event-related* fields and non–phase-locked responses as *induced* or *rhythmic* fields. Averaging is most commonly calculated by the sum of the magnetic fields across trials for each sample point divided by the total number of trials. A main assumption for using averaging to increase the SNR is that the wanted ERF has a consistent amplitude and phase that is phase locked to an event, whereas the noise has a random phase relation to the event. If the noise is stationary (has similar means and variances and doesn't covary across trials) and stochastic with respect to repeated events, then the noise amplitude in the averaged waveform will be reduced by the square root of the total number of trials in the average. This is known as the "square-root" rule of averaging (Hamalainen et al. 1993; Picton, Lins, and Scherg 1995). The more trials averaged, the better is the noise reduction and therefore the greater is the SNR. Figure 5.7 shows that for averaged auditory ERFs to an 80 decibel (SPL) 40 Hz amplitude-modulated tone, increasing the number of trials decreases the noise and thus increases the SNR. The black lines are the average of the

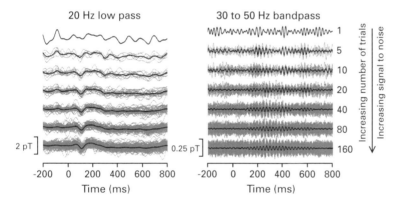

Figure 5.7
Effect of the number of trials on the signal-to-noise ratio for auditory event-related fields to a 40 Hz amplitude modulated tone. The noise level in an averaged response will decrease by the square root of the number of trials ($\sqrt{N}$); therefore the signal to noise will increase with an increase in the number of trials on average. For example, the prestimulus noise is substantially larger in averages of 1 to 10 trials than the signal between 100 and 200 ms (a indiscernible P1m–N1m–P2m transient). An auditory transient response (P1m–N1m–P2m) is visibly larger than the prestimulus noise in averages of 20 or more trials (*left panel*); and a 40 Hz auditory steady-state response is observably larger than the prestimulus noise in averages of 40 or more trials (*right panel*). This illustrates the importance of collecting a sufficient number of trials in order to clearly identify event-related fields.

individual trials (gray lines) for increasing numbers of trials from top to bottom. To demonstrate how to estimate the number of trials needed to obtain adequate SNR (SNR ≥ 2), we will take the example of the 20 Hz low-pass filtered response amplitudes from those in figure 5.7. The initial noise level in the prestimulus baseline is estimated to be about 675 fT and the final signal of the N1m auditory response is 350 fT (measured as the peak at 100 ms in the 160 trial averaged response). To get a final SNR of 2, the noise floor should be less than 175 fT (350 fT divided by 2). At least 15 trials are therefore needed to reduce the initial 675 fT noise level to a 175 fT level. As can bee seen in figure 5.7, the N1m in the 20 Hz transient ERF (left panel) is clearly larger by about two to three times than the prestimulus noise level in averaged waveforms of 20 or more trials, whereas the 40 Hz ASSR (right panel) is not clearly resolved until around 40 trials. In general, initial SNRs (at trial 1) are smaller for higher frequency responses, and thus more trials are needed to get the noise floor to a level that a stable signal can be measured. Having a SNR of at least 2 also increases the probability of measuring stable and thus more valid response amplitudes because the noise will have little affect on the signal. The example above is for an auditory ERF from a single condition, but most MEG paradigms are designed to contrast conditions; for example, the mismatch negativity (MMN) response is a subtraction of deviant responses from standard responses (Naatanen et al. 2007). A MMN response for single subject of about 150 fT would require at least 100 trials to obtain a SNR of 2 if the single-trial noise was about 750 fT.

There are, however, trade-offs for increasing the number of stimuli/events, such as participant vigilance, fatigue, and learning. Increasing the number of stimuli will increase the SNR if the ERFs remain stable, but fatigue and decreased vigilance will decrease the ERF stability and amplitude. Thus researchers should be aware of and not extend the study duration to when participants' vigilance decreases and fatigue sets in for the experimental protocols. In general, most typically developed adults (university students) performing simple perceptual or cognitive tasks can remain vigilant for 40 to 60 minutes in the MEG, depending on the number of rest periods and stimuli presented. Children of different ages and abilities have various levels of cognitive capabilities and thus vigilance duration in the MEG varies dramatically. Pilot testing is always recommended for particularly new study designs in order to estimate when participant's vigilance and fatigue levels occur. A possible solution to increasing the number of stimulus presentations is to reduce the stimulus onset asynchrony (SOA) or interstimulus interval (ISI). However, caution should be taken because the frequency of stimulus events can dramatically affect the recorded ERFs. For example, Hari and colleagues showed that decreasing the ISI from 8.8 to 1.1 s decreases the auditory N1m ERF amplitudes from approximately 800 to 200 fT (Hari et al. 1987). Overlap of long-latency ERFs can also occur with short SOA/ISI and will thus alter the ERF amplitudes. Additionally, if the SOA is consistent for all trials, then oscillatory responses at the

SOA's frequency or its harmonics might be in phase with the stimulus onset and thus not reduced by averaging procedures. Furthermore a consistent SOA can cause participants to expect when stimulus onsets occur, and thus the response amplitude will be affected by expectancy and attention. This can lead to misinterpretation of the results as was the case for the expectancy response being subtracted out twice when calculating audiovisual integration in a multisensory processing paradigm (Teder-Salejarvi et al. 2002). Randomizing the SOA or ISI is an effective means to counteract these effects. Another important factor that possibly covaries with the number of stimulus presentations is learning. If learning occurs across the study session, and thus stimulus presentations, then increasing the number of stimuli could yield greater ERFs for later trials as compared to earlier trials. In summary, researchers should understand the potential confounds in the averaging procedure and to be aware of which ones will affect the ERFs when designing a study.

Averaging sensor data across a group of individuals (group-participant averaging) is generally not appropriate for MEG because participants' head positions are in different locations in the dewar, and thus fields from a specific generator will not always be recorded at the same sensor location across all participants. Spatial smearing of the MEG fields may result, thereby reducing its spatial resolution. A solution, albeit not simple, is to perform group-participant averaging of the source-modeled signals because the locations of the modeled sources can be transformed into a common template space. The modeled data must therefore be a good representation (i.e., fit) of the recorded data.

Artifact Removal and Reduction   Several methods have been developed and verified to be useful for attenuating or removing electric and magnetic artifacts in order to improve the SNR of the EEG or MEG. We discuss three of them here. For artifacts that are transient from trial to trial, an artifact rejection approach could be performed. This procedure simply rejects a trial from subsequent analyses if the MEG signal at any time point within a trial or within a specified time interval exceeds an a priori defined threshold (e.g., 2 pT). This can be performed automatically by most software packages or manually by an experienced human user searching through the data. An advantage of the later is that the researcher can become familiar with the data and its general noise level. Furthermore artifacts that are just subthreshold might be missed by automatic procedures and the user will be able to better identify and reject these trials. A potential problem with the artifact rejection procedure is that it can result in poor SNRs if there are too few remaining trials after rejection. A general guideline for artifact rejection is that the number of rejected trials should be within 10 to 15 percent of the total trials. The trials can be sorted based on the trials noise level and then the top 10 to 15 percent of the noisiest trials can be rejected. The main reason for this guideline is the issue of efficiency in averaging the data. The more trials that are rejected, the less the total number of trials can be added for averaging out non–phase-locked activity and noise. The non–phase-locked activity will be reduced by the inverse of the square root of the number of trials. Thus rejecting more trials will lead to less reduction in noise levels and thus poorer SNR. The trade-off between rejecting and accepting trials can be determined for each data set by estimating the initial noise within a single trial without rejection and using one over the square root of the noise to determine the crossover point when rejecting trials becomes inefficient for averaging. But this estimation is generally not performed, and rejecting 10 to 15 percent of the trials is usually applied.

Another method to deal with artifacts is to utilize a source modeling approach that uses ECD or beamforming techniques to identify where the noise is being generated. Once the location and orientation of the source for the artifact is determined, it is incorporated into the source model for the signal space projection (Berg and Scherg 1991). Essentially this attenuates the MEG signal that could result from activity at the modeled artifact's spatial location, and thus leaving the remaining MEG variance attributable to the brain signal. The ECD modeling works extremely well for eye movements and blinks because the sources of such activity can be modeled with a high level of accuracy and confidence (Berg and Scherg 1991). This approach is effective when modeling EEG/MEG recording from an eye movement localizer task in which participants are asked to move their eyes azimuthally and vertically across the screen and to blink. This five-minute procedure can be easily added to the beginning or end of a recording session. A comparable procedure is to search through the MEG and mark eye blinks and eye movements and then average these events in order to model the eye movement related activity. Although this later procedure is appropriate, it is harder to identify saccade-related fields within the experimental data than from the eye-artifact localizer data because in the eye-artifact localizer data the researcher knows with a high level of certainty when a saccade is being performed. Using beamforming can also help extract brain signal from unwanted noise because it will end up localizing the noise to regions near the noise source.

A third approach uses principle component analysis (PCA) to reduce artifacts (Picton et al. 2000). It works by identifying and removing from each trial all principal components in the MEG signal that exceed a set threshold (e.g., 2 picoT). All PCA components that have peak activity exceeding the threshold are removed and the other PCA components are then summated to yield the artifact-corrected MEG signals. Figure 5.8 shows the topographies and overlaid sensor waveforms for using a PCA artifact correction method to reduce artifacts from dental implants (a–b) and a blink (c–d). The dental implant (figure 5.8a) creates persistently large deflections in the sensor waveforms that are distributed over the frontal and lower temporal sensors shown in the topography above. After PCA correction (figure 5.8b) the dental artifact distortions are absent and a visual ERF is visible in the topography over the

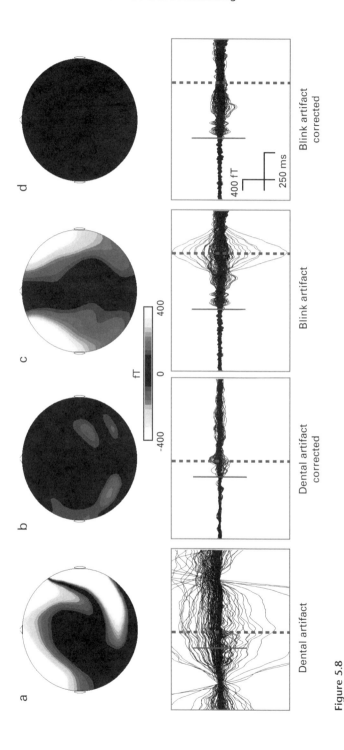

Figure 5.8

Artifact reduction using principle component analysis (PCA) on dental implant (a–b) and eye-blink (c–d) artifacts. The waveforms from 151 sensors are overlaid in an butterfly plot in the bottom graphs with the corresponding topographies (top view with the nose pointing toward top of page, left ear on left side, and right ear on right side) at the time designated by the red dotted line. The red solid line designates stimulus onset of a visual object presented at foveal fixation. The dental artifacts (a) distributed over the frontal and lower temporal sensors produce large magnetic fields that obscure any underlying neuromagnetic responses. Once the principle components related to the dental artifacts are removed, visual event-related field are clearly observed in the waveforms and topography (b). A blink artifact (c) can also be reduced by using the PCA procedure as observed in comparing (c) before correction with (d) after correction. (See plate VIII.)

posterior sensors and in the sensor waveforms at 180 ms (red dotted line) after stimulus onset (red solid line). PCA correction also works well for eye-blink artifacts. A typical blink artifact is evident in the uncorrected topography and sensor waveforms (figure 5.8c), which is then absent in the corrected topography and sensor waveforms (figure 5.8d).

Even though researchers should make all attempts to remove paramagnetic and ferromagnetic materials from participants before recording, sometimes it is not feasible. Source modeling and PCA approaches for artifact reduction might be useful. A caveat to the source modeling and PCA artifact removal methods is that the spread function of the modeled/removed noise component might overlap with spatial distributions from neural generators, especially in the orbital frontal regions for eye related artifacts. Thus real brain signal might be undesirably removed and caution should be taken to limit this by possibly using the traditional artifact rejection approach.

Time–Frequency Response   Sometimes one researcher's noise is another researcher's treasure. Not all activity in the prestimulus or pre-event period is noise. The brain is constantly active and for a large part, neural populations oscillate together. For example, the alpha rhythm (7–13 Hz) is well known to be modulated by opening and closing the eyes. In response to a visual stimulus, the alpha rhythm is reduced in the poststimulus interval as compared to prestimulus interval, but the alpha rhythm is not phase locked to the stimulus onset and thus is not evident in the ERF.

Time–frequency response (TFR) analyses are a group of specialized tools that are generally used to estimate changes in neural oscillations by calculating the temporal-spectral energy and phase of the MEG in specific frequency bands. TFR analyses can be performed on continuous, epoched, and averaged data and can be applied to sensor data as well as source modeled data. Generally, TFR analyses are used to investigate power changes in oscillations that are time locked (i.e., event-related) but not necessarily phase locked to an event (i.e., induced activity).

Methods have been developed to identify increases and decreases in spectral energy of oscillations that are induced by an event, referred to as event-related synchronization (ERS) and desynchronization (ERD) respectively (Pfurtscheller and Aranibar 1977; Pfurtscheller 2001). These are not to be confused with ERFs, which traditionally refer to activity that is both time locked and phase locked to an event. To calculate ERS/ERD, a wavelet or Hilbert transform can be used to determine the magnitude of spectral energies within narrow frequencies bands for a range of frequencies. These magnitudes represent changes in power of the oscillatory magnetic fields, which can then be normalized to a prestimulus baseline or resting interval. Increases and decreases in these normalized power changes are classified as ERS and ERD respectively, and are assumed to represent increases or decreases in synchronicity of firing of neural ensembles that are oscillating at a specific frequency. Figure 5.9 depicts an example using a wavelet

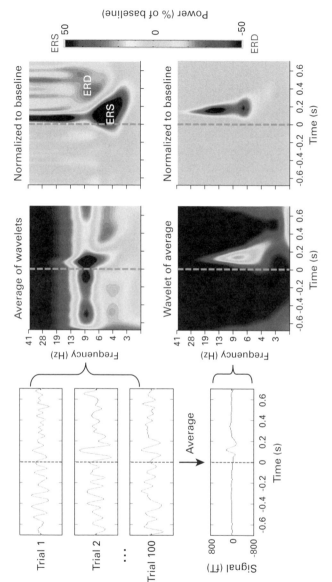

Figure 5.9

Time–frequency analyses of single-trial (*top left*) and averaged trial (*bottom left*) induced and evoked auditory responses in a sensor over the temporal parietal junction. The single-trial waveforms show a classical alpha (7–13 Hz) rhythm that is suppressed after the tone onset. This is clearly seen in the wavelet coefficients (*top middle*) as a dark red band across the prestimulus interval that is reduced in the poststimulus interval after about 250 ms. This rhythm has been termed an event-related desynchronization (ERD), and it is evident in the normalized to baseline map (*top right*). An event-related synchronization (ERS) is also visible and is most likely related to the evoked responses, which can be seen in the bottom middle and left plots. (See plate IX.)

to estimate the temporal-spectral energy of epoched and averaged responses to a tone. TFRs are calculated using wavelets for the single-trial waveforms (upper left) that are then averaged (upper middle). Large power is visible across the alpha (7–9 Hz) band in the prestimulus interval and a reduction in the poststimulus interval. This reduction, an ERD (blue), becomes evident when the response power is normalized to the prestimulus interval (upper right TFR plot). An ERS (red) is also visible in the theta (3–7 Hz) band of the normalized TFR plot. The wavelet results of the averaged data (bottom right) show only an ERS around 200 ms, which represents the change in power of the evoked fields. This is consistent with the theta ERS in single-trial TFR results (upper right). As is evident, the single-trial TFR analyses can provide added information regarding the non–phase-locked activity, an ERD in this example.

Salmelin and Hari developed a method, called temporal spectral evolution (TSE) that is computationally less intensive for calculating changes in cortical rhythms than using wavelets (Hari et al. 1997; Salmelin and Hari 1994). Additionally the units for TSE are the same as those for the ERFs (Tesla) and thus easily comparable. The steps for calculating TSE are to narrowband filter the signal, rectify (take absolute values) the filtered signal, average the rectified amplitudes across trials, and then normalize them to baseline (typically a prestimulus interval). Both these methods provide information regarding the changes in oscillatory power with respect to an event. An important aspect to note about these TFR analyses is the trade-off between spectral and temporal resolutions. The spectral resolution is inversely proportional to the temporal resolution. Thus, if one wishes to obtain temporally discrete information (e.g., within a 10 ms interval), the spectral resolution will be broad (e.g., a band width of at least 100 Hz). Conversely, in order for one to accurately estimate power within a narrow frequency band (e.g., 7–12 Hz; bandwidth = 5 Hz), the time interval will be long (e.g., at least 1/5 Hz = 200 ms). Additionally at least one cycle of the lowest frequency in the band of interest should be measured. For example, to estimate changes in the alpha band (7–12 Hz), at least 143 ms (duration of one cycle of a 7 Hz oscillation) would need to be used, but because the bandwidth is 5 Hz, at least 200 ms would be needed. A more conservative approach is to double the time interval needed to resolve the lowest frequency—rationalized by defining rhythmic activity as at least two or more cycles of an oscillation.

Head Modeling and Anatomical Co-Registration

A good head model is imperative to obtaining precise and accurate source localization from both EEG and MEG data. Because brain tissue, skull, and skin do not attenuate or distort magnetic fields to the same extent as electric fields, obtaining electrical conductivities for boundaries between these tissues is mostly unnecessary for MEG. A single sphere model is therefore typically used for MEG source modeling. However, where this sphere is placed relative to the brain surface will affect the source model. The sphere can thus be shifted to different locations to get a more accurate result. The issue is then where should a single sphere be positioned relative to brain anatomy? One approach is to use multiple spheres shifted in position based on a best fit to the head shape using the outer scalp surface, or preferably the boundary with the largest change in conductivity such as the inner skull surface. These surfaces can be obtained from structural MRIs. Making sure that the fiducials (reference-coil locations) from the head shapes match those of the anatomical images is highly important for precise co-registration of the functional source-reconstructed images to the structural images. A substantial part of co-registration error is in the reapplication of the fiducial markers (head localization coils in the MEG and vitamin E markers in the MRI). An effective means to minimize this error is to acquire MEG data and then structural images (usually using MRI) without reestablishing fiducial locations. If the MEG and MRI scans must be done at different facilities or on different days, then a good alternative is to take a photograph of the fiducial locations in order to accurately replicate placement.

In some situations MRI scans might be impractical and thus the participant's MRI image will be unavailable for head shape extraction and co-registration. A participant's headshape can usually be measured by collecting points on the scalp using a spatial-digitizing device (e.g., a Polhemus 3D digitizer). This headshape can then be matched to headshapes created from MRIs in a database (Holliday et al. 2003). This allows reasonably accurate functional-to-structural co-registration, less than 15 mm error. Another option is to warp (i.e., normalize) the headshapes and functional images to a template headshape from a single template MRI that best matches that population's anatomy (Beg et al., submitted). This approach has the advantage of not requiring MRI scanning or having a large MRI database. There are, however, at least three caveats to not obtaining MRIs from each participant. First and foremost, a participant's anatomy can be significantly different from a matched MRI or a template MRI, thereby providing insufficient information to interpret function-to-structure mapping at an individual level. Second, fiducial-location error between the MEG data and a matched or template MRI can be sufficient enough to introduce large shifts in source locations when using a three-fiducial placement system (nasion, left ear, and right ear). For example, an error of 1 cm in superior/inferior plane for the ear fiducials can cause an error of 2 cm in source location within the posterior occipital lobe. Averaging across participants' functional images with such an error would lead to invalid spatially normalized, group-averaged source images. Thus it is important to consistently and accurately place fiducials at head features (e.g., nasion, inion, and temporal-mandibular joint) that can be clearly located on the structural MRI. Third, the lack of direct co-registration of the participant's anatomy and function will limit the use of cortically constrained source modeling procedures (Auranen et al. 2007; Baillet,

Mosher, and Leahy 2001; Joshi et al. 2005). Because of these limitations, beamforming procedures and interpretation of the results will benefit most by obtaining each participant's MRI.

Beamforming

The equivalent current dipole or ECD is the best-known and most frequently used model for brain source activity (Nunez 1981). It is based on the assumption that activation of a specific cortical region involves populations of functionally interconnected neurons (macrocolumns) within a relatively small area. When measured from a distance, this local population activity can be modeled by a vector sum or "equivalent" current dipole that represents the aggregate activity of these neurons. Traditionally ECD analysis proceeds by estimating a priori the number of equivalent dipoles and their approximate locations, and then adjusting the dipole parameters (location and orientation) by a nonlinear search that minimizes differences between the field computed from the dipole model and the measured field. This approach has proved useful for modeling simple configurations of focal brain activity, yet is compromised by interaction between closely spaced sources, and may produce incorrect solutions due to unknown sources that are not included in the model. This makes the localization of distributed or complex patterns of brain activity associated with higher cognitive functions that may involve multiple active brain regions difficult and prone to error. Distributed current models such as those based on the minimum-norm method, first proposed for MEG by Hämäläinen and Ilmoniemi, can overcome some of these limitations by modeling extended continuous patterns of brain activity (Hamalainen and Ilmoniemi 1984). Moreover such linear source estimation techniques are attractive because they eliminate the need for performing nonlinear fitting of user-defined models to the data required by dipole modeling approaches. However, minimum-norm based methods are inherently biased toward solutions close to the sensors and require additional constraints to prevent biased estimates of source location, particularly in the presence of noise. A number of constrained or spatially weighted minimum-norm techniques have been developed for neuromagnetic source reconstruction and vary in their computational complexity and methodological approach to providing unbiased distributions of source activity in the brain. These have been described in the literature under a variety of names, including dynamic SPM (Dale et al. 2000; David et al. 2006), FOCUSS (Gorodnitsky, George, and Rao 1995), magnetic field tomography (Ioannides, Bolton, and Clarke 1990; Pascual-Marqui, Michel, and Lehmann 1994), LORETA (Pascual-Marqui, Michel, and Lehmann 1994), and SLORETA (Pascual-Marqui 2002).

A recent technique introduced to the neuromagnetic source modeling literature is a spatial filtering approach based on the array processing technique known as *beamforming*. The beamforming method reduces the influence of unknown sources by removing spatial correlations in the data that do not correspond to source activity at the location of interest. Thus beamforming techniques can be used as a method of scanning through source space to produce accurate three-dimensional volumetric images of source activity.

The concept of spatial filtering as a source reconstruction method in MEG and EEG has received only moderate attention since its introduction in the early 1990s. However, more recent techniques based on the minimum-variance beamforming algorithm, combined with appropriate spatial normalization techniques, have shown a great deal of promise as flexible, yet accurate approaches to source localization in MEG. Various beamforming algorithms have been introduced in the last decade that have been successfully applied to imaging both focal and distributed brain activity without the requirement for a priori source models. These beamforming algorithms are based on the familiar concept of linear source estimation, but they differ from the more conventional minimum-norm techniques in that they are *adaptive*, data-dependent spatial filters that do not require user defined models of source covariance. Linear source estimation in turn is based on the assumption that the measured data covariance can be used to derive the contributions of a limited number of sources needed to reconstruct the total spatial distribution of source activity with minimal crosstalk or interference between sources. In contrast, minimum-norm methods can in some instances be considered a form of data independent or *non-adaptive* spatial filtering (Greenblatt, Ossadtchi, and Pflieger 2005) and must account for a large number of possible configurations of sources resulting in high-dimensional solutions requiring various regularization techniques and relatively noise-free data (because the noise sources are not included in the model). Minimum-variance beamforming methods are computationally much simpler but also highly data dependent, and thus caution must be taken in the selection of data to avoid failure to accurately reconstruct all sources due to insufficient signal-to-noise or excessive source correlation (Brookes et al. 2007). Even under these circumstances, however, beamforming methods tend to be biased toward false negatives and are less likely to produce spurious or false solutions in comparison to conventional dipole modeling techniques. This is supported by a recent comparison of the LCMV beamformer, MUSIC, and minimum-norm estimation techniques based on receiver-operating characteristics (ROC), showing that beamformers performed the highest among the three methods in terms of sensitivity,that is, the highest true-positive rate relative to false negatives (Darvas et al. 2004).

Beamforming is an array signal-processing method used in radar and communications applications to improve the signal detection capability of multiple antenna arrays through the selective nulling of interference signals (Godara 1997; Van Veen and Buckley 1988) and has recently been adapted to the problem of neuromagnetic source reconstruction (Van Veen et al. 1997). A beamformer can be thought of as a spatial filter designed to detect a signal corresponding to a specified location while simultaneously attenuating signals from all other locations. For localization of brain activity the signal of interest is defined by the forward solution for a current dipole source at a specified location. In addition *adaptive* beamforming (based on the minimum-variance beamforming algorithm) does not require specifying the number of interference sources or their forward solutions. Various types of beamforming algorithms have been recently adapted to neuromagnetic measurements to take advantage of the high dimensionality of signal space afforded by currently available multi-channel MEG systems (Gross et al. 2001; Robinson and Vrba 1999; Sekihara et al. 2001). Although these different applications of the beamforming method to neuromagnetic source reconstruction have evolved independently and vary somewhat in the details of their implementation, they are similar in their mathematical basis. A number of recent reviews describe in detail mathematical similarities and differences between minimum-variance beamforming and other linear estimation techniques and also describe the relative performance of these methods for simulated data (Greenblatt, Ossadtchi, and Pflieger 2005; Hillebrand et al. 2005; Sekihara, Sahani, and Nagarajan 2005). It has also been shown that beamforming methods can be directly related to other linear estimation techniques, such as minimum-norm, differing primarily in the method of determining the source covariance (Mosher, Baillet, and Leahy, 2003). The appendix provides a brief description to the computation of spatial filters based on beamforming algorithms.

Correlated Activity

A main assumption to beamforming is that there is little to no correlated activity between brain regions. This assumption is not always valid, especially for spatially distinct regions that are driven by a common generator or stimulus such as in the case of bilateral activation of the auditory cortices (Brookes et al., 2007; Herdman et al. 2003; Van Veen et al. 1997). However, most brain correlations are not high (<80 percent) and generally persist for less than a few hundred milliseconds; thus a beamformer still works moderately well in such situations of moderately correlated activities (Van Veen et al. 1997). Several approaches, however, have been developed to compensate for the beamformer's inherent reduction of correlated sources (Brookes et al. 2007; Dalal, Sekihara, and Nagarajan 2006; Herdman et al. 2003; Popescu et al. 2008). One approach for dealing with correlated activity between auditory cortices calculates beamformer weights by using partial-sensor coverage, only sensors over each hemisphere, instead of full-sensor coverage (Herdman et al. 2003). Figure 5.10 shows the spatial distribution of the source magnitudes for each voxel calculated using the full-sensor and partial-sensor coverage for an axial slice at the level of a participant's auditory cortices. The left and right partial-sensor maps have been amalgamated into one map for easier visualization. Larger and narrower peaks are evident in the maps using

a. Whole array beamforming

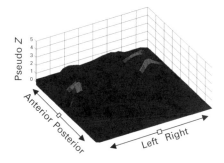

b. Half array beamforming

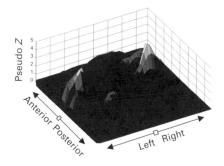

c. Hemispheric peaks

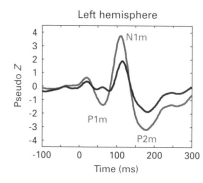

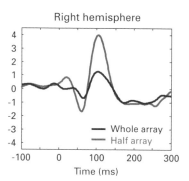

Figure 5.10
Beamformer outputs. Shown in the top graphs are the beamformer approaches for a single axial slice at the level the participant's auditory cortices for the whole array (a) and half array (b). Note the narrower and larger source powers (pseudo-Z values) for the half array method. The source waveforms (c) for the hemispheric peaks are shown in the lower graphs. The half array beamformer waveforms (red lines) are larger and represent the traditionally P1m–N1m–P2m morphology better than the whole array beamformer waveforms.

the partial-sensor than full-sensor approach. Additionally the source waveforms at the locations of the left- and right-hemispheric peaks in the spatial maps show an attenuated (P1m–N1m–P2m) response when calculating the beamformer weights using the full-sensor (black line) than the partial-sensor (red line) method. Figure 5.10a shows that correlated bilateral auditory activity can still be localized using the full-sensor approach, but it is attenuated because it accounts for the correlated hemispheric activity; whereas responses using the partial-sensor approach are less attenuated. This example is simply an illustration of the potential problem with beamformer suppression of correlated sources; there are however at least three caveats to using the partial-sensor approach: (1) full suppression of interference source in contralateral hemisphere is not guaranteed; (2) the degrees of freedom are reduced, thereby limiting the number of real and interfering sources allowable in the estimates of the beamformer weights; and (3) medial sources might be underrepresented, mislocalized, or absent where their resultant MEG fields that cross the midline are used in separate beamformer calculations (Popescu et al. 2008). In simulated auditory data, Popescu et al. (2008) showed substantial errors in estimates of source location, amplitude, and phase using the partial-sensor coverage approach, whereas the method of multiple-constrained minimum-variance beamformers with coherent source region suppression had little to no errors in estimates of source location, amplitude, or phase. This later method is similar to other approaches that are also effective at accurately localizing source activity and work by incorporating one or many locations (e.g., a volume) of correlated sources into the forward model, thereby removing its suppression from the beamformer calculations (Brookes et al. 2007; Dalal, Sekihara, and Nagarajan 2006). These methods work best when a priori information is given about what correlated sources can be acceptably added to the forward model. Such a priori information can be based on previous literature or searching for correlated sources within the data, which can be computationally intensive depending on the number of source locations to be searched. In summary, one must recognize the assumptions made to constrain the data used in beamformer calculations, and thus the results should be interpreted accordingly. Beamforming methods are continually advancing, and they provide researchers with improved accuracy in localizing source activities.

Signal to Noise

In general, the procedures as discussed above to obtain a good SNR data for ERF and TFR analyses are applicable to beamforming. Taking the appropriate steps to reduce the noise and increase the signal is important because the spatial resolution of a minimum-variance beamformer—such as synthetic aperture magnetometry (SAM)—is dependent on the data's SNR (Robinson and Vrba 1999). As evident in figure 5.11, the spread function of the SAM beamformer output and the number of spurious sources in the auditory event-related beamforming (ERB) images for an N1m response are

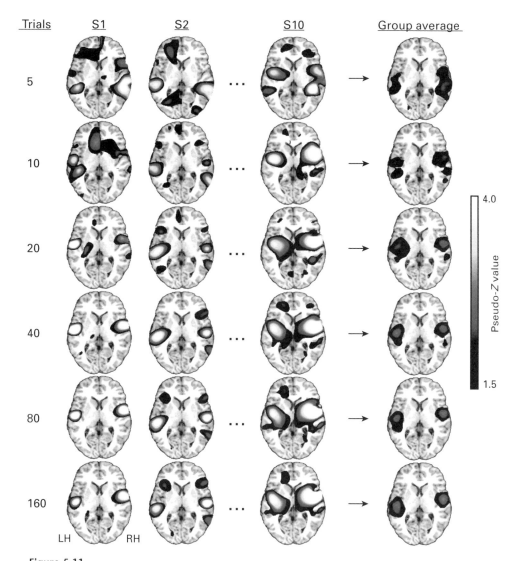

Figure 5.11

Effects of the number of trials used to calculate the event-related beamformer (SAM) images for ERFs to an 80 dB SPL tone. ER-SAM images were transformed into common anatomical space. Then a threshold of 1.5 (statistical threshold of $p < 0.01$ for the group average of 160 trials) was applied, and the resulting images were overlaid onto a template brain. ER-SAM maps for participant's S1, S2, and S10 that have less than 20 trials show inconsistent localizations of the auditory generators and several extra sources. The group-averaged images (*far right*) show bilateral activations for all trial averages, but it is not until 20 or more trials that the localizations accurately depict only one auditory generator in each hemisphere. (See plate X.)

reduced with increasing the number of trials that are used. The 160 trial ERB images clearly show two bilaterally discrete sources within the auditory cortices for the individual-participant and group-averaged ERB images. For less than 40 trials there are broadly distributed sources with large spread functions and extra sources throughout the brain. Furthermore auditory sources are not present, or they are localized to areas outside the auditory belt region for participant S1 and S2 in the 5 trial averaged images. On a positive note, auditory sources are present in all participants' images with at least 20 trials and the group-averaged images show two distinct auditory sources. This is where group averaging can help reduce the noise due to intersubject variability. Even though beamforming is used to spatially attenuate noise, thereby increasing SNR, an adequate number of trials are still needed to provide a sufficient SNR in order to properly estimate the beamformer weights for localizing ERFs.

Differential and Event-Related Beamforming

Two different applications of beamformer source imaging currently used in MEG are what we term here differential beamforming (Robinson and Vrba 1999) and event-related beamforming (Cheyne, Bakhtazad, and Gaetz 2006). Several studies have successfully implemented both differential and event-related beamformers in localizing auditory (e.g., Brookes et al. 2007; Herdman et al. 2003; Popescu et al. 2008), visual (e.g., Barnes et al. 2004; Brookes et al. 2005; Itier et al. 2006), somatosensory (e.g., Bardouille and Ross 2008; Cheyne et al. 2007; Gaetz and Cheyne 2003; Hashimoto et al. 2001; Ishii et al., 2002; Robinson 2004; Schulz et al. 2004), motor (e.g., Cheyne, Bakhtazad, and Gaetz 2006; Hillebrand et al. 2005; Ishii et al. 2002; Teismann et al. 2007), multisensory (e.g., Herdman et al. 2006), saccades (e.g., Herdman and Ryan 2007), mental effort (e.g., Ishii et al. 1999), language (e.g., Herdman et al. 2007; Hirata et al. 2004; Liu et al. 2008; Singh et al. 2002), and other related processes. Both differential and event-related beamformer methods similarly use the minimum-variance beamforming equations (see the appendix).

A *differential* beamformer compares outputs between two time intervals, generally expressed as active and control time intervals, for a specific frequency band. Thus a differential beamformer can be used to localize the changes in total response power (induced + evoked) relative to an event by comparing a poststimulus (active) interval to a prestimulus (control) interval. The choice of the time–frequency intervals for active and control states are user selected but they should adhere to the time–frequency trade-off principles as discussed above for TFR analyses. Additionally a differential beamformer will have estimates of both induced and evoked activity and thus should be interpreted accordingly. A detailed review of the differential beamforming technique is given by Hillebrand and colleagues (2005).

Although the beamformer output at the location of an active brain source will be correct, a normalized value such as the *neural activity index* (Van Veen et al. 1997) or the pseudo–*Z statistic* (Robinson and Vrba 1999) must be used to make volumetric images of source power throughout the brain. This is due to the nonhomogeneous amplification of noise throughout the image due to rapidly decreasing signal strength with increasing distance from the MEG sensors (see the appendix). Robinson and Vrba (1999) have presented a statistical estimate of the differential beamformer, termed the pseudo–*T* statistic. Figure 5.12 shows a differential beamformer localization (using the pseudo–*T* statistic for SAM) of an alpha-band event-related desynchronization (ERD) in the occipital cortices in response to a visual stimulus.

For an event-related beamformer (ERB), weights are estimated from one time interval across a broad frequency band (Cheyne, Bakhtazad, and Gaetz 2006; Cheyne et al. 2007). These weights are then applied to the averaged MEG data to calculate the total source power at a given voxel location and time point. A similar approach was proposed by Sekihara and colleagues (2001), which they termed a *spatiotemporal* beamformer. An implementation of an event-related or spatiotemporal beamformer was recently described by Cheyne et al. (2006) and termed *event-related SAM* because it was computationally similar to the SAM beamformer algorithm introduced by Robinson and Vrba (1999). The latter introduced the concept of using a scalar instead of a vector beamforming approach (single rather than multiple orthogonal sources at each brain location) by searching for the optimal source orientation based on single trial data. A more recent hybrid approach was also described (Cheyne et al. 2007) that derives source orientation directly from a vector beamformer. Both procedures can produce four-dimensional images (volume by time) of the event-related activity. However, the ERB method arbitrarily assigns the polarity of the source power (current flow away or toward to the cortical surface) across each voxel because the source orientation determined by the beamformer is not unique (i.e., could be either 37° or 217°). This makes the maps ambiguous and, more important, averaging across participants inappropriate unless

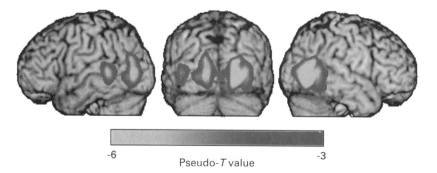

-6   Pseudo-*T* value   -3

Figure 5.12

A differential beamformer image of an alpha (7–12 Hz) event-related desynchronization (ERD) between 300 to 6,000 ms after a visual stimulus (a word) was presented at the screen's center. The ERD was calculated as pseudo-*T* values and projected to the surface of 3D MRI. (See plate XI.)

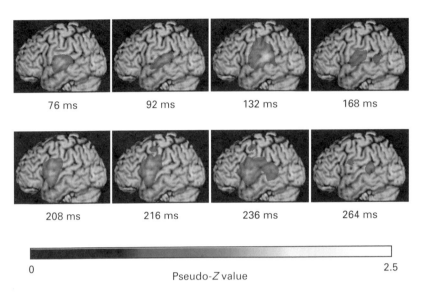

76 ms   92 ms   132 ms   168 ms

208 ms   216 ms   236 ms   264 ms

0   Pseudo-Z value   2.5

Figure 5.13
Event-related beamformer (ER-SAM) images projected to the surface of a 3D MRI at the peak latencies of 76 to 264 ms of the event-related fields with respect to a spoken noun from which participants had to generate a semantically related action word. Note that the spread of source locations from the transverse temporal gyrus at 76 ms to the inferior frontal gyrus at 208 ms follow the path described for the classical language network. (See plate XII.)

the source polarities are flipped to be in a consistent direction across the group. Flipping the polarity of thousands of sources in a brain volume is not practical. A simple alternative is to take the absolute values of the beamformer output to construct the ERB images. Figure 5.13 shows group-averaged ERB 3D maps for an auditory task in which participants generated an action word associated with a noun spoken to them (Herdman et al. 2007). The ERB maps show a spread of activation from the primary auditory cortex (76–132 ms) to the posterior-superior temporal sulcus (132–168 ms), and then to the insula/frontal operculum and precentral sulcus (208–236 ms). These regions and flow of activity are consistent with feed-forward pathway of the classically defined language network. This example illustrates the usefulness of the ERB method to localize processes related to audition, as well as language.

Group-Averaging
Each person's head and brain anatomy are unique but are grossly consistency across individuals of similar age, gender, ethnicity, and development. Because of anatomical variability across individuals, locations of function will also be variable. In order to group-average beamformer images, it is necessary to transform each individual's

functional maps into a common anatomical space (Barnes and Hillebrand 2003). This step was initially developed for PET and fMRI data and can be accomplished using several software packages, such as the Statistical Parametric Mapping (SPM) software from University College of London(www.fil.ion.ucl.ac.uk/spm/) or the FSL software from the University of Oxford, UK (http://www.fmrib.ox.ac.uk/fsl/). The first step is to define a template to be used as a common anatomical space. Typically the Talaraich-Tourneoux (Talaraich and Tournoux 1988) or MNI (Montreal Neurological Institute; www.bic.mni.mcgill.ca) template brains are used to allow comparisons across studies and labs. The next step is to calculate a transformation matrix for the normalizing each individual's structural data to the common anatomical space. This transformation matrix is then applied to the beamformer images in order to normalize them to a common space. Averaging and statistical analyses can then be applied to these normalized beamformer images.

Statistical Analyses

Subtracting Beamformer Images A common practice in neuroimaging is to subtract responses among conditions and/or participant groups. Because beamformer outputs are an estimate of the SNR, differences could be due to signal and/or noise differences between conditions. Thus, when calculating differential beamforming or ERB between two conditions, the researcher should ensure that the noise levels are similar across conditions. Using the same number of trials for each condition will generally produce similar noise levels, but the noise floor should be quantitatively evaluated for each condition. Statistically comparing the means and variances of the beamformer outputs within a baseline (control) time interval should be performed to determine if significant differences exist in noise levels between conditions. If differences exist, then the researcher should attempt to equate the noise levels by possibly altering the number of trials in one condition and/or to ensure that artifacts are not contaminating one condition more than another.

Furthermore special consideration needs to be taken when estimating the beamformer weights for the ERB method. Here we outline three approaches and their caveats to comparing ERB outputs across conditions. One method is to subtract the single-trial sensor data for condition B from condition A with equal number of trials per condition and then calculate the ERB on the difference data. This will ensure that the magnitude and phase differences between conditions remain in the data before ERB calculation. Importantly, this approach is not wrought with having different noise estimates in the ERB weights because the ERB calculations are performed on one data set, the difference waveforms. This should theoretically result in a better source estimate for the underlying physiological processes involved in modulating a source component or the addition of another source component in one condition (i.e., a difference component).

However, subtracting data sets alters the background noise, which therefore affects the beamformer weights. This procedure needs further investigation to determine its validity in localizing difference components, such as mismatch negativity. A second method is to concatenate the single-trial data for all conditions into one data set, then calculate the ERB weights for the concatenated data set yielding an estimate of the overall source activity, then applying the weights to each condition's averaged data, and finally subtracting the ERB rectified outputs between conditions. The caveat to this approach is that the weights are based on the amalgamation of the signal variances among conditions and could lead to not finding additional source generators if the single-state responses dominate estimating the weights. A third method is to calculate the ERB weights for each condition individually and then subtract the ERB rectified outputs. The additional problem with this approach is the problem discussed above if noise levels are different between conditions. This could lead to finding false sources because the spatial spread function of an ERB map is related to the data's SNR. Differences in ERB maps could simply result from larger noise in one condition yielding a broader spatial distribution than in the other condition and when subtracted the difference map could have spatial maxima that are related to noise differences, not signal differences. For this later method a conservative position would be to only contrast the ERB outputs at the location of the spatial maxima for each condition and not spatial maxima in the difference ERB maps.

Calculating Significance Thresholds A main objective for statistical analyses of beamformer images is to obtain a confidence level or threshold that identifies which source locations have activity that is greater than noise. For this purpose a null distribution of the noise needs to be estimated and then test if each beamformer voxel's magnitude exceeds a given threshold determined by the user-defined alpha level (usually $P < 0.01$). Several methods have been developed to assess the statistical significance of functional maps. One way to estimate noise distribution is using permutation analyses (Chau et al. 2005). The basic permutation method rearranges the active and control beamformer outputs for one individual's map, averages this map with the other participants, and then repeats this procedure for all individuals. Thus a full matrix of permuted images for the null distribution will be 2^n (where n is the number of individual images). Values from all permutations across all voxels and participants can be used to construct the null distribution. Confidence levels can then be estimated from this distribution and used as statistical thresholds for beamformer image. Thus voxels with beamformer outputs exceeding a set threshold are considered significant. This does not mean that each voxel contains source activity but rather that it is an estimate of the SNR and the probability of a source being resident at that location. For the ERB method, the null distribution could simply be calculated from the beamformer images of a prestimulus interval or of a plus/minus reference. For the prestimulus interval, the assumption is that it contains only noise, and thus poststimulus beamformer outputs are considered significant if they exceed a confidence level (i.e., threshold) determined from the noise distribution of a prestimulus interval.

Once beamformer images are thresholded, locations of maximal ERB output can be identified by finding peaks that are spatially separated by a preset amount (e.g., 1–2 cm). These images can then be visualized using one of many commercial or custom software packages for visualizing functional and structural brain images. A peak location has the highest probability of being the generator location and can then be used as a location to extract the time–domain beamformer outputs for single or averaged trial data. These time–domain data from peak ERB locations can then be used for further analyses, such as TFR analyses as described for ERFs above.

Concluding Comments

MEG provides a means to directly and noninvasively measure the electromagnetic activity from neurons in the human brain. Although measuring MEG requires specialized instrumentation and procedures, it can be used to record from typically and atypically developing children and adults, as well as from clinical populations (e.g., epilepsy). Like most neuroimaging techniques, participant factors, collection procedures, and analysis methods should be carefully considered when designing MEG studies in order to obtain the highest quality data possible. Once the data are collected, latest advances in source modeling procedures, such as beamforming, can provide a means to estimate MEG activity from neural networks with exquisite temporal (<1 ms) and good spatial specificity (5–20 mm). Current advancements in neuroimaging are using MEG and beamforming techniques to understand the complexity by which the neural populations in the human brain dynamically interact through short- and long-range connections. Thus the field of neuroimaging is helping to gain significant ground on understanding the underlying neural processes involved in perception and cognition and their relationships with behavior.

Appendix: Minimum-Variance Beamforming

We denote the measured magnetic field magnitude as a function of time t for the mth detector as $b_m(t)$ and the measured field as the vector $\mathbf{m}(t)$, where

$$\mathbf{m}(t) = [b_1(t), b_2(t), \ldots, b_M(t)]. \tag{1}$$

We then define a beamformer spatial filter for a given brain location, expressed as the three-dimensional position vector $\mathbf{r}$ ($= x, y, z$) with a unique set of coefficients or weights (one weight per MEG detector) denoted $\mathbf{w}(\mathbf{r})$. The total power projected by the filter for this location $S^2(\mathbf{r})$ over some interval of time $\mathbf{T}$ is given by the temporal integration of the measured data as a function of time multiplied by the weights

$$S^2(\mathbf{r}) = \int_{\mathbf{T}} \left| \mathbf{w}^T(\mathbf{r})\mathbf{m}(t) \right|^2 dt, \tag{2}$$

where T denotes transpose. If the weights must account for more than one source at each location, we replace $\mathbf{w}(r)$ with a multidimensional weight matrix $\mathbf{W}(r)$ and the expression above can be more conveniently written as

$$S^2(\mathbf{r}) = tr\{\mathbf{W}^T(\mathbf{r})\mathbf{C}_m\mathbf{W}(\mathbf{r})\}, \tag{3}$$

where $\mathbf{C}_m$ represents the measured data covariance matrix computed over the time interval $\mathbf{T}$ and $tr\{\cdot\}$ represents the trace of the resulting $N \times N$ matrix for a $N \times M$-dimensional spatial filter given by $\mathbf{W}^T$. To derive a spatial filter that minimizes contributions from all sources, yet passes activity for the source of interest with known magnitude, we seek weights that will minimize total power output of the spatial filter given by (3), while retaining unity gain for the forward solution for the target source. This can be expressed as the following minimization problem:

$$\min_{\mathbf{W}(\mathbf{r})} S^2(\mathbf{r}) = \mathbf{W}^T(\mathbf{r})\mathbf{C}_m\mathbf{W}(\mathbf{r}) \tag{4}$$

subject to

$$\mathbf{W}^T(\mathbf{r})\mathbf{H}(\mathbf{r}) = \mathbf{I}, \tag{5}$$

where $\mathbf{H}(\mathbf{r})$ represents the N by M matrix of forward solutions with N as the number of forward solution vectors, one forward solution for current flow in each orthogonal direction. When a spherical model is used, only tangentially flowing currents contribute to the MEG signal, and $\mathbf{H}(\mathbf{r})$ is represented by two orthogonal tangential dipoles with forward solutions denoted $\mathbf{B}(\mathbf{r}, \mathbf{u}_\theta)$ and $\mathbf{B}(\mathbf{r}, \mathbf{u}_\phi)$ such that $\mathbf{H}(\mathbf{r}) = [\mathbf{B}(\mathbf{r}, \mathbf{u}_\theta), \mathbf{B}(\mathbf{r}, \mathbf{u}_\phi)]$. The solution to (5) can be solved using the associated Lagrange multiplier function, resulting in what is commonly referred to as the *linearly constrained minimum-variance* or LCMV beamformer (Van Veen et al. 1997) because it involves minimization of the signal power or variance with multiple linear constraints for response of the filter to sources with orthogonal orientations at location $\mathbf{r}$. The solution is given by

$$\mathbf{W}(\mathbf{r}) = \mathbf{C}_m^{-1}\mathbf{H}(\mathbf{r})\left[\mathbf{H}^T(\mathbf{r})\mathbf{C}_m^{-1}\mathbf{H}(\mathbf{r})\right]^{-1}, \tag{6}$$

where $\mathbf{C}_m$ the data covariance matrix based on the measured signals for the data segments of interest, and $\mathbf{W}(\mathbf{r})$ is the resulting $N \times M$ weight matrix.

The solution for the beamformer weights given by (6) requires computing the measurement covariance matrix inverse, $\mathbf{C}_m^{-1}$ and thus assumes this matrix is well estimated and nonsingular. In some cases this may not be true (e.g., in the case of averaged data) and regularization of the covariance matrix may be required prior to computing the beamformer weights, typically by replacing $\mathbf{C}_m^{-1}$ with $[\mathbf{C}_m + \mu\mathbf{I}]^{-1}$, where μ is a parameter that determines the amount of regularization and $\mathbf{I}$ is the identity matrix.

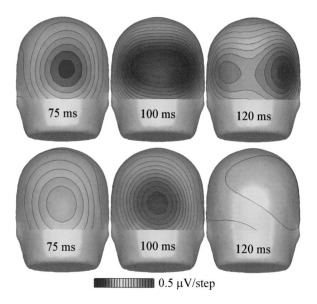

Plate I

Topographic maps indicating the scalp distribution of the VEP (*top row*) and the VESPA (*bottom row*) at 75, 100, and 120 ms. Activity at 100 ms is much more focused over the midline for the VESPA. The bilateral spread evident at 120 ms for the VEP is not manifest in the VESPA.

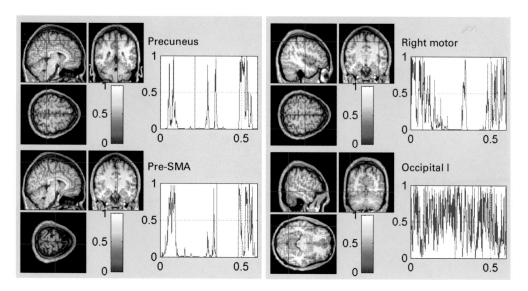

Plate II

Temporally adjusted *p*-values for some motor and nonmotor areas. The voxels are indicated by the intersection of the blue crosses at the left of each panel. The temporal evolution of the *p*-value after temporal adjustment is depicted on the right. The horizontal axis depicts the time in seconds with key pressing occurring at 0.4 s.

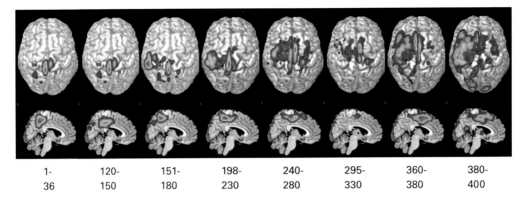

| 1- | 120- | 151- | 198- | 240- | 295- | 360- | 380- |
| 36 | 150 | 180 | 230 | 280 | 330 | 380 | 400 |

Plate III

Spatiotemporal sequence of brain voxels that statistically differ ($p < 0.05$, adjusted) between left and right self-paced finger tapping. The picture is constructed by selecting periods when the same pixels remained differentially activated over time and computing for each of these periods the mean over time of the $(1 - p)$-value.

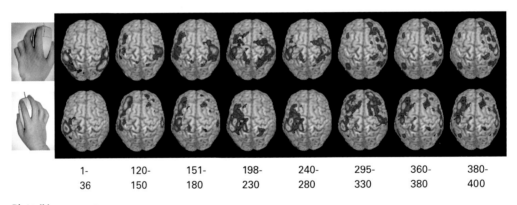

| 1- | 120- | 151- | 198- | 240- | 295- | 360- | 380- |
| 36 | 150 | 180 | 230 | 280 | 330 | 380 | 400 |

Plate IV

Electrical neuroimaging (ELECTRA inverse solution) results for the analysis procedure based on ERPs obtained for left-hand (*top plot*) and right-hand finger tapping (*bottom*). The temporal periods presented are identical to those in plate III.

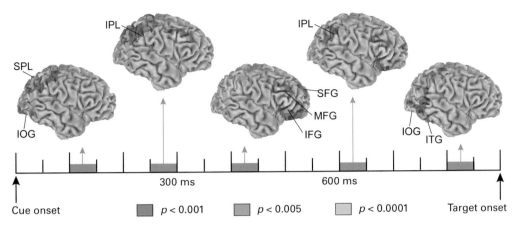

Plate V

Statistical nonparametric mapping of EEG beamformer output. Shown are SnPMs of theta-band activity for five time intervals during the cue-target interval of a spatial cueing task. Only the statistically significant ($p < 0.005$) activity is displayed. Adapted from Green and McDonald (2008).

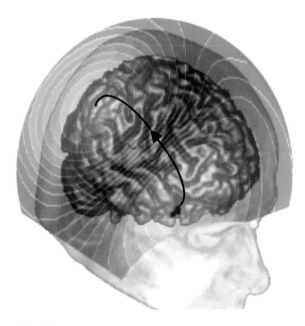

Plate VI

Topography of an auditory event-related field (an N1m) represented on a helmet's surface overlaying a participant's head. A green arrowed line depicts the directions of the outgoing (blue) and ingoing (red) magnetic fields. An active auditory source, estimated with an event-related beamformer technique, is projected to the cortical surface lying along the Sylvian fissure.

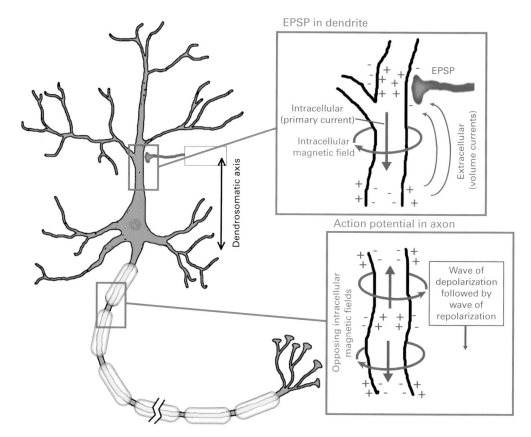

Plate VII

Neurophysiological events underlying the generation of the MEG signal. Excitatory postsynaptic potentials (EPSPs) in the apical dendrites of a pyramidal neuron create intracellular current flow (blue arrowed line) toward the soma. This current will create a magnetic field (red arrowed line) perpendicular to the dendrosomatic axis, similar to current flowing in a wire (see plate VI) that is recordable in far-field MEG measurements. Action potentials in the axon also create larger intracellular current flow along the length of the axon and perpendicular magnetic fields. However, depolarization and repolarization of the axonal membrane create opposing magnetic fields that are in close proximity to each other (represented as a quadrapole); therefore action potentials result in minimal far-field MEG signals.

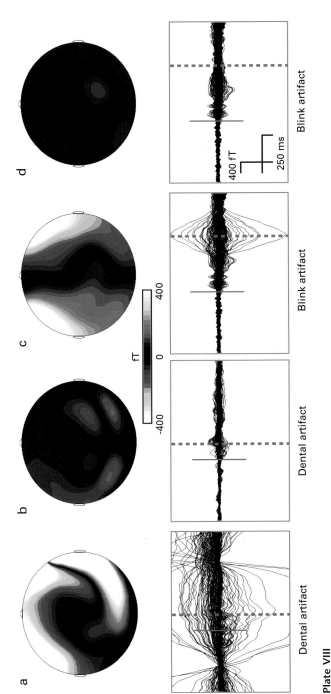

Plate VIII

Artifact reduction using principle component analysis (PCA) on dental implant (a–b) and eye-blink (c–d) artifacts. The waveforms from 151 sensors are overlaid in an butterfly plot in the bottom graphs with the corresponding topographies (top view with the nose pointing toward top of page, left ear on left side, and right ear on right side) at the time designated by the red dotted line. The red solid line designates stimulus onset of a visual object presented at foveal fixation. The dental artifacts (a) distributed over the frontal and lower temporal sensors produce large magnetic fields that obscure any underlying neuromagnetic responses. Once the principle components related to the dental artifacts are removed, visual event-related field are clearly observed in the waveforms and topography (b). A blink artifact (c) can also be reduced by using the PCA procedure as observed in comparing (c) before correction with (d) after correction.

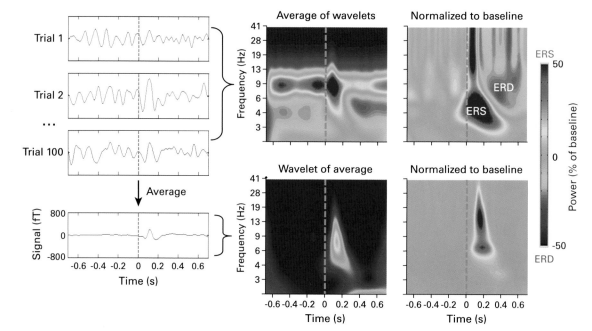

Plate IX

Time–frequency analyses of single-trial (*top left*) and averaged trial (*bottom left*) induced and evoked auditory responses in a sensor over the temporal parietal junction. The single-trial waveforms show a classical alpha (7–13 Hz) rhythm that is suppressed after the tone onset. This is clearly seen in the wavelet coefficients (*top middle*) as a dark red band across the prestimulus interval that is reduced in the poststimulus interval after about 250 ms. This rhythm has been termed an event-related desynchronization (ERD), and it is evident in the normalized to baseline map (*top right*). An event-related synchronization (ERS) is also visible and is most likely related to the evoked responses, which can be seen in the bottom middle and left plots.

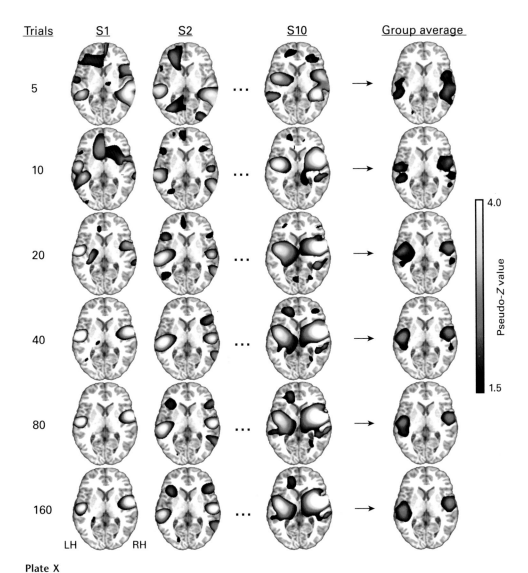

Plate X

Effects of the number of trials used to calculate the event-related beamformer (SAM) images for ERFs to an 80 dB SPL tone. ER-SAM images were transformed into common anatomical space. Then a threshold of 1.5 (statistical threshold of $p < 0.01$ for the group average of 160 trials) was applied, and the resulting images were overlaid onto a template brain. ER-SAM maps for participant's S1, S2, and S10 that have less than 20 trials show inconsistent localizations of the auditory generators and several extra sources. The group-averaged images (*far right*) show bilateral activations for all trial averages, but it is not until 20 or more trials that the localizations accurately depict only one auditory generator in each hemisphere.

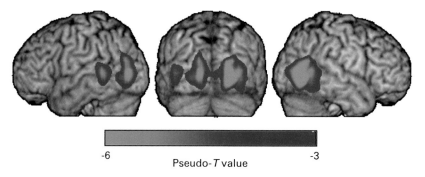

-6   Pseudo-*T* value   -3

Plate XI

A differential beamformer image of an alpha (7–12 Hz) event-related desynchronization (ERD) between 300 and 6,000 ms after a visual stimulus (a word) was presented at the screen's center. The ERD was calculated as pseudo-*T* values and projected to the surface of 3D MRI.

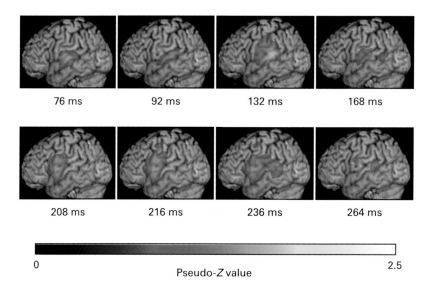

| 76 ms | 92 ms | 132 ms | 168 ms |

| 208 ms | 216 ms | 236 ms | 264 ms |

0   Pseudo-*Z* value   2.5

Plate XII

Event-related beamformer (ER-SAM) images projected to the surface of a 3D MRI at the peak latencies of 76 to 264 ms of the event-related fields with respect to a spoken noun from which participants had to generate a semantically related action word. Note that the spread of source locations from the transverse temporal gyrus at 76 ms to the inferior frontal gyrus at 208 ms follow the path described for the classical language network.

It is important to point out here that increasing the amount of regularization of $\mathbf{C}_m$ decreases the spatial selectivity of the beamformer as it decreases the contribution of the spatial correlation between sensors (i.e., the off-diagonals of $\mathbf{C}_m$). Thus regularization of $\mathbf{C}_m$ acts as a trade-off between spatial resolution of the filter and sensitivity to noise. With no regularization ($\mu = 0$) the beamformer provides maximal resolution and therefore optimal ability to separate closely spaces sources.

Since the covariance matrix $\mathbf{C}_m$ is often computed only over the time period of interest, a convenient estimate of the total source power over this interval at the voxel location $\mathbf{r}$ is given by

$$\hat{S}^2(\mathbf{r}) = tr\left\{\mathbf{W}(\mathbf{r})^\top \mathbf{C}_m \mathbf{W}(\mathbf{r})\right\}. \tag{7}$$

It might be noted here that if we only desire source power over the covariance time window, we can substitute (6) into (7)—in which case the weight vector terms cancel and the source power is given by $S^2(\mathbf{r}) = tr\{[\mathbf{H}(\mathbf{r})\mathbf{C}_m^{-1}\mathbf{H}(\mathbf{r})]^{-1}\}$—without computing the weights directly. In the case of a *scalar* beamformer where a single dominant current orientation can be estimated for each brain location, the weight matrix $\mathbf{W}(\mathbf{r})$ simplifies to a single column vector $\mathbf{w}(\mathbf{r})$, making it more convenient to compute the output of the beamformer filter in units of source amplitude or moment (i.e., Ampere-meters) as a single time series (sometimes referred to as a "virtual sensor" or "virtual electrode") for each brain location $\mathbf{r}$ as a function of time t given by

$$S(\mathbf{r}, t) = \mathbf{w}(\mathbf{r})^\top \mathbf{m}(t). \tag{8}$$

Since spatial filters based on beamforming coefficients with maximal spatial resolution should result in reduced or minimal crosstalk between multiple sources, the output of these filters can be used to create a volumetric source image by computing arrays of spatial filters at fixed spacing over a large region of the brain. However, the beamformer weights computed using equations (7) and (8) are unable to suppress *uncorrelated* noise, which will be amplified in a spatially non-uniform manner by the weights due to rapidly decreasing signal strength with increasing distance from the sensors, resulting in spatial distortions in the beamformer images (Van Veen et al. 1997). Fortunately this distortion can be effectively removed by normalizing the beamformer output by an estimated amount of the uncorrelated noise projected through the weights, by taking the ratio of projected signal power to projected noise power. The result is beamformer output that is scaled to units of noise variance. This has been termed the *neural activity index* (Van Veen et al. 1997) or *pseudo–Z* statistic (Robinsonand Vrba 1999). If Σ_n is a diagonal matrix of estimated sensor noise variance the pseudo–Z statistic is given by

$$Z^2(\mathbf{r}) = \frac{tr\left\{\mathbf{W}(\mathbf{r})^\top \mathbf{C}_m \mathbf{W}(\mathbf{r})\right\}}{tr\left\{\mathbf{W}(\mathbf{r})^\top \sum_n \mathbf{W}(\mathbf{r})\right\}}. \tag{9}$$

Similarly *weight vector normalized* beamformers may be employed (Huang et al. 2004; Sekihara et al. 2001) where the beamformer coefficients (equation 6) are normalized by the square of the weight vector matrix, that is, by the gain of the weights. The estimate of source power directly from the weights is then free from spatial distortions, although output of such beamformers will be in arbitrary units.

References

Auranen T, Nummenmaa A, Hamalainen MS, et al. 2007. Bayesian inverse analysis of neuromagnetic data using cortically constrained multiple dipoles. *Hum Brain Mapp* 28:979–94.

Baillet S, Mosher JC, Leahy RM. 2001. Electromagnetic brain mapping. 14–30.

Bardouille T, Ross B. 2008. MEG imaging of sensorimotor areas using inter-trial coherence in vibrotactile steady-state responses. *NeuroImage* 42(1):323–31.

Barnes GR, Hillebrand A. 2003. Statistical flattening of MEG beamformer images. *Hum Brain Mapp* 18:1–12.

Barnes GR, Hillebrand A, Fawcett IP, Singh KD. 2004. Realistic spatial sampling for MEG beamformer images. *Hum Brain Mapp* 23:120–7.

Beg F, Wong S, Cheung T, Virji-Babul N, Herdman AT. (submitted) External landmark and headshape based functional data normalization. *NeuroImage*.

Berg P, Scherg M. 1991. Dipole modelling of eye activity and its application to the removal of eye artefacts from the EEG and MEG. *Clin Phys Physiol Meas* 12 (suppl):A49–54.

Brookes MJ, Gibson AM, Hall SD, et al. 2005. GLM-beamformer method demonstrates stationary field, alpha ERD and gamma ERS co-localisation with fMRI BOLD response in visual cortex. *NeuroImage* 26:302–8.

Brookes MJ, Stevenson CM, Barnes GR, et al. 2007. Beamformer reconstruction of correlated sources using a modified source model. *NeuroImage* 34:1454–65.

Chau W, Mcintosh AR, Robinson SE, Schulz M, Pantev C. 2004. Improving permutation test power for group analysis of spatially filtered MEG data. *NeuroImage* 23:983–96.

Cheyne D, Bakhtazad L, Gaetz W. 2006. Spatiotemporal mapping of cortical activity accompanying voluntary movements using an event-related beamforming approach. *Hum Brain Mapp* 27:213–29.

Cheyne D, Bostan AC, Gaetz W, Pang EW. 2007. Event-related beamforming: a robust method for presurgical functional mapping using MEG. *Clin Neurophysiol* 118:1691–1704.

Cohen D. 1968. Magnetoencephalography: evidence of magnetic fields produced by alpha-rhythm currents. *Science* 161:784–6.

Dalal SS, Sekihara K, Nagarajan SS. 2006. Modified beamformers for coherent source region suppression. *IEEE Trans Biomed Eng* 53:1357–63.

Dale AM, Liu AK, Fischl BR, et al. 2000. Dynamic statistical parametric mapping: combining fMRI and MEG for high-resolution imaging of cortical activity. *Neuron* 26:55–67.

Darvas F, Pantazis D, Kucukaltun-Yildirim E, Leahy RM. 2004. Mapping human brain function with MEG and EEG: methods and validation. *NeuroImage* 23(suppl 1):S289–99.

David O, Kiebel SJ, Harrison LM, Mattout J, Kilner JM, Friston KJ. 2006. Dynamic causal modeling of evoked responses in EEG and MEG. *NeuroImage* 30:1255–72.

Gaetz WC, Cheyne DO. 2003. Localization of human somatosensory cortex using spatially filtered magnetoencephalography. *Neurosci Lett* 340:161–4.

Godara LC. 1997. Application of antenna array to mobile communications. Part II: Beam-forming and direction-of-arrival considerations. *Proc IEEE* 85:1195–1245.

Gorodnitsky IF, George JS, Rao BD. 1995. Neuromagnetic source imaging with FOCUSS: a recursive weighted minimum norm algorithm. *Electroencephalogr Clin Neurophysiol* 95:231–51.

Greenblatt RE, Ossadtchi A, Pflieger M. 2005. Local linear estimators for the bioelectromagnetic inverse problem. *IEEE Trans Sign Process* 53:3403–12.

Gross J, Kujala J, Hamalainen M, Timmermann L, Schnitzler A, Salmelin R. 2001. Dynamic imaging of coherent sources: studying neural interactions in the human brain. *Proc Natl Acad Sci USA* 98:694–69.

Hamalainen M, Hari R, Ilmoniemi RJ, Knuutila J, Lounasmaa OV. 1993. Magnetoencephalography: theory, instrumentation, and applications to noninvasive studies of the working human brain. *Rev Mod Phys* 65:413–96.

Hamalainen MS, Ilmoniemi RJ. 1984. *Interpreting Measured Magnetic Fields of the Brain: Estimates of Current Distribution.* tkk-f-a559.

Hari R, Pelizzone M, Makela JP, Hallstrom J, Leinonen L, Lounasmaa OV. 1987. Neuromagnetic responses of the human auditory cortex to on- and offsets of noise bursts. *Audiology* 26:31–43.

Hari R, Salmelin R, Makela JP, Salenius S, Helle M. 1997. Magnetoencephalographic cortical rhythms. *Int J Psychophysiol* 26:51–62.

Hashimoto I, Kimura T, Iguchi Y, Takino R, Sekihara K. 2001. Dynamic activation of distinct cytoarchitectonic areas of the human SI cortex after median nerve stimulation. *Neuroreport* 12:1891–187.

Herdman AT, Fujioka T, Chau W, Ross B, Pantev C, Picton TW. 2006. Cortical oscillations related to processing congruent and incongruent grapheme-phoneme pairs. *Neurosci Lett* 399:61–6.

Herdman AT, Pang EW, Ressel V, Gaetz W, Cheyne D. 2007. Task-related modulation of early cortical responses during language production: an event-related synthetic aperture magnetometry study. *Cerebr Cortex* 17:2536–43.

Herdman AT, Ryan JD. 2007. Spatio-temporal brain dynamics underlying saccade execution, suppression, and error-related feedback. *J Cogn Neurosci* 19:420–32.

Herdman AT, Wollbrink A, Chau W, Ishii R, Ross B, Pantev C. 2003. Determination of activation areas in the human auditory cortex by means of synthetic aperture magnetometry. *NeuroImage* 20:995–1005.

Hillebrand A, Singh KD, Holliday IE, Furlong PL, Barnes GR. 2005. A new approach to neuroimaging with magnetoencephalography. *Hum Brain Mapp* 25:199–211.

Hirata M, Kato A, Taniguchi M, et al. 2004. Determination of language dominance with synthetic aperture magnetometry: comparison with the Wada test. *NeuroImage* 23:46–53.

Holliday IE, Barnes GR, Hillebrand A, Singh KD. 2003. Accuracy and applications of group MEG studies using cortical source locations estimated from participants' scalp surfaces. *Hum Brain Mapp* 20:142–7.

Huang MX, Shih JJ, Lee RR, et al. 2004. Commonalities and differences among vectorized beamformers in electromagnetic source imaging. *Brain Topogr* 16:139–58.

Ioannides AA, Bolton JPR, Clarke CJS. 1990. Continuous probabilistic solutions to the biomagnetic inverse problem. *Inverse Probl* 6:523–42.

Ishii R, Schulz M, Xiang J, et al. 2002. MEG study of long-term cortical reorganization of sensorimotor areas with respect to using chopsticks. *Neuroreport* 13:2155–9.

Ishii R, Shinosaki K, Ukai S, et al. 1999. Medial prefrontal cortex generates frontal midline theta rhythm. *Neuroreport* 10:675–69.

Itier RJ, Herdman AT, George N, Cheyne D, Taylor MJ. 2006. Inversion and contrast-reversal effects on face processing assessed by MEG. *Brain Res* 1115:108–20.

Joshi AA, Shattuck DW, Thompson PM, Leahy RM. 2005. A framework for registration, statistical characterization and classification of cortically constrained functional imaging data. *Info Process Med Imag Proc Conf* 19:186–96.

Liu Y, Xiang J, Wang Y, Vannest JJ, Byars AW, Rose DF. 2008. Spatial and frequency differences of neuromagnetic activities in processing concrete and abstract words. *Brain Topogr* 20:123–9.

Lu Z, Kaufman L. 2003. *Magnetic Source Imaging of the Human Brain*. Mahwah, NJ: Erlbaum.

Marinkovic K, Cox B, Reid K, Halgren E. 2004. Head position in the MEG helmet affects the sensitivity to anterior sources. *Neurol Clin_Neurophysiol NCN*:30.

Mosher JC, Baillet S, Leahy RM. 2003. Equivalence of linear approaches in bioelectromagnetic inverse solutions. IEEE Workshop on Statistical Signal Processing, St. Louis, MO.

Naatanen R, Paavilainen P, Rinne T, Alho K. 2007. The mismatch negativity (MMN) in basic research of central auditory processing: a review. *Clin Neurophysiol* 118:2544–90.

Nellhaus G. 1968. Head circumference from birth to eighteen years. Practical composite international and interracial graphs. *Pediatrics* 41:106–14.

Niedermeyer E, Lopes da Silva FH. 2005. *Electroencephalography: Basic Principles, Clinical Applications, and Related Fields*. Philadelphia: Lippincott Williams Wilkins.

Nunez PL. 1981. *Electric Fields of the Brain*. New York: Oxford University Press.

Pantazis D, Nichols TE, Baillet S, Leahy RM. 2005. A comparison of random field theory and permutation methods for the statistical analysis of MEG data. *NeuroImage* 25:383–94.

Pantev C, Dinnesen A, Ross B, Wollbrink A, Knief A. 2006. Dynamics of auditory plasticity after cochlear implantation: a longitudinal study. *Cerebr Cortex* 16:31–6.

Pascual-Marqui RD. 2002. Standardized low-resolution brain electromagnetic tomography (sLORETA): technical details. *Meth Findings Exp Clin Pharmacol* 24(suppl D):5–12.

Pascual-Marqui RD, Michel CM, Lehmann D. 1994. Low resolution electromagnetic tomography: a new method for localizing electrical activity in the brain. *Int J Psychophysiol* 18:49–65.

Pfurtscheller G. 2001. Functional brain imaging based on ERD/ERS. *Vision Res* 41:1257–60.

Pfurtscheller G, Aranibar A. 1977. Event-related cortical desynchronization detected by power measurements of scalp EEG. *Electroencephalogr Clin Neurophysiol* 42:817–26.

Picton TW, Lins OG, Scherg M. 1995. The recording and analysis of event-related potentials. In: Boller F, Grafman J, eds. *Handbook of Neurophysiology*. New York: Elsevier, 3–73.

Picton TW, van Roon P, Armilio ML, Berg P, Ille N, Scherg M. 2000. The correction of ocular artifacts: a topographic perspective. *Clin Neurophysiol* 111:53–65.

Popescu M, Popescu EA, Chan T, Blunt SD, Lewine JD. 2008. Spatio-temporal reconstruction of bilateral auditory steady-state responses using MEG beamformers. *IEEE Trans Biomed Eng* 55:1092–1102.

Robinson SE. 2004. Localization of event-related activity by SAM(erf). *Neurol Clin Neurophysiol* NCN:109.

Robinson SE, Vrba J. 1999. Functional neuroimaging by synthetic aperture magnetometry (SAM). In: Yoshimoto T, Kotani M, Kuriki S, Karibe H, Nakasato N, eds. *Recent Advances in Biomagnetism*. Sendai: Tohoku University Press, 302–5.

Salmelin R, Hari R. 1994. Characterization of spontaneous MEG rhythms in healthy adults. *Electroencephalogr Clin Neurophysiol* 91:237–48.

Schulz M, Chau W, Graham SJ, et al. 2004. An integrative MEG-fMRI study of the primary somatosensory cortex using cross-modal correspondence analysis. *NeuroImage* 22:120–33.

Sekihara K, Nagarajan SS, Poeppel D, Marantz A, Miyashita Y. 2001. Reconstructing spatio-temporal activities of neural sources using an MEG vector beamformer technique. *IEEE Trans Biomed Eng* 48:760–71.

Sekihara K, Sahani M, Nagarajan SS. 2005. Localization bias and spatial resolution of adaptive and non-adaptive spatial filters for MEG source reconstruction. *NeuroImage* 25:1056–67.

Sekihara K, Nagarajan S. 2008. *Adaptive Spatial Filters for Electromagnetic Brain Imaging*. Berlin: Springer.

Singh KD, Barnes GR, Hillebrand A, Forde EM, Williams AL. 2002. Task-related changes in cortical synchronization are spatially coincident with the hemodynamic response. *NeuroImage* 16:103–14.

Talaraich J, Tournoux P. 1988. *Co-planar Stereotaxic Atlas of the Human Brain: 3-Dimensional Proportional System—An Approach to Cerebral_Imaging*. New York: Thieme.

Teder-Salejarvi W, McDonald JJ, Russo FD, Hillyard SA. 2002. An analysis of audio-visual crossmodal integration by means of event-related potential (ERP) recordings. *Cogn Brain Res* 14:106–14.

Teismann IK, Steinstraeter O, Stoeckigt K, et al. 2007. Functional oropharyngeal sensory disruption interferes with the cortical control of swallowing. *BMC Neurosci* 8:62.

Van Veen BD, Buckley KM. 1988. Beamforming: a versatile approach to spatial filtering. *IEEE Trans Sign Process* 5:4–24.

Van Veen BD, van Drongelen W, Yuchtman M, Suzuki A. 1997. Localization of brain electrical activity via linearly constrained minimum variance spatial filtering. *IEEE Trans Biomed Eng* 44:866–80.

6 Dynamic Causal Modeling for Evoked Responses

Stefan J. Kiebel, Marta I. Garrido, and Karl J. Friston

A key topic in M/EEG methods research is to identify models that describe the mapping from the underlying neuronal system to the observed M/EEG response. These models should incorporate known or assumed constraints (David and Friston 2003; Sotero et al. 2007). By way of biophysically and neuronally informed forward models, we can use the M/EEG to make explicit statements about the underlying biophysical and neuronal parameters (David et al. 2006).

In past years there have been three important developments in M/EEG analysis. First, standard computers are now powerful enough to perform sophisticated analyses in a routine fashion (David et al. 2006). This and other analyses would have been impractical ten years ago, even for low-density EEG measurements. Second, the way methods researchers describe their M/EEG models has changed dramatically in the last decade. Recent descriptions tend to specify the critical assumptions underlying the model, followed by the inversion technique. This is useful because models for M/EEG can be complex; specifying the model explicitly also makes a statement about how one believes data were generated (Daunizeau et al. 2007; Kiebel et al. 2008). Model development has become more effective and transparent as a result because fully specified models can be compared to other models.

The third substantial advance is the advent of empirical or hierarchical Bayesian approaches to M/EEG model inversion. Bayesian approaches allow for constraints to be introduced that ensure robust parameter estimation (e.g., Auranen et al. 2007; Nummenmaa et al. 2007; Penny et al. 2007; Zumer et al. 2007). The introduction of constraints is vital once the model is complex enough to generate ambiguities (conditional dependencies) among groups of parameters. Although correlations among parameter estimates could be avoided by using less complex models, further research into the mechanisms behind the M/EEG would be precluded as a consequence. An empirical Bayesian formulation allows the data to resolve model ambiguities and uncertainties. The traditional argument against the use of Bayesian methods is that the priors introduce "artificial" or "biased" information not solicited by the data. Essentially the claim is that the priors enforce solutions that are desired by the researcher. This argument can be discounted for three reasons. First, in empirical Bayesian procedures the weight afforded by the priors is determined by the data, not the analyst. Second, Bayesian analysis provides the posterior distribution, which encodes uncertainty about the parameters, after observing the data. If the posterior is similar to the prior, then the data do not contain sufficient information to enable qualitative inference. This deduction can be tested explicitly using the model evidence (see below); the fact that a parameter cannot be resolved is informative in itself. Third, Bayesian analysis usually explores a selection of models, followed by model comparison (Garrido et al. 2007b). For example, one can invert a model[1] derived from one's favorite cognitive neuroscience theory, along with other alternative models. The best model can then be found by comparing model evidences using standard decision criteria (Penny et al. 2004).

In summary, we argue that the combination of these developments allow for models that are sophisticated enough to capture the full richness of the data. The Bayesian approach is central to this new class of models, without which it is not possible to constrain complex models or deal with inherent correlations among parameter estimates. Bayesian model comparison represents the important tool of selecting the best among competing models, which is central to the scientific process.

Dynamic causal modeling (DCM) provides a generative spatiotemporal model for M/EEG responses. The idea central to DCM is that M/EEG data are the response of a dynamic input–output system to experimental inputs. It is assumed that the sensory inputs are processed by a network of discrete but interacting neuronal sources. For each source we use a neural mass model that describes responses of neuronal subpopulations. Each population has its own (intrinsic) dynamics governed by the neural mass equations but also receives extrinsic input, either directly as sensory input or from other sources. The whole set of sources and their interactions are fully specified by a set of first-order differential equations that are formally related to other neural mass models used in computational models of M/EEG (Breakspear et al. 2006; Rodrigues et al. 2006). We assume that the depolarization of pyramidal cell populations gives rise to observed M/EEG data; one specifies how these depolarizations are expressed in the sensors through a conventional lead field. The full spatiotemporal model takes the form of a nonlinear state-space model with hidden states modeling (unobserved) neuronal dynamics, while the observation (lead field) equation is instantaneous and linear in the states. In other words, the model consists of a temporal and spatial part with temporal (e.g., connectivity between two sources) and spatial parameters (e.g., lead field parameters like equivalent current dipole (ECD) locations). In the next section we describe the DCM equations and demonstrate how the ensuing model is inverted using Bayesian techniques. We illustrate inference using evoked responses from a multi-subject EEG data set. In particular, we will motivate the use of Bayesian priors to derive better M/EEG models by exploiting symmetry assumptions about the way the data were generated. We conclude with a discussion about current DCM algorithms and point to some promising future developments.

Dynamic Causal Modeling: Theory

The intuition behind the DCM scheme is that a designed perturbation of neuronal dynamics can be promulgated and distributed throughout a system of coupled anatomical sources to produce region-specific responses. This system is modeled using a dynamic input–state output system with multiple inputs and outputs. Responses are evoked by deterministic inputs that correspond to experimental manipulations (i.e., presentation of stimuli). Experimental factors (i.e., stimulus attributes or context) can also change the parameters or causal architecture of the system producing these responses. The state variables cover both the neuronal activities and other neurophysiological or biophysical variables needed to form the outputs. Outputs are those components of neuronal responses that can be detected by MEG/EEG sensors. In our model these components are depolarizations of a "neural mass" of pyramidal cells. DCM starts with a reasonably realistic neuronal model of interacting cortical regions. This model is supplemented with a spatial forward model of how neuronal activity is transformed into measured responses, here M/EEG scalp-averaged responses. This enables the parameters of the neuronal model (e.g., effective connectivity) to be estimated from observed data. For M/EEG data this spatial model is a forward model of electromagnetic measurements that accounts for volume conduction effects (Mosher et al. 1999).

Hierarchical MEG/EEG Neural Mass Model

DCMs for M/EEG adopt a neural mass model (David and Friston 2003) to explain source activity in terms of the ensemble dynamics of interacting inhibitory and excitatory subpopulations of neurons, based on the model of Jansen and Rit (1995). This model emulates the activity of a source using three neural subpopulations, each assigned to one of three cortical layers; an excitatory subpopulation in the granular layer, an inhibitory subpopulation in the supragranular layer and a population of deep pyramidal cells in the infragranular layer. The excitatory pyramidal cells receive excitatory and inhibitory input from local interneurons (via intrinsic connections confined to the cortical sheet) and send excitatory outputs to remote cortical sources via extrinsic connections. See also Grimbert and Faugeras (2006) for a bifurcation analysis of this model.

   In David et al. (2005) we developed a hierarchical cortical model to study the influence of forward, backward, and lateral connections on evoked responses. This model embodies directed extrinsic connections among a number of sources, each based on the Jansen model (Jansen and Rit 1995), using the connectivity rules described in Felleman and Van Essen (1991). By these rules, it is straightforward to construct any hierarchical cortico-cortical network model of cortical sources. Under simplifying assumptions, directed connections can be classified as (1) bottom-up or forward connections that originate in the infragranular layers and terminate in the granular layer, (2) top-down or backward connections that connect infragranular to agranular layers, or (3) lateral connections that originate in infragranular layers and target all layers. These long-range or extrinsic cortico-cortical connections are excitatory and are mediated through the axonal processes of pyramidal cells. For simplicity, we do not consider thalamic connections, but model thalamic afferents as a function encoding subcortical input (see below).

The Jansen and Rit model emulates the MEG/EEG activity of a cortical source using three neuronal subpopulations. A population of excitatory pyramidal (output) cells receives inputs from inhibitory and excitatory populations of interneurons, via intrinsic connections. Within this model, excitatory interneurons can be regarded as spiny stellate cells found predominantly in layer 4 and in receipt of forward connections. Excitatory pyramidal cells and inhibitory interneurons occupy agranular layers and receive both intrinsic and extrinsic backward and lateral inputs. The ensuing DCM is specified in terms of its state equations and an observer or output equation

$$\begin{aligned} \dot{x} &= f(x, u, \theta), \\ h &= g(x, \theta), \end{aligned} \tag{1}$$

where x are the neuronal states of cortical sources, u are exogenous inputs, and h is the system's response. θ are quantities that parameterize the state and observer equations (see also below the discussion of prior assumptions). The state equations are ordinary first-order differential equations, and these are derived from the behavior of the three neuronal subpopulations that operate as linear damped oscillators. The integration of the differential equations pertaining to each subpopulation can be expressed as a convolution of the exogenous input to produce the response (David and Friston 2003). This convolution transforms the average density of presynaptic inputs into an average postsynaptic membrane potential, where the convolution kernel is given by

$$p(t)_e = \begin{cases} \dfrac{H_e}{\tau_e} t \exp\left(-\dfrac{t}{\tau_e}\right), & t \geq 0, \\ 0, & t < 0. \end{cases} \tag{2}$$

In this expression the subscript e stands for excitatory. Similarly subscript i is used for inhibitory synapses. H controls the maximum postsynaptic potential, and τ represents a lumped rate constant. An operator S transforms the potential of each subpopulation into firing rate, which is the exogenous input to other subpopulations. This operator is assumed to be an instantaneous sigmoid nonlinearity of the form

$$S(x) = \frac{1}{1 + \exp(-\rho_1(x - \rho_2))} - \frac{1}{1 + \exp(\rho_1 \rho_2)}, \quad (3)$$

where the free parameters ρ_1 and ρ_2 determine its slope and translation. Interactions among the subpopulations depend on internal coupling constants, $\gamma_{1,2,3,4}$, which control the strength of intrinsic connections and reflect the total number of synapses expressed by each subpopulation (see figure 6.1). The integration of this model, to form predicted responses, rests on formulating these two operators (equations 2 and 3) in terms of a set of differential equations as described in (David and Friston 2003). These equations, for all sources, can be integrated using the matrix exponential of the systems Jacobian as described in the appendices of (David et al. 2006). Critically the integration scheme allows for conduction delays on the con-

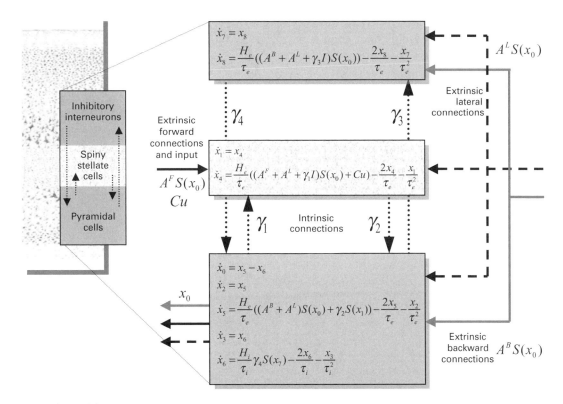

Figure 6.1
Neuronal state equations. A source consists of three neuronal subpopulations connected by four intrinsic connections with weights $\gamma_{1,2,3,4}$. Mean firing rates (equation 3) from other sources arrive via forward A^F, backward A^B, and lateral connections A^L. Similarly exogenous input Cu enters receiving sources. The output of each subpopulation is its transmembrane potential (equation 2).

nections, which are free parameters of the model. A DCM, at the network level, obtains by coupling sources with extrinsic forward, backward, and lateral connections as described above.

Event-Related Input and Event-Related Response-Specific Effects

To model event-related responses, the network receives inputs from the environment via input connections. These connections are exactly the same as forward connections and deliver inputs u to the spiny stellate cells in layer 4 of specified sources. In the present context, inputs u model afferent activity relayed by subcortical structures and is modeled with two components: The first is a gamma density function (truncated to peri-stimulus time). This models an event-related burst of input that is delayed with respect to stimulus onset and dispersed by subcortical synapses and axonal conduction. Being a density function, this component integrates to one over peri-stimulus time. The second component is a discrete cosine set modeling systematic fluctuations in input, as a function of peri-stimulus time. In our implementation peri-stimulus time is treated as a state variable, allowing the input to be computed explicitly during integration. The event-related input is exactly the same for all ERPs. The effects of experimental factors are mediated through event-related response (ERR)-specific changes in connection strengths. Figure 6.1 gives a summary of the resulting differential equations.

We can model differential responses to different stimuli in two ways. The first is when the effects of experimental factors are mediated through changes in extrinsic connection strengths (David et al. 2006). For example, this extrinsic mechanism can be used to explain ERP (event-related potential) differences by modulating forward (bottom-up) or backward (top-down) coupling. The second mechanism involves changing the intrinsic architecture; of the sort mediating local adaptation. Changes in connectivity are expressed as differences in intrinsic, forward, backward, or lateral connections that confer a selective sensitivity on each source, in terms of its response to others. The experimental or stimulus-specific effects are modeled by coupling gains

$$A_{ijk}^{F} = A_{ij}^{F} B_{ijk},$$
$$A_{ijk}^{B} = A_{ij}^{B} B_{ijk},$$
$$A_{ijk}^{L} = A_{ij}^{L} B_{ijk}.$$

(4)

Here A_{ij} encodes the strength of a connection to the ith source from the jth and B_{ijk} encodes its gain for the kth ERP. The superscripts (F, B, or L) indicate the type of connection, namely forward, backward, or lateral (see also figure 6.1). By convention, we set the gain of the first ERP to unity so that the gains of subsequent ERPs are relative to the first. The reason we model extrinsic modulations in terms of gain (a multiplicative factor), as opposed to additive effects, is that by construction, connections should always be positive. This is assured provided that both the connection and its gain are positive. In this context a (positive) gain of less than one represents a decrease in connection strength.

Note that if we considered the gains as elements of a gain matrix, the intrinsic gain would occupy the leading diagonal. Intrinsic modulation can explain important features of typical evoked responses, which are difficult to model with a modulation of extrinsic connections (Kiebel et al. 2007). We model the modulation of intrinsic connectivity by a gain on the amplitude H_e of the synaptic kernel (equation 2). A gain greater than one effectively increases the maximum response that can be elicited from a source. For the ith source

$$H_{ek}^{(i)} = H_e^{(i)} B_{iik}. \tag{5}$$

The Spatial Forward Model

The dendritic signal of the pyramidal subpopulation of the ith source $x_0^{(i)}$ is detected remotely on the scalp surface in M/EEG. The relationship between scalp data h and source activity is assumed to be linear and instantaneous:

$$h = g(x, \theta) = L(\theta^L) x_0, \tag{6}$$

where L is a lead field matrix (i.e., spatial forward model) that accounts for passive conduction of the electromagnetic field (Mosher et al. 1999). In this expression we assume that the spatial expression of each source is caused by one equivalent current dipole (ECD). Of course, one could use different source models, such as extended patches on the cortical surface (Daunizeau et al., in preparation). The head model for the dipoles is based on four concentric spheres, each with homogeneous and isotropic conductivity. The four spheres approximate the brain, skull, cerebrospinal fluid, and scalp. The parameters of the model are the radii and conductivities for each layer. Here we use as radii 71, 72, 79, and 85 mm, with conductivities 0.33, 1.0, 0.0042, and 0.33 S/m respectively. The potential at the sensors requires an evaluation of an infinite series, which can be approximated using fast algorithms (Mosher et al. 1999; Zhang 1995). The lead field of each ECD is then a function of three location and three orientation or moment parameters $\theta^L = \{\theta^{pos}, \theta^{mom}\}$. For the ECD forward model we used a Matlab (Mathworks) routine that is freely available as part of the FieldTrip package (http://neuroimaging.ruhosting.nl/fieldtrip/), under the GNU general public license.

Data Reduction

For computational expediency we generally reduce the dimensionality of the sensor data: in previous versions of DCM (David et al. 2006; Kiebel et al. 2006), we projected the data onto the principal eigenvectors of the sample covariance matrix of the data. This projection retained the maximum amount of information in the reduced data. However, the projection is not informed about which data can be explained by the model. Effectively, the projection spans data that cannot be generated by the model. In more recent versions of our software we use the principal components of the prior covariance of the data, as these are a function of, and only of, the model.

The prior covariance of the signal in sensor space C^h follows from (6),

$$
\begin{aligned}
C^h &= \langle hh^T \rangle_{p(\theta)} = \langle Lx_0 x_0^T L^T \rangle_{p(\theta)} \\
&= \left\langle \sum_{ij} \Delta\theta_i \frac{\partial L}{\partial \theta_i} C^x \frac{\partial L^T}{\partial \theta_j} \Delta\theta_j \right\rangle_{p(\theta)} = \sum_{ij} C_{ij}^L \frac{\partial L}{\partial \theta_i} C^x \frac{\partial L^T}{\partial \theta_j},
\end{aligned}
$$

$$
C_{ij}^L = \langle \Delta\theta_i \Delta\theta_j \rangle_{p(\theta)},
$$

$$
C^x = \langle x_0 x_0^T \rangle_{p(\theta)},
$$

$$
\Delta\theta_i = \theta_i - \mu_i,
$$

(7)

where C^x and C^L correspond to the prior covariances of the pyramidal cell depolarization and the lead field parameters respectively. For simplicity, we assume that $C^x = 1$ and compute the principal components of C^h from equation (7). We then retain a specified number of components or spatial modes. This procedure furnishes a subspace that spans signals, which can be explained by the model. Below, in the second study, we used twelve modes for all inversions. Note that generally this projection results in different data subspaces for models that differ in the number and (prior) placement of the sources. To facilitate model comparison, we used the same projection in all model inversions. This is because the model evidence pertains to the data explained by the model.

The Observation or Likelihood Model

In summary, our DCM comprises a state equation that is based on neurobiological heuristics and an observer equation based on an electromagnetic forward model. By integrating the state equation and passing the ensuing states through the observer equation, we generate a predicted measurement. This procedure corresponds to a generalized convolution of the inputs to generate a response $h(\theta)$ (equation 6). The generalized convolution gives an observation model for the vectorized data y and the associated likelihood

$$
y = \text{vec}(h(\theta) + X\theta^X) + \varepsilon,
$$

$$
p(y|\theta, \lambda) = N(\text{vec}(h(\theta) + X\theta^X), \text{diag}(\lambda) \otimes V).
$$

(8)

Measurement noise, ε, is assumed to be zero-mean Gaussian and independent over channels, that is, $\text{Cov}(\text{vec}(\varepsilon)) = \text{diag}(\lambda) \otimes V$, where λ is an unknown vector of channel-specific variances. V represents the error's temporal autocorrelation matrix, which we assume is the identity matrix. This is tenable because we down-sample the data to about 8 ms. Low-frequency noise or drift components are modeled by X, which is a block diagonal matrix with a low-order discrete cosine set for each evoked response and channel. The order of this set can be determined by Bayesian model selection (see below). This model is fitted to data by tuning the free parameters θ to minimize the discrepancy between predicted and observed MEG/EEG time series under model complexity constraints (more formally, the parameters minimize the variational free energy; see below). In addition to minimizing prediction error, the parameters are constrained by a prior specification of the range they are likely to lie in (Friston et al. 2003). These constraints, which take the form of a prior density $p(\theta)$, are combined with the likelihood, $p(y|\theta)$, to form a posterior density $p(\theta|y) \propto p(y|\theta)p(\theta)$ according to Bayes's rule. It is this posterior or conditional density we want to estimate. Gaussian assumptions about the errors in (8) enable us to compute the likelihood from the prediction error. The only outstanding quantities we require are the priors, which are described next.

Model Priors and Symmetry Constraints

The connectivity architecture is constant over peri-stimulus time and defines the dynamical behavior of the DCM. We have to specify prior assumptions about the connectivity parameters to estimate their posterior distributions. Priors have a dramatic impact on the landscape of the objective function to be optimized: precise prior distributions ensure that the objective function has a global minimum that can be attained robustly. Under Gaussian assumptions the prior distribution $p(\theta_i)$ of the ith parameter is defined by its mean and variance. The mean corresponds to the prior expectation. The variance reflects the amount of prior information about the parameter. A tight distribution (small variance) corresponds to precise prior knowledge. The parameters of the state equation can be divided into six subsets: (1) extrinsic connection parameters, which specify the coupling strengths among sources; (2) intrinsic connection parameters, which reflect our knowledge about canonical micro-circuitry within a source; (3) conduction delays; (4) synaptic and sigmoid parameters controlling the dynamics within an source; (5) input parameters, which control the subcortical delay and dispersion of event-related responses; and importantly (6) intrinsic and extrinsic gain parameters. Table 6.1 list the priors for these parameters (see also David et al. 2006 for details). Note that we fixed the values of intrinsic coupling parameters as described in Jansen and Rit (1995). Interlaminar conduction delays are usually fixed at 2 ms, and interregional delays have a prior expectation of 16 ms.

In classical ECD models often symmetry constraints are used to model homologous pairs of dipoles in both hemispheres. These constraints are biologically well motivated by assumptions about symmetric activation of bilateral sensory sources due to bilateral

Table 6.1
Prior densities of parameters for connections to the ith source from the jth, in the kth-evoked response

Extrinsic coupling parameters	$A_{ijk}^{F} = A_{ij}^{F} B_{ijk}$ $\qquad$ $A_{ij}^{F} = 32 \exp(\theta_{ij}^{F})$ $\quad$ $\theta_{ij}^{F} \sim N\left(0, \frac{1}{2}\right)$ $A_{ijk}^{B} = A_{ij}^{B} B_{ijk}$ $\qquad$ $A_{ij}^{B} = 16 \exp(\theta_{ij}^{B})$ $\quad$ $\theta_{ij}^{B} \sim N\left(0, \frac{1}{2}\right)$ $A_{ijk}^{L} = A_{ij}^{L} B_{ijk}$ $\qquad$ $A_{ij}^{L} = 4 \exp(\theta_{ij}^{L})$ $\quad$ $\theta_{ij}^{L} \sim N\left(0, \frac{1}{2}\right)$ $\qquad\qquad\qquad B_{ijk} = \exp(\theta_{ijk}^{B})$ $\quad$ $\theta_{ij}^{B} \sim N\left(0, \frac{1}{2}\right)$ $\qquad\qquad\qquad C_{i} = \exp(\theta_{i}^{C})$ $\quad$ $\theta_{i}^{C} \sim N\left(0, \frac{1}{2}\right)$		
Intrinsic coupling parameters	$\gamma_1 = 128$ $\qquad\qquad\qquad \gamma_2 = \frac{4}{5}\gamma_1 \qquad\qquad \gamma_3 = \frac{1}{4}\gamma_1 \quad \gamma_4 = \frac{1}{4}\gamma_1$		
Conduction delays (ms)	$\Delta_{ii} = 2$ $\qquad\qquad\qquad \Delta_{ij} = 16 \exp(\theta_{ij}^{\Delta}) \quad \theta_{ij}^{\Delta} \sim N\left(0, \frac{1}{16}\right)$		
Synaptic parameters (ms)	$H_{e,k}^{(i)} = B_{iik} H_{e}^{(i)}$ $\qquad$ $T_{e}^{(i)} = 8 \exp(\theta_{i}^{T}) \quad \theta_{i}^{T} \sim N\left(0, \frac{1}{8}\right)$ $H_{e}^{(i)} = 4 \exp(\theta_{i}^{H}) \quad \theta_{i}^{H} \sim N\left(0, \frac{1}{8}\right)$ $T_{i} = 16 \qquad\qquad H_{i} = 32$		
Sigmoid parameters	$\rho_1^{(i)} = \frac{2}{3} \exp(\theta_{i}^{\rho_1}) \quad \theta_{i}^{\rho_1} \sim N\left(0, \frac{1}{8}\right)$ $\rho_2^{(i)} = \frac{1}{3} \exp(\theta_{i}^{\rho_2}) \quad \theta_{i}^{\rho_2} \sim N\left(0, \frac{1}{8}\right)$		
Input parameters (s)	$u(t) = b(t, \eta_1, \eta_2) + \sum \theta_{i}^{c} \cos(2\pi(i-1)t) \quad \theta_{i}^{c} \sim N(0, 1)$ $\eta_1 = \exp(\theta_1^{\eta}) \qquad\qquad\qquad\qquad\qquad \theta_1^{\eta} \sim N\left(0, \frac{1}{16}\right)$ $\eta_2 = 16 \exp(\theta_2^{\eta}) \qquad\qquad\qquad\qquad \theta_2^{\eta} \sim N\left(0, \frac{1}{16}\right)$		
Spatial (ECD) parameters (mm)	$\theta_{i}^{pos} \sim N(L_{i}^{pos}, 32 I_3)$ $\theta_{i}^{mom} \sim N(0, 8 I_3)$		

sensory input. In classical approaches these constraints are "hard"; that is, the parameters of homologous dipoles are shared. Here, in the context of DCM, we illustrate the use of informed Bayesian priors to implement "soft" symmetry constraints that are expressed in the posterior estimates only when supported by the data. We will use the term "hard symmetry constraint" by which we mean that two parameters are set to be equal. "Soft symmetry constraints" refers to the use of informative priors so that two parameters will be similar but not necessarily equal. For both hard and soft symmetry constraints we render the prior variances of the two parameters the same. A hard constraint is implemented by setting covariances equal to the variance or the negative variance. This makes the covariance matrix rank-deficient (by one dimension), which is equivalent to removing a parameter from the model. The rank deficiency is accommodated by the DCM inversion routine by projecting to a full-rank parameter subspace. As a desired side effect this projection makes the pair of parameters coupled such they will have the same posterior mean (or one posterior mean is the negative of the other).

Soft constraints are implemented by setting the covariances of a pair of parameters to a value less than the variance (or negative variance). This will induce a positive (or negative) correlation in the posterior distribution. The closer the absolute of the covariance is to the absolute of the variance, the higher is the induced positive or negative correlation in the posterior. Throughout the chapter we will construct soft priors by multiplying the variance by 0.9 (−0.9) to derive the covariances.

Inference and Model Comparison

For a given DCM, say model m, parameter estimation corresponds to approximating the moments of the posterior distribution given by Bayes's rule

$$p(\theta|y, m) = \frac{p(y|\theta, m)p(\theta, m)}{p(y|m)}. \tag{9}$$

The estimation procedure employed in DCM is described in (Friston et al. 2003). The posterior moments (mean η and covariance Σ) are updated iteratively using variational Bayes under a fixed-form Laplace (i.e., Gaussian) approximation to the conditional density $q(\theta) = N(\eta, \Sigma)$. This procedure can be regarded as an expectation-maximization (EM) algorithm that employs a local linear approximation of equation (8) about the current conditional expectation. The **E**-step conforms to a Fisher-scoring scheme (Fahrmeir and Tutz 1994) that performs a descent on the variational free energy $F(q, \lambda, m)$ with respect to the conditional moments. In the **M**-step, the error variances λ are updated in exactly the same way. The estimation scheme can be summarized as follows:

Repeat until convergence

E-step $q \leftarrow \min\limits_q F(q, \lambda, m)$

M-step $\lambda \leftarrow \min\limits_\lambda F(q, \lambda, m)$ (10)

$$F(q, \lambda, m) = \langle \ln q(\theta) - \ln p(y|\theta, \lambda, m) - \ln p(\theta|m) \rangle_q$$
$$= D(q\|p(\theta|y, \lambda, m)) - \ln p(y|\lambda, m).$$

Note that the free energy is simply a function of the log-likelihood and the log-prior for a particular DCM and $q(\theta)$. The expression $\langle \cdot \rangle_q$ denotes the expectation under the density q. $q(\theta)$ is the approximation to the posterior density $p(\theta|y, \lambda, m)$ that we require. The **E**-step updates the moments of $q(\theta)$ (these are the variational parameters η and Σ) by minimizing the variational free energy. The free energy is the Kullback-Leibler divergence (denoted by $D(\cdot \| \cdot)$) between the real and approximate conditional density minus the log-likelihood. This means that the conditional moments or variational parameters maximize the marginal log-likelihood, while minimizing the discrepancy between the true and approximate conditional density. Because the divergence does not depend on the covariance parameters, minimizing the free energy in the **M**-step is equivalent to finding the maximum likelihood estimates of the covariance parameters. This scheme is identical to that employed by DCM for functional magnetic resonance imaging (Friston et al. 2003). The source code for this routine can be found in the Statistical Parametric Mapping software package (see the Software Note at the end of this chapter), in the function "spm_nlsi_N.m."

Bayesian inference proceeds using the conditional or posterior density estimated by iterating equation (10). Usually Bayesian inference involves specifying a parameter or compound of parameters as a contrast, $c^T\eta$. Inferences about this contrast are made using its conditional covariance, $c^T\Sigma c$. For example, one could compute the probability that any contrast is greater than zero or some meaningful threshold, given the data. This inference is conditioned on the particular model specified. In other words, given the data and model, inference is based on the probability that a particular contrast is bigger than a specified threshold. In some situations one may want to compare different models. This entails Bayesian model comparison.

Different models are compared using their evidence (Penny et al. 2004). The model evidence is

$$p(y|m) = \int p(y|\theta, m)\, p(\theta|m)\, d\theta.$$ (11)

Note that the model evidence is simply the normalization constant in equation (9). The evidence can be decomposed into two components: an accuracy term, which quantifies the data fit, and a complexity term, which penalizes models with a large number of parameters. Therefore the evidence embodies the two conflicting requirements of a good model; that is, it explains the data and is as simple as possible. In the following we approximate the model evidence for model m, under a normal approximation (Friston et al. 2003) by

$$\ln p(y|m) \approx \ln p(y|\lambda, m). \tag{12}$$

This expression is simply the maximum value of the objective function attained by EM (see the **M**-step in equation 10). The most likely model is the one with the largest log evidence. This enables Bayesian model selection. Model comparison rests on the likelihood ratio B_{ij} (i.e., the Bayes factor) of the evidence or relative log evidence for two models. For models i and j,

$$\ln B_{ij} = \ln p(y|m = i) - \ln p(y|m = j). \tag{13}$$

Conventionally strong evidence in favor of one model requires the difference in log evidence to be three or more (Penny et al. 2004). This threshold criterion plays a similar role as a p-value of $0.05 = 1/20$ in classical statistics (used to reject the null hypothesis in favor of the alternative model). A difference in log-evidence of greater than three (i.e., a Bayes factor more than $\exp(3) \sim 20$) indicates that the data provide strong evidence in favor of one model over the other. This is a standard way to assess the differences in log evidence quantitatively.

Illustrative Examples

Mismatch Negativity

In this section we illustrate the use of DCM for evoked responses by analyzing EEG data acquired under a mismatch negativity (MMN) paradigm. DCM allows us to test hypotheses about the changes in connectivity between sources. In this example study we will test a specific hypothesis (see below) about the MMN generation and compare various models over a group of subjects. The results shown here are a part of a series of papers that consider in detail the MMN and its underlying mechanisms (Garrido et al. 2007b).

Novel sounds, or oddballs, embedded in a stream of repeated sounds, or standards, produce a distinct response that can be recorded noninvasively with MEG and EEG. The MMN is the negative component of the waveform obtained by subtracting the event-related response to a standard from the response to an oddball, or deviant. This response to sudden changes in the acoustic environment peaks at about 100 to 200 ms from change onset (Sams et al. 1985) and exhibits an enhanced negativity that is distributed over frontotemporal areas, with prominence in frontal regions.

The MMN is believed to be an index of automatic change detection reflecting a pre-attentive sensory memory mechanism (Tiitinen et al. 1994). There have been several compelling mechanistic accounts of how the MMN might arise. The most common interpretation is that the MMN can be regarded as a marker for error detection, caused by a break in a learned regularity or familiar auditory context. The early work by Näätänen and colleagues suggested that the MMN results from a comparison between the auditory input and a memory trace of previous sounds. In agreement with this theory, others (Naatanen and Winkler 1999; Sussman et al. 1999; Winkler et al. 1996) have postulated that the MMN would reflect online modifications of the auditory system, or updates of the perceptual model, during incorporation of a newly encountered stimulus into the model—*the model-adjustment hypothesis*. Hence the MMN would be a specific response to stimulus change and not to stimulus alone. This hypothesis has been supported by Escera et al. (2003), who provide evidence that the prefrontal cortex is involved in a top-down modulation of a deviance detection system in the temporal cortex. In light of the Näätänen model, it has been claimed that the MMN is caused by two underlying functional processes: a sensory memory mechanism related to temporal generators and an automatic attention-switching process related to the frontal generators (Giard et al. 1990). Accordingly it has been shown that the temporal and frontal MMN sources have distinct behaviors over time (Rinne et al. 2000) and that these sources interact with each other (Jemel et al. 2002). Thus the MMN could be generated by a temporofrontal network (Doeller et al. 2003; Opitz et al. 2002), as revealed by M/EEG and fMRI studies. This work has linked the early component (about 100–140 ms) to a sensorial or noncomparator account of the MMN, elaborated in the temporal cortex, and a later component (about 140–200 ms) to a cognitive part of the MMN, involving the frontal cortex (Maess et al. 2007).

Using DCM, we modeled the MMN generators with a frontotemporal network comprising bilateral sources over the primary and secondary auditory and frontal cortex. Following the model-adjustment hypothesis, we assumed that the early and late component of the MMN could be explained by an interaction of temporal and frontal sources or network nodes. The MMN itself is defined as the difference between the responses to the oddball and the standard stimuli. Here we modeled both evoked responses and explained the MMN, namely differences in the two ERPs, by a modulation of DCM parameters. There are two kinds of parameters that seem appropriate to induce the difference between oddballs and standards: (1) modulation of extrinsic connectivity between sources and (2) modulation of intrinsic parameters in each source. Modulation of intrinsic parameters would correspond to a mechanism that is more akin to an *adaptation* hypothesis, namely that the MMN is generated by local adaptation of populations. This is the hypothesis considered by (Jaaskelainen et al. 2004), who report evidence that the MMN is explained by differential adaptation of two pairs of bilateral temporal sources. In a recent paper (Garrido et al. 2007a) we have compared models derived from both hypotheses: (1) the model-adjustment hypothesis and (2) the adaptation hypothesis. Here we will constrain ourselves to demonstrate inference based on DCMs derived from the model-adjustment hypothesis only, which involves a frontotemporal network.

Experimental Design

We studied a group of 13 healthy volunteers aged 24 to 35 (5 females). Each subject gave signed informed consent before the study, which proceeded under local ethical committee guidelines. Subjects sat on a comfortable chair in front of a desk in a dimly illuminated room. Electroencephalographic activity was measured during an auditory "oddball" paradigm in which subjects heard of "standard" (1,000 Hz) and "deviant" tones (2,000 Hz), occurring 80 percent (480 trials) and 20 percent (120 trials) of the time, respectively, in a pseudorandom sequence. The stimuli were presented binaurally via headphones for 15 minutes every 2 seconds. The duration of each tone was 70 ms with 5 ms rise and fall times. The subjects were instructed not to move, to keep their eyes closed, and to count the deviant tones.

EEG was recorded with a Biosemi system with 128 scalp electrodes. Data were recorded at a sampling rate of 512 Hz. Vertical and horizontal eye movements were monitored using EOG (electro-oculograms) electrodes. The data were epoched offline, with a peri-stimulus window of –100 to 400 ms, down-sampled to 200 Hz, band-pass filtered between 0.5 and 40 Hz, and re-referenced to the average of the right and left ear lobes. Trials in which the absolute amplitude of the signal exceeded 100 μV were excluded. Two subjects were eliminated from further analysis because of excessive trials containing artifacts. In the remaining subjects an average 18 percent of trials were excluded.

Specification of Dynamic Causal Model

In this section we specify three plausible models defined under a given architecture and dynamics. The network architecture was motivated by recent electrophysiological and neuroimaging studies looking at the sources underlying the MMN (Doeller et al. 2003; Opitz et al. 2002). We assumed five sources, modeled as equivalent current dipoles (ECDs), over left and right primary auditory cortices (A1), left and right superior temporal gyrus (STG), and right inferior frontal gyrus (IFG); see figure 6.2. Our mechanistic model attempts to explain the generation of each individual response, that is, responses to standards and deviants. Therefore left and right primary auditory cortex (A1) were chosen as cortical input stations for processing the auditory information. (Opitz et al. 2002) identified sources for the differential response, with fMRI and EEG measures, in both the left and right superior temporal gyrus (STG) and in the right inferior frontal gyrus (IFG). Here we employ the coordinates reported by (Opitz et al. 2002) (for the left and right STG and the right IFG) and (Rademacher et al. 2001) (for the left and right A1) as prior source location means, with a prior variance of 32 mm. We converted these coordinates, given in the literature in Talairach space, to MNI space using the algorithm described in http://imaging.mrc-cbu.cam.ac.uk/imaging/MniTalairach. The moment parameters had prior mean of 0 and a variance

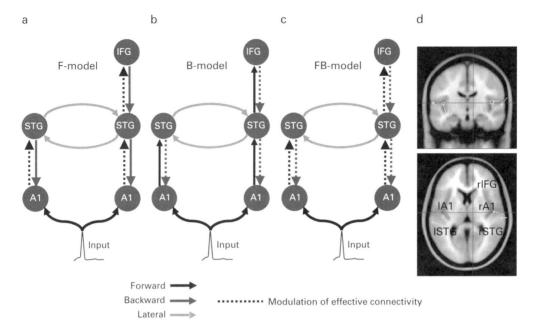

Figure 6.2
Model specification. The sources comprising the network are connected with forward (dark gray), backward (gray), or lateral (light gray) connections as shown. A1: primary auditory cortex; STG: superior temporal gyrus; IFG: inferior temporal gyrus. Three different models were tested within the same architecture (a–c), allowing for learning-related changes in forward **F**, backward **B**, and forward and backward **FB** connections respectively. The broken lines indicate the connections we allowed to change. (d) Sources of activity, modeled as dipoles (estimated posterior moments and locations), are superimposed in an MRI of a standard brain in MNI space.

of 8 in each direction. We have used these parameters as priors to estimate, for each individual subject, the posterior locations and moments of the ECDs (table 6.2). Using these sources and prior knowledge about the functional anatomy, we constructed the following DCM: An extrinsic input entered bilaterally to A1, which were connected to their ipsilateral STG. Right STG was connected with the right IFG. Interhemispheric (lateral) connections were placed between left and right STG. All connections were reciprocal (i.e., connected with forward and backward connections or with bilateral connections). Given this connectivity graph, specified in terms of its nodes and connections, we tested three models. These models differed in the connections that could show putative learning-related changes, namely differences between listening to standard or deviant tones. Models F, B, and FB allowed changes in forward, backward, and both forward and backward connections respectively (see figure 6.2). All three models

Table 6.2
Prior coordinates for the locations of the equivalent current dipoles in Montreal Neurology Institute (MNI) space (in mm)

Left primary auditory cortex (**lA1**)	−42, −22, 7
Right primary auditory cortex (**rA1**)	46, −14, 8
Left superior temporal gyrus (**lSTG**)	−61, −32, 8
Right superior temporal gyrus (**rSTG**)	59, −25, 8
Right inferior frontal gyrus (**rIFG**)	46, 20, 8

were compared against a baseline or null model. The null model had the same architecture described above but precluded any coupling changes between standard and deviant trials.

Results

The difference between the ERPs evoked by the standard and deviant tones revealed a standard MMN. This negativity was present from 90 to 190 ms and had a broad spatial pattern, encompassing electrodes previously associated with auditory and frontal areas. Four different DCMs—forward only (F-model), backward only (B-model), forward and backward (FB-model), and the null model—were inverted for each subject. Figure 6.3 illustrates the model comparison based on the increase in log evidence over the null model, for all subjects. Figure 6.3a shows the log evidence for the three models, relative to the null model, for each subject, revealing that the three models were significantly better than the null in all subjects. The diamond attributed to each subject identifies the best model on the basis of the highest log evidence. The FB-model was significantly better in 7 out of 11 subjects. The F-model was better in four subjects but only significantly so in three (for one of these subjects [subject 6], model comparison revealed only weak evidence in favor of the F-model over the FB-model, though still very strong evidence over the B-model). In all but one subject, the F-model and the FB-model were better than the B-model. Figure 6.3b shows the log evidences for the three models at the group level. The log evidence for the group is the sum of the log evidences from all subjects because of the independent measures over subjects. Both F and FB are clearly more likely than B, and over the subjects there is very strong evidence in favor of model FB over model F. Figure 6.4a shows, for the best model FB, the predicted responses at each node of the network for each trial type (i.e., standard or deviant) for a single subject (subject 9). For each

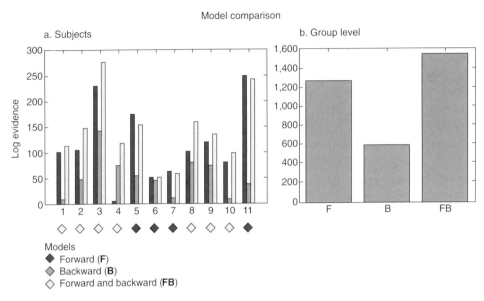

Figure 6.3
Bayesian model selection among DCMs for the three models **F**, **B**, and **FB**, expressed relative to a DCM in which no connections were allowed to change (null model). The graphs show the free energy approximation to the log evidence. (a) Log evidence for models **F**, **B**, and **FB** for each subject (relative to the null model). The diamond attributed to each subject identifies the best model on the basis of the subject's highest log evidence. (b) Log evidence at the group level, pooled over subjects, for the three models.

connection in the network the plot shows the coupling gains and the conditional probability that the gains are different from one. For example, a coupling change of 2.04 from lA1 to lSTG means that the effective connectivity increased 104 percent for rare events relative to frequent events. The response, in measurement space, of the three principal spatial modes is shown on the right (figure 6.4b). This figure shows a remarkable agreement between predicted (solid) and observed (dotted) responses. Figure 6.5 summarizes the conditional densities of the coupling parameters for the F-model (figure 6.5a) and FB-model (figure 6.5b). For each connection in the network the plot shows the coupling gains and the conditional probability that the gains are different from one, pooled over subjects. For the F-model the effective connectivity has increased in all connections with a conditional probability of almost 100 percent. For the FB-model the effective connectivity has changed in all forward and backward connections with a probability of almost 100 percent. Equivalently, and in accord with theoretical predictions, all extrinsic connections (i.e., influences) were modulated for rare events as compared to frequent events.

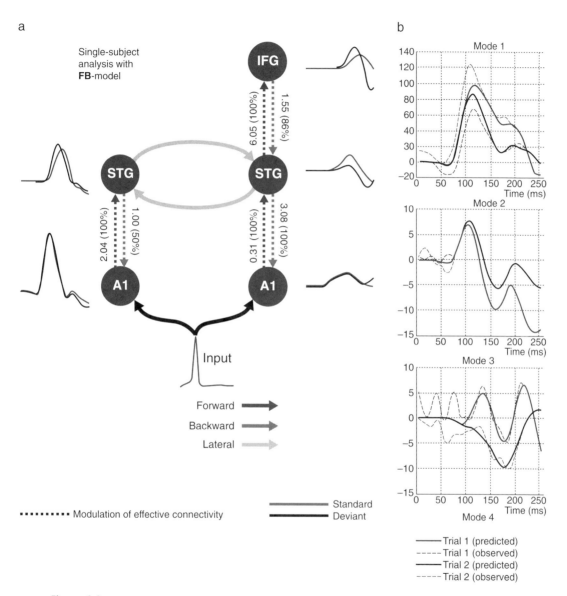

Figure 6.4

DCM results for a single subject—subject 9, an **FB**-model. (a) Reconstructed responses for each source and changes in coupling during oddball processing relative to standards. The numbers next to each connection are the gain modulation in connection to strength and the posterior probability that the modulation is different from one. The mismatch response is expressed in nearly every source. (b) Predicted (*solid*) and observed (*broken*) responses in measurement space that result from a projection of the scalp data onto their first three spatial modes.

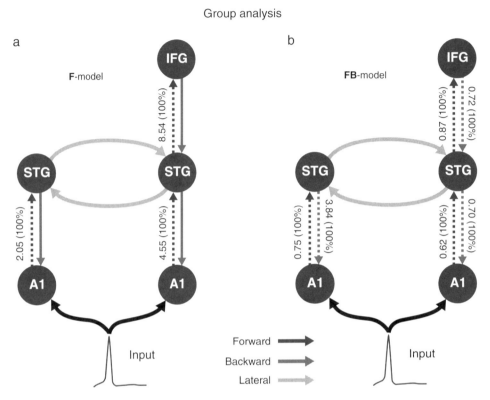

Figure 6.5
Coupling gains and their posterior probability estimated over subjects for each connection in the network for the **F**-model (a) and the **FB**-model (b). There are widespread learning-related changes in all connections, expressed as modulations of coupling for deviants relative to standards.

Symmetry Constraints

Specification of Dynamic Causal Model

To illustrate the use of DCM symmetry constraints, we use the same data as above, where we excluded an additional subject due to too many missing channels. Also we assume only four of the sources above to be part of the model (left and right primary auditory cortex, and left and right superior temporal gyrus: lA1, rA1, lSTG, rSTG). However, while we use this four-source model as an example how one can incorporate symmetry constraints, we do not want to compare four and five source models for these data. For the four sources, we assume the same prior locations as for the first application (table 6.2). For each spatial or temporal parameter, we introduce symmetry constraints between the left and right hemisphere version of this parameter. For example, a "hard" symmetry constraint on the feedforward connectivity parameter from A1 to STG means that the posterior mean of the connectivity parameter in the left hemisphere (lA1 to lSTG) is the same as for the homologue parameter in the right hemisphere (rA1 to rSTG).

With DCM the symmetry constraints can be deployed in either the temporal or spatial components of the model. This feature enables one to test for symmetry in temporal (neural-mass) parameters in the presence of nonsymmetric spatial expressions of homologous sources, and vice versa. For the mismatch negativity data, the use of symmetry priors, both for the temporal and spatial parameters, is biologically well motivated because subjects received bilateral auditory input. Therefore it might be assumed, for example, that the spatial parameters of the A1 sources reflect anatomically symmetric sources. Symmetry in temporal parameters would indicate that the functional processes, which evolve over peri-stimulus time, appear identical. Importantly, in contrast to conventional approaches, the Bayesian approach allows us to use "soft" priors, which embody our knowledge that the parameters are probably not entirely symmetric but close to symmetry. For example, soft spatial priors are appropriate, if one assumes that the spatial parameters of two homologous dipoles, and in particular, dipole moments, are similar to each other.

We used nine models where each model was a mixture of three levels of spatial symmetry constraints (hard/soft/none) and three levels of temporal symmetry constraints (hard/soft/none); see table 6.3. For example, the model SpaceS/TimeH has soft symmetry constraints on all homologue pairs of spatial parameters, and hard symmetry constraints on all homologue pairs of temporal parameters. Hard and soft symmetry constraints were implemented as described above by manipulating the prior covariance matrix of the parameters. The "no symmetry constraint" was implemented

Table 6.3
Symmetry constraints

	Temporal hard symmetry	Temporal soft symmetry	No temporal symmetry
Spatial hard symmetry	**SpaceH/TimeH**	**SpaceH/TimeS**	**SpaceH/Time0**
Spatial soft symmetry	**SpaceS/TimeH**	**SpaceS/TimeS**	**SpaceS/Time0**
No spatial symmetry	**Space0/TimeH**	**Space0/TimeS**	**Space0/Time0**

Note: We used nine different models to fit each single-subject data sets of a multi-subject EEG study. Each model had one of three levels of symmetry constraints (hard/soft/no) for spatial and temporal parameters. See text for a description of how these symmetry constraints were implemented.

by assuming prior independence, which is the default setting for DCM. For the spatial symmetry constraints, we coupled the three moment and location parameters in x, y, and z. For the temporal symmetry constraints, we coupled all temporal parameters, namely the remainder of the DCM parameters.

Results

After inverting all models (i.e., fitting each of the nine models to each single subject), we calculated the log evidence for each model (summed over subjects), relative to the overall mean over models (table 6.4). Although the overall results are not unequivocal, there are some clear trends. First, the SpaceS/TimeH and SpaceS/TimeS both have high log model evidences and were the best models for a relatively high number of subjects. This indicates a trend for models with soft or even hard symmetry constraints on both temporal and spatial parameters. Among the worst three models are the most constrained (SpaceH/TimeH) and the least constrained model (Space0/Time0). These models represent two extremes in our model space. This is important because it means that the best models, for the real data, use soft constraints; namely informative Bayesian priors. The results in table 6.4 also indicate that some spatial constraints are appropriate for our data because there is only one instance (subject 1), for which a spatially unconstrained model is the winning model (table 6.5). Conversely, there are only two subjects (3 and 7) for which temporally constrained models were not among the winning models. In summary, our results suggest that for the auditory evoked response data here, the best models are those that have some symmetry constraints on both spatial and temporal parameters.

A typical group analysis would now proceed with analyzing data, over subjects, for the best model found at the group level. In our case this would be the SpaceS/TimeS (four sources).

Table 6.4
Group results for symmetry study

	Temporal hard symmetry	Temporal soft symmetry	No temporal symmetry
Spatial hard symmetry	−161.77 (1)	57.03 (1)	−102.78 (0)
Spatial soft symmetry	87.97 (4)	114.44 (3)	14.08 (2)
No spatial symmetry	2.85 (1)	10.83 (1)	−22.65 (2)

Note: We inverted nine different DCMs for each of ten data sets. The entries show, for each model, the log-evidence summed over subjects, relative to their overall mean, over models. The best model is highlighted in gray. The numbers in brackets indicate how often a model was the best, for each of the ten data sets.

Table 6.5
Single-subject results for the symmetry study

	SpaceH/TimeH	SpaceS/TimeH	SpaceO/TimeH	SpaceH/TimeS	SpaceS/TimeS	SpaceO/TimeS	SpaceH/TimeO	SpaceS/TimeO	SpaceO/TimeO
S 1	−16.05	1.09	−19.85	7.25	11.83	26.60	−19.41	−7.80	16.33
S 2	−18.90	17.11	12.56	16.83	20.59	−4.89	−18.45	−3.70	−21.14
S 3	−6.59	−10.37	−20.76	1.86	3.58	6.20	−0.34	11.86	14.57
S 4	0.52	10.16	0.32	−0.40	5.80	−3.73	−4.93	0.84	−8.59
S 5	−6.71	14.56	6.28	9.96	8.24	−7.64	−3.80	−4.11	−16.76
S 6	9.19	16.42	1.65	5.22	11.20	−7.14	−11.51	−2.51	−22.52
S 7	−61.30	5.98	−1.69	−12.42	2.51	25.84	14.63	41.68	−15.23
S 8	−78.91	1.57	20.93	21.38	23.62	14.86	−13.04	5.14	4.43
S 9	22.85	18.99	7.03	19.37	12.38	−28.97	−36.26	−37.19	21.80
S 10	−5.83	12.43	−3.63	−12.04	14.65	−10.29	−9.63	9.87	4.46

Note: Individual log-evidences, for each model and subject. The values are relative to the mean over subjects. The best models (gray highlight) have log-evidences that are greater than three, relative to the other models.

Discussion

Dynamic causal modeling (DCM) for M/EEG entails the inversion of informed spatio-temporal models of observed responses. The idea is to model condition-specific responses over channels and peri-stimulus time with the same model, where the differences among conditions are explained by changes in only a few key parameters. The face and predictive validity of DCM have been established, and this makes it a potentially useful tool for group studies (David et al. 2006; Garrido et al. 2007b; Kiebel et al. 2006). In principle, the same approach can be applied to the analysis of single trials, where one would use a parametric modulation of parameters to model the effects of trial-to-trial changes in an experimental variable (e.g., reaction time or forgotten vs. remembered).

One can also view DCM for evoked responses as a source reconstruction device using biophysically informed temporal constraints. This is because DCM has two components; a neural-mass model of the interactions among a small number of dipole sources and a classical electromagnetic forward model that links these sources to extracranial measurements. Inverting the DCM implicitly optimizes the location and moments of the dipole sources. This is in contrast to traditional equivalent current dipole-fitting approaches, where dipoles are fitted sequentially to the data; using user-selected periods and/or channels of the data. Classical approaches have to proceed in this way because there is usually too much spatial and temporal dependency among the sources to identify the parameters precisely. With our approach we place temporal constraints on the model that are consistent with the way that signals are generated biophysically. As we have shown, these allow simultaneous fitting of multiple dipoles to the data.

We used the equivalent current dipole (ECD) model because it is analytic, fast to compute, and a quasi-standard when reconstructing evoked responses. However, the ECD model is just one candidate for spatial forward models. Given the lead field, one can use any spatial model in the observation equation (equation 6). A further example would be some linear distributed approach (Baillet et al. 2001; Daunizeau et al. 2006; Phillips et al. 2005) where a "patch" of dipoles, confined to the cortical surface, would act as the spatial expression of one area (Daunizeau et al., in preparation). With DCM one could also use different forward models for different areas (hybrid models). For example, one could employ the ECD model for early responses while using a distributed forward model for higher areas.

Given our findings from the symmetry study, we suggest that evoked responses, due to bilateral sensory input (e.g., visually or auditory), could be analyzed using DCMs with symmetry priors. We recommend soft constraints on both temporal and spatial parameters for routine analysis. One should not use models with hard (fixed) symmetry priors on both spatial and temporal parameters (SpaceH/TimeH) without caution. This model turned out to be the worse for real EEG data. Although this model reduces the number of parameters to nearly a quarter of the full Space0/Time0 model, it seems to introduce too many constraints to be a useful explanation of the data.

In practice, one can use Bayesian model comparison to test hypotheses about the symmetry of neuronal processes in the two hemispheres. This class of questions has been asked in auditory processing, language, vision, and other cognitive research areas (Coan and Allen 2003; Hagemann 2004; Harmon-Jones et al. 2008; Yasin 2007). The approach advocated here is to test competing hypotheses directly by formulating appropriate models and performing model comparison to identify the best model. It provides for a more principled methodology than fitting an overinclusive model and making inference using the posterior distribution of parameters. For example, if one wants to test for hemispheric symmetry of some temporal parameters, one can formulate a symmetric and a nonsymmetric model and perform model comparison. This is different from inverting a single unconstrained model and computing some statistic on the ratio or difference of the homologous parameter estimates. The latter approach is typically used in M/EEG research but, as shown above, could be replaced by formal model comparison.

We anticipate that Bayesian model comparison will become a ubiquitous tool in M/EEG. This is because further development of M/EEG models and their fusion with other imaging modalities requires more complex models embodying useful constraints. The appropriateness of such models for any given data cannot necessarily be intuited but can be assessed formally using Bayesian model comparison. The key is to compute the model evidence $p(y|m)$ (equation 11) for using a variational approach (see above) or as described in (Sato et al. 2004), or employ sampling approaches like the Monte Carlo–Markov chain (MCMC) techniques as in Auranen et al. (2007) and Jun et al. (2005, 2008). In principle, one can compare models based on different concepts, or indeed inversion schemes, for a given data set y. For example, one can easily compare different types of source reconstruction (ECD vs. source imaging) with DCM. This cannot be done with classical, non-Bayesian approaches for which model comparisons are only feasible under certain constraints ("nested models"), precluding comparisons among qualitatively different models. Although other approximations to the model evidence exist, such as the Akaike information criterion, they are not generally useful with informative priors (Beal 2003).

Software Note

All procedures have been implemented as Matlab (MathWorks) code. The source code is freely available in the DCM and neural model toolboxes of the Statistical Parametric Mapping package (SPM8) under http://www.fil.ion.ucl.ac.uk/spm/.

Acknowledgments

This work was supported by the Wellcome Trust.

Note

1. Model "inversion'" is a technical term and stands for "fitting the model," namely by computing the posterior distributions of the model parameters.

References

Auranen T, Nummenmaa A, Hamalainen MS, Jaaskelainen IP, Lampinen J, Vehtari A, Sams M. 2007. Bayesian inverse analysis of neuromagnetic data using cortically constrained multiple dipoles. *Hum Brain Mapp* 28:979–94.

Baillet S, Mosher JC, Leahy RM. 2001. Electromagnetic brain mapping. *IEEE Sign Process* 18:14–30.

Beal MJ. 2003. Variational algorithms for approximate Bayesian inference. PhD diss. University College, London.

Breakspear M, Roberts JA, Terry JR, Rodrigues S, Mahant N, Robinson PA. 2006. A unifying explanation of primary generalized seizures through nonlinear brain modeling and bifurcation analysis. *Cereb Cortex* 16:1296–1313.

Coan JA, Allen JJ. 2003. Frontal EEG asymmetry and the behavioral activation and inhibition systems. *Psychophysiology* 40:106–14.

Daunizeau J, Grova C, Marrelec G, Mattout J, Jbabdi S, Pelegrini-Issac M, Lina JM, Benali H. 2007. Symmetrical event-related EEG/fMRI information fusion in a variational Bayesian framework. *Neuroimage* 36:69–87.

Daunizeau J, Mattout J, Clonda D, Goulard B, Benali H, Lina JM. 2006. Bayesian spatio-temporal approach for EEG source reconstruction: conciliating ECD and distributed models. *IEEE Trans Biomed Eng* 53:503–16.

David O, Friston KJ. 2003. A neural mass model for MEG/EEG: coupling and neuronal dynamics. *Neuroimage* 20:1743–55.

David O, Harrison L, Friston KJ. 2005. Modelling event-related responses in the brain. *Neuroimage* 25:756–70.

David O, Kiebel SJ, Harrison LM, Mattout J, Kilner JM, Friston KJ. 2006. Dynamic causal modeling of evoked responses in EEG and MEG. *Neuroimage* 30:1255–72.

Doeller CF, Opitz B, Mecklinger A, Krick C, Reith W, Schroger E. 2003. Prefrontal cortex involvement in preattentive auditory deviance detection: neuroimaging and electrophysiological evidence. *Neuroimage* 20:1270–82.

Escera C, Yago E, Corral MJ, Corbera S, Nunez MI. 2003. Attention capture by auditory significant stimuli: semantic analysis follows attention switching. *Eur J Neurosci* 18:2408–12.

Fahrmeir L, Tutz G. 1994. *Multivariate Statistical Modelling Based on Generalized Linear Models.* New York: Springer.

Felleman DJ, Van Essen DC. 1991. Distributed hierarchical processing in the primate cerebral cortex. *Cereb Cortex* 1:1–47.

Friston KJ, Harrison L, Penny W. 2003. Dynamic causal modelling. *Neuroimage* 19:1273–1302.

Garrido MI, Kilner JM, Kiebel SJ, Friston KJ. 2007a. Evoked brain responses are generated by feedback loops. *Proc Natl Acad Sci USA* 104:20961–6.

Garrido MI, Kilner JM, Kiebel SJ, Stephan KE, Friston KJ. 2007b. Dynamic causal modelling of evoked potentials: a reproducibility study. *Neuroimage* 36:571–80.

Giard MH, Perrin F, Pernier J, Bouchet P. 1990. Brain generators implicated in the processing of auditory stimulus deviance: a topographic event-related potential study. *Psychophysiology* 27:627–40.

Grimbert F, Faugeras O. 2006. Bifurcation analysis of Jansen's neural mass model. *Neural Comput* 18:3052–68.

Hagemann D. 2004. Individual differences in anterior EEG asymmetry: methodological problems and solutions. *Biol Psychol* 67:157–82.

Harmon-Jones E, Abramson LY, Nusslock R, Sigelman JD, Urosevic S, Turonie LD, Alloy LB, Fearn M. 2008. Effect of bipolar disorder on left frontal cortical responses to goals differing in valence and task difficulty. *Biol Psychiat* 63:693–8.

Jaaskelainen IP, Ahveninen J, Bonmassar G, Dale AM, Ilmoniemi RJ, Levanen S, Lin FH, May P, Melcher J, Stufflebeam S, Tiitinen H, Belliveau JW. 2004. Human posterior auditory cortex gates novel sounds to consciousness. *Proc Natl Acad Sci USA* 101:6809–14.

Jansen BH, Rit VG. 1995. Electroencephalogram and visual evoked potential generation in a mathematical model of coupled cortical columns. *Biol Cybern* 73:357–66.

Jemel B, Achenbach C, Muller BW, Ropcke B, Oades RD. 2002. Mismatch negativity results from bilateral asymmetric dipole sources in the frontal and temporal lobes. *Brain Topogr* 15:13–27.

Jun SC, George JS, Kim W, Pare-Blagoev J, Plis S, Ranken DM, Schmidt DM. 2008. Bayesian brain source imaging based on combined MEG/EEG and fMRI using MCMC. *Neuroimage* 40:1581–94.

Jun SC, George JS, Pare-Blagoev J, Plis SM, Ranken DM, Schmidt DM, Wood CC. 2005. Spatio-temporal Bayesian inference dipole analysis for MEG neuroimaging data. *Neuroimage* 28:84–98.

Kiebel SJ, Daunizeau J, Phillips C, Friston KJ. 2008. Variational Bayesian inversion of the equivalent current dipole model in EEG/MEG. *Neuroimage* 39:728–41.

Kiebel SJ, David O, Friston KJ. 2006. Dynamic causal modelling of evoked responses in EEG/MEG with lead field parameterization. *Neuroimage* 30:1273–84.

Kiebel SJ, Garrido MI, Friston KJ. 2007. Dynamic causal modelling of evoked responses: the role of intrinsic connections. *Neuroimage* 36:332–45.

Maess B, Jacobsen T, Schroger E, Friederici AD. 2007. Localizing pre-attentive auditory memory-based comparison: magnetic mismatch negativity to pitch change. *Neuroimage* 37:561–71.

Mosher JC, Leahy RM, Lewis PS. 1999. EEG and MEG: forward solutions for inverse methods. *IEEE Trans Biomed Eng* 46:245–59.

Naatanen R, Winkler I. 1999. The concept of auditory stimulus representation in cognitive neuroscience. *Psychol Bull* 125:826–59.

Nummenmaa A, Auranen T, Hamalainen MS, Jaaskelainen IP, Lampinen J, Sams M, Vehtari A. 2007. Hierarchical Bayesian estimates of distributed MEG sources: theoretical aspects and comparison of variational and MCMC methods. *Neuroimage* 35:669–85.

Opitz B, Rinne T, Mecklinger A, von Cramon DY, Schroger E. 2002. Differential contribution of frontal and temporal cortices to auditory change detection: fMRI and ERP results. *Neuroimage* 15:167–74.

Penny WD, Kilner J, Blankenburg F. 2007. Robust Bayesian general linear models. *Neuroimage* 36:661–71.

Penny WD, Stephan KE, Mechelli A, Friston KJ. 2004. Comparing dynamic causal models. *Neuroimage* 22:1157–72.

Phillips C, Mattout J, Rugg MD, Maquet P, Friston KJ. 2005. An empirical Bayesian solution to the source reconstruction problem in EEG. *Neuroimage* 24:997–1011.

Rademacher J, Morosan P, Schormann T, Schleicher A, Werner C, Freund HJ, Zilles K. 2001. Probabilistic mapping and volume measurement of human primary auditory cortex. *Neuroimage* 13:669–83.

Rinne T, Alho K, Ilmoniemi RJ, Virtanen J, Naatanen R. 2000. Separate time behaviors of the temporal and frontal mismatch negativity sources. *Neuroimage* 12:14–19.

Rodrigues S, Terry JR, Breakspear M. 2006. On the genesis of spike-wave oscillations in a mean-field model of human thalamic and corticothalamic dynamics. *Phys Lett* A355:352–7.

Sams M, Paavilainen P, Alho K, Naatanen R. 1985. Auditory frequency discrimination and event-related potentials. *Electroencephalogr Clin Neurophysiol* 62:437–48.

Sato MA, Yoshioka T, Kajihara S, Toyama K, Goda N, Doya K, Kawato M. 2004. Hierarchical Bayesian estimation for MEG inverse problem. *Neuroimage* 23: 806–26.

Sotero RC, Trujillo-Barreto NJ, Iturria-Medina Y, Carbonell F, Jimenez JC. 2007. Realistically coupled neural mass models can generate EEG rhythms. *Neural Comput* 19:478–512.

Sussman E, Winkler I, Ritter W, Alho K, Naatanen R. 1999. Temporal integration of auditory stimulus deviance as reflected by the mismatch negativity. *Neurosci Lett* 264:161–4.

Tiitinen H, May P, Reinikainen K, Naatanen R. 1994. Attentive novelty detection in humans is governed by pre-attentive sensory memory. *Nature* 372:90–2.

Winkler I, Karmos G, Naatanen R. 1996. Adaptive modeling of the unattended acoustic environment reflected in the mismatch negativity event-related potential. *Brain Res* 742:239–52.

Yasin I. 2007. Hemispheric differences in processing dichotic meaningful and nonmeaningful words. *Neuropsychologia* 45:2718–29.

Zhang Z. 1995. A fast method to compute surface potentials generated by dipoles within multilayer anisotropic spheres. *Phys Med Biol* 40:335–49.

Zumer JM, Attias HT, Sekihara K, Nagarajan SS. 2007. A probabilistic algorithm integrating source localization and noise suppression for MEG and EEG data. *Neuroimage* 37:102–15.

7 Synchronization Analysis in EEG and MEG

Lawrence M. Ward and Sam M. Doesburg

Cognition requires cooperation between neural populations within and across brain areas. Such cooperation moreover must be dynamic in order to accommodate the demands of particular tasks, and to organize features of various percepts. It is clear that many routine cognitive acts require the coordination of activity among specific brain areas. For example, consider what typically occurs when one discovers that they have misplaced their keys. First, a cluttered table or desktop might be subjected to a serial visual search as objects are examined in turn. This requires activation of, and functional integration within, a task-dependant network of brain areas including prefrontal cortex, frontal eye fields, parietal cortex, and inferior temporal regions, that is, those areas relevant for visual attention control and object recognition (Corbetta and Schulman 2002; Gazzaniga et al. 2002). If that search yields no fruit, one might shift one's attention to recalling the events of the night before in search of some record of the missing keys' fate. This requires that a new assembly of neural regions becomes active and functionally coupled as attention is disengaged from the visual search and directed toward recent memory. This new task involves coordinated activity in the prefrontal cortex, hippocampus, and parahippocampal cortical areas (Fell et al. 2001; Gazzaniga et al. 2002). The attention search network moreover must be decoupled because neural populations involved in that task must be freed up for new duties (in this case prefrontal cortex). Rapid reorganization of such large-scale functional networks in the brain requires that connectivity between brain regions be dynamically realized. Such transient coupling and decoupling of brain areas must occur faster than anatomical connectivity can be altered.

Synchronization of neural oscillations been proposed as a mechanism for selective functional integration of neural populations mediating perceptual binding and cognitive brain networks (e.g., Engel and Singer 2001; Varela et al. 2001; Ward 2003). In this view neurons that oscillate in synchrony exchange information more effectively, relative to nonsynchronously oscillating neurons, as they are able to consistently exchange bursts of action potentials during the depolarized phase of the target neurons' ongoing membrane potential fluctuations (Fries 2005). Synchronization of task relevant neural populations appears to be a very general mechanism for dynamic functional organization in the nervous system. A wide variety of cognitive processes, including associative learning, mental rotation, conscious recollection, visual working memory, and coherent perception, have all been shown to coincide with increased neural synchronization between relevant brain regions (e.g., Tallon-Baudry et al. 1998; Miltner et al. 1999; Rodriguez et al. 1999; Bhattacharya et al. 2001; Burgess and Ali 2002; Gruber et al. 2002). Moreover various pathological conditions, including schizophrenia, autism, dyslexia, Alzheimer's disease, and essential tremor, are accompanied by disturbances of oscillatory synchronization (e.g., Llinás et al. 2005; Schnitzler and Gross 2005). Such results strongly suggest that synchronization among brain areas is critical for the task-dependent organization of neural activity, and that the disruption of normal rhythmicity is responsible for a plethora of neurological conditions. Accordingly the calculation of synchronization between electrodes/sensors and reconstructed sources of EEG/MEG activation has become an increasingly popular and promising tool in cognitive neuroscience.

Synchronization: A Physical Concept

Synchronization is a physical concept that was probably first observed by Christiaan Huygens, who in 1665 described how the pendula of two clocks hanging from the same wooden beam came to be swinging exactly contrary to each other even if one of them was disturbed (Pikovsky, Kurths, and Rosenblum 2001). Clock pendula are oscillators, and in order to understand the concept of phase synchronization, we need to understand something about oscillators. This is because phase synchronization only makes sense if it continues for a little while—single events can be simultaneous but not synchronized. For present purposes we define synchronization generally to be *the adjustment of rhythms of self-sustained oscillating systems caused by their interaction*. The definition of phase synchronization between neural systems will be given after we describe oscillators and phase.

Oscillators and Phase

An oscillator is a system that repeatedly returns to the same state. The prototype is a pendulum clock, whose pendulum oscillates between two extreme positions with a fixed period (except for energy losses from friction and air resistance, necessitating the addition of an energy source, usually a dangling weight in early clocks). The oscillation of a pendulum in a pendulum clock is periodic, where the *period* (T) is the time it takes to swing away from and return to a particular position (figure 7.1). Oscillators are characterized by their *amplitude* (A), which measures how far from a particular position or state the oscillation takes the system, and the *frequency* (f), which measures how many cycles from and to a given state the oscillation makes in a given time

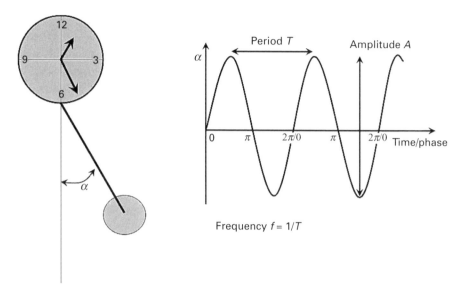

Figure 7.1
Sinusoidal wave (here a sine wave) generated by a pendulum clock, with definitions of period, amplitude, and frequency.

period, usually one second, meaning that frequency is usually measured in cycles per second, or Hertz (Hz).

The exact state of *any* self-sustained periodic oscillator can be described precisely by specifying its *phase* (ϕ), which measures where the oscillation is in its cycle. Phase is measured in radians, from 0 to 2π. One cycle, or period, increments phase by 2π, and phase is said to grow linearly with time. Phase is usually treated as a cyclic variable; that is, it jumps back to zero after it reaches 2π and thus can be visualized as going around a circle. Phase can also be designated in degrees, from 0 to 360, where 0 and 360 are again the same as are 0 and 2π radians. We will use the radian measure of phase in this chapter. Phase is the key concept of synchronization theory because synchronization between two oscillators is defined in terms of the relationship between their phases. Oscillators that have the same phase for some period of time are said to be *in phase* during that time, whereas oscillators whose phase persistently differs by exactly π are said to be *anti-phase*. In both cases, and indeed in any situation where two oscillators maintain a fixed phase difference, $\phi_1 - \phi_2 = c$, for some period of time, the oscillators are said to be *synchronized*. We also say that such oscillators are *phase locked*. When the phases of two oscillators change independent of each other, the oscillators are not synchronized, or phase locked, although they may occasionally have the same phase.

Oscillatory Synchronization

In order for oscillators to synchronize, they must be *coupled*. This means that each influences the other by perturbing (advancing or retarding) its phase. When this situation persists for long enough, the mutual influences result in *synchronization* during which the weak coupling maintains the phases of the oscillators in a fixed relationship. For example, with two pendulum clocks suspended from the same wooden board, as in Huygens's original demonstration, the minute vibrations caused by each clock's mechanism are transmitted through the board and influence the other clock. This is *weak coupling*. When oscillators are weakly coupled, they may experience synchronization if their natural frequencies of oscillation are not too different. For any given strength of coupling, there is a range of frequency mismatch over which synchronization may take place. Once the oscillators are synchronized, they oscillate with the same common frequency and a fixed relationship between their phases, in the case of Huygens's clocks in anti-phase. If the coupling becomes too strong, however, then the synchronized oscillators become essentially one oscillator, and synchronization is no longer an issue. For example, if the pendula of two clocks are directly connected by a metal bar, then the two clocks are essentially one. The boundary between weak and strong coupling is vague and depends on what we are studying. In general, the criterion to use is the independence of the two systems—for example, if one ceases oscillating, then the other should not be forced also to cease. In the case of brain areas this is usually not an issue—brain areas oscillate independently of each other even in the event of brain damage to several of the areas.

Natural systems are noisy. This means that the parameters of natural oscillators, such as neurons, vary somewhat randomly, and thus they cannot achieve exact synchronization for any significant period of time. In particular, the phase of natural oscillators exhibits *phase diffusion*, or random perturbations, because of noise. Fortunately we can define average parameter values (average period and thus average frequency) over relatively long time periods, and speak of *stochastic phase locking*, where because of phase diffusion we can only identify a tendency for the phase difference to remain near a particular value. Even when we find evidence of stochastic phase locking, in a very noisy system the noise will sometimes cause large jumps of 2π in phase. These are called *phase slips*, and they do occur in the context of EEG and MEG synchronization.

Synchronization of Relaxation Oscillators

Synchronized groups of neurons show some of the characteristics of simple phase oscillators, like pendulum clocks, but individual neurons are more usefully described as *relaxation oscillators*. Relaxation oscillators display more complicated cycles than do simpler oscillators. In particular, they display periods of slow and fast motion within a single cycle, making their cycles resemble a sequence of pulses. This is exactly what the rhythm of a neuron looks like, with action potentials, or spikes (fast), separated by periods of slow buildup of potential toward the spike threshold (caused by internal processes and also by postsynaptic potentials). Synchronization can occur via three different mechanisms in relaxation oscillators, including neurons. These are (1) phase resetting by pulses, (2) threshold variation, and (3) natural frequency variation (Pikovsky et al. 2001). Any of these could occur in neurons as a result of synaptic input, although they might have different signatures and be used for different purposes in the brain. As yet we have no way to differentiate reliably among them in EEG and MEG data.

Fourier Analysis: Spectral Power and Phase

The critical quantities to obtain from the time series of electrical or magnetic recordings, whether from sensors or inferred from source localization algorithms, are spectral power and phase at the various functionally relevant frequencies of oscillation (classically and in this chapter defined in bands of width increasing with frequency—delta band: 1 Hz to 3 Hz; theta band: 4 Hz to 7 Hz; alpha band: 8 Hz to 14 Hz; beta band: 15 Hz to 29 Hz; gamma band: 30 Hz to 50 Hz—see Ward 2003). Spectral power is a measure of the amplitude of an oscillation, whereas phase is a measure of where an oscillation is in its cycle. With respect to EEG/MEG signals, spectral power indexes local synchronization (as described in a later section), and phase is used to compute phase locking between more distant sources. Classically these quantities can be obtained from Fourier analysis of the signal, that is, when the signal is transformed from the time to the frequency domain via the Fourier transform. The Fourier transform represents a time-varying signal, like an EEG or MEG recording, in the frequency domain as a set of sine and cosine waves or as a set of cosine waves with various phase offsets. Of course, we are working with real sampled data, so we use the discrete Fourier transform, which estimates the Fourier transform of a function from a finite number of its sampled points. Moreover we use the fast Fourier transform (FFT) so that computations are feasible (see Ramirez 1985 for a readable introduction). Thus at this point we will describe how we obtain phase offset and amplitude (the square root of spectral power) of the cosine components from the FFT of the recorded time series.

Before we define the discrete Fourier transform, however, we need to realize that if a continuous function $h(t)$ is sampled at some interval, Δ, and that if it is also bandwidth limited to frequencies smaller than some cutoff frequency f_c (which is true of all EEG and MEG data because of the filters implemented by the amplifiers), then the samples, h_n, completely determine the function. In other words, we have

$$h(t) = \Delta \sum_{n=-\infty}^{\infty} h_n \frac{\sin[2\pi f_c(t - n\Delta)]}{\pi(t - n\Delta)}, \tag{1}$$

where f_c is the *Nyquist* frequency, which is defined as

$$f_c = \frac{1}{2\Delta}.$$

For example, for a sampling rate of 500 Hz, which means a sampling interval of 0.002 s, the Nyquist frequency is 1/0.004 or 250 Hz. To avoid a phenomenon called *aliasing*, whereby all of the variation of the signal above the Nyquist frequency is folded into the recorded signal, the sampling rate should always be set to give at least two sample points per cycle for the highest frequency recorded. In other words, set the analog filter on the amplifier to filter out frequencies higher than the sampling frequency divided by 2, or set the sampling frequency to at least twice the amplifier's low-pass filter cutoff. See Press et al. (1992) for more on this. Also remember that once you have limited yourself to this range of frequencies, you are stuck with it.

The discrete Fourier transform is defined as

$$H_n \equiv \sum_{k=0}^{N-1} h_k e^{2\pi i k n/N}, \tag{2}$$

where $h_k = h(t_k)$ represents the sampled points of the function $h(t)$ at times $t_k = k\Delta$, $k = 0, 1, 2, \ldots, N-1$, and $n = -N/2, -(N-1)/2, \ldots, (N-1)/2, N/2$, the discrete frequencies at which the transform is defined, and $-N/2$ and $N/2$ represent the Nyquist frequency limits. For practical reasons we consider only positive frequencies $0 \leq f \leq f_c$, and thus values of n from 0 to $N/2$. Luckily there is a very fast way to compute this transform and thus to obtain the complex numbers H_n. It is called the fast Fourier transform, and it is used thousands of times every day.

One issue that emerges with Fourier analysis is that the function $h(t)$ is assumed to be complex (i.e., to consist of real and imaginary parts), and so is its Fourier transform, whether discrete or continuous. Complex numbers are defined as vectors in a two-dimensional space called the Argand plane. The real part is simply a real number, and the imaginary part is a real number as well, but multiplied by $i = \sqrt{-1}$. Because i doesn't exist (you can't take the square root of a negative number), this complicates matters. Algebraic operations are defined differently for complex numbers, and such numbers are written differently from real numbers, as a somewhat confusing sum: $x + iy$. A less confusing way to write them would be as a pair (x, y), but the computational rules are more intuitive for the standard way. Another slight complication is that the numbers that we record in EEG or MEG are real numbers, not complex numbers. We consider them to be simply represented by $x + i0$, meaning their imaginary component is zero. Even in this case the output of a FFT, however, is a set of complex numbers called the *Fourier series*.

How could the Fourier series, which is comprised of a set of sine and cosine waves of various amplitudes and phases, arise from equation (2), which has only the sum of a set of exponential functions? This wondrous result arises from a formula discovered in 1714 by Roger Coates and popularized by Leonard Euler somewhat later. Euler proved that

$$e^{i\phi} = \cos\phi + i\sin\phi. \tag{3}$$

In equation (3), ϕ again stands for phase, as it is portrayed in figure 7.2. Both sides of the equation can be represented by infinite series, and Euler proved that these infinite series are equal. Equation (3) represents a way to translate between Cartesian and polar coordinates in the Argand plane. This is done by noting that we write any complex number as $z = x + iy$, as above, where x and y are Cartesian coordinates in the Argand plane. Now Euler's formula implies that

$$z = x + iy = |z|(\cos\phi + i\sin\phi) = |z|e^{i\phi}, \tag{4}$$

where x is the real part and y is the imaginary part of the complex number, and its magnitude is $|z| = \sqrt{x^2 + y^2}$. Basically the numbers $\sin\phi$ and $\cos\phi$ respectively represent the Cartesian coordinates of the phase angle in a "unit space," that is, a space where the points can only be along the unit circle (as in figure 7.2).

Notice that the cosine and sine are the same function, simply shifted by $\pi/2$ radians (or 90°) with respect to each other. The parts of the complex number then simply multiply these coordinates to create their actual magnitude. On the other hand, the

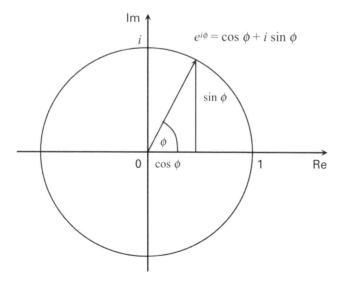

Figure 7.2
Phase ϕ represented in the Argand (complex) plane, with polar and Cartesian coordinates shown as equivalent (Euler's identity).

quantity $e^{i\phi}$ represents this same point in polar coordinates; in other words, in terms of the phase angle alone, and the magnitude of z represents the length of the vector that has that angle with the x axis (in radians).

So we could rewrite equation (2) as

$$H_n = \sum_k \left(A_n \cos\left(\frac{2\pi nk}{N}\right) + B_n \sin\left(\frac{2\pi nk}{N}\right) \right) = \sum_k \left(M_n \cos\left(\left[\frac{2\pi nk}{N}\right] + P_n\right) \right), \qquad (5)$$

where A_n and B_n are called the "Fourier coefficients," $M_n = \sqrt{A_n^2 + B_n^2}$ is the magnitude, and $P_n = \tan^{-1}(B_n/A_n)$ is the phase offset (or simply phase). Note that the term $2\pi nk/N$ represents the steady progression of the phase of the sine or cosine wave with sample k ($k = 1, 2, \ldots, N$, which stands for time here), whereas P_n represents a phase offset, unique to each frequency, n. So we can represent the wave at a particular frequency as a cosine wave that has its usual progression as well as a phase offset, or initial phase, that represents a phase advance or retardation for the entire time period over which we have considered the signal. This is the relevant aspect of the phase that we wish to use. So if we Fourier analyzed two signals and compared their phases at a particular frequency, we would actually be comparing these phase offsets.

The longer the sampled set of inputs, the better the Fourier series approximates the actual Fourier transform of the (assumed) data function. The algorithm of the FFT also works better on sequences of samples that equal an integer power of 2. Therefore data are usually *zero-padded* (zeros are added to the end of the data set until the number of samples equals an integer power of 2). This both speeds up the algorithm and also increases the accuracy of the result.

A further complication is that the FFT is computed not for individual integer frequencies but for logarithmically spaced frequency intervals. Thus the result is somewhat fuzzy in the frequency domain. Moreover the FFT actually computed in most EEG and MEG work concerning the temporal dynamics of brain activity is the short-time Fourier transform. In EEG and MEG data the typical Fourier analysis assumption that the signal is the same for all time, that is that it is *stationary*, is sure to be violated. Indeed we are most interested in the changes in the signal over time. This means that the entire signal, usually a meaningful epoch, is divided into several overlapping time windows, and the FFT done for each of these. This yields as a result a time–frequency analysis of both spectral power (the square of the magnitude of the Fourier coefficient) and phase. There are two problems here: both the time and frequency intervals make the resolution fuzzy, and worse, the resolution of each quantity trades off with the other. The smaller the time windows, the better the temporal resolution but the worse the frequency resolution (as there are fewer cycles of each frequency to analyze), whereas the larger the time windows, the better the frequency resolution but the worse the temporal resolution (since the average is taken over the entire window). Clearly, also the larger the window, the less precisely can the estimate of phase be applied temporally. This problem can be ameliorated somewhat by taking moderate size windows but overlapping them to a large extent, but there is still the remaining frequency resolution problem. Phase is not a meaningful quantity for broad band signals, as there are many frequencies in such signals and an average phase across them applies not very well to any one of them. For this reason, although Fourier analysis is often used to analyze EEG and MEG data for spectral power changes over time, where precise timing information can be obtained for somewhat broad frequency ranges indicative of local synchronization in those ranges, it is seldom used for analysis of long-distance synchronization, where precise phase information is required. To obtain phase information that is useful simultaneously with relevant amplitude information, we must use wavelet analysis or use the analytic signal method. These will be described in a later section when we discuss phase locking across longer distances.

Synchronization of Action Potentials and Local Field Potentials

Early experimental evidence that neural synchronization serves to functionally couple neural groups came from studies using electrodes implanted in cat cortex. It was initially demonstrated that gamma-band synchronization of local field potentials (LFPs) and multi-unit activity (MUA) is increased between columns representing features belonging to a common object (Gray et al. 1989). Columnar synchronization in the gamma frequency range moreover was shown to organize discrete neural assemblies to segregate the representations of objects that overlap one another in the visual scene (Engel, König, and Singer 1991). The prevalence of recurrent collaterals from pyramidal cells gives rise to a coherent population oscillation within a cortical column, and during waking such columnar oscillations occur at a relatively high frequency and are spatially segregated, properties arising from the interaction of cellular and network dynamics (Nunez 1995). Given that tuning parameters of columns in primary visual cortex refer to basic stimulus properties, these results suggest that a gamma-synchronous neural assembly dynamically integrates features into perceptual objects (figure 7.3). It also seems that synchronization of oscillatory rhythms is the mechanism by which features of perceptual objects are bound across visual cortical regions, including those represented in association cortex, because stimulus-specific gamma synchronization has been observed between monkey V1 and V2, between V1 and extra-striate motion areas, and between left and right hemisphere V1s of cats (Engel, König, et al. 1991; Engel, Kreiter, et al. 1991; Frein et al. 1994; Gray and Singer 1989). Such observations have culminated in the hypothesis that such selective neural synchronization may be a fundamental brain mechanism for object representation, and a neural substrate for sensory awareness (Tallon-Baudry and Bertrand 1999; Engel and Singer 2001).

The integrative and organizing role of neural synchronization is not limited to sensation and perception, but rather it is a pervasive feature of central nervous system activity. Visuo-motor integration during a Go/NoGo task, for example, is reflected by

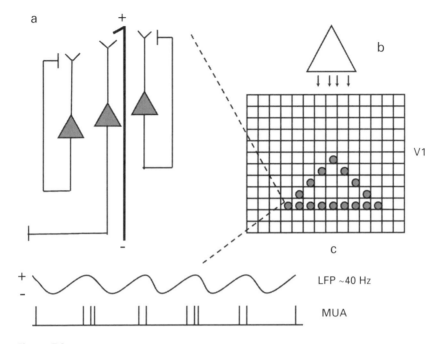

Figure 7.3
(a) Schematic representation of pyramidal neurons within a cortical column. Note the prevalence of recurrent collaterals that project back to the dendrites of neurons within the same cortical column, giving rise to a coherent columnar dynamic that, during wakefulness, exhibits fast (~40 Hz) oscillations. Below is a typical roughly 40 Hz oscillation recorded from primary visual cortex wherein multi-unit activity (MUA) is locked to the cycle of the columnar local field potential (LFP). (b) A simple visual object. (c) Typical object representation across synchronously oscillating columns on the retinotopically organized surface of primary visual cortex. Circles represent columns that oscillate synchronously at around 40 Hz when the triangle is (b) is viewed.

synchronization between visual and motor cortex of cats that varies according to task demands (Roelfsema et al. 1997). This role of neural synchronization extends to neural activity of a purely motor nature, as evidenced by the occurrence of cortico-spinal coherence that is sensitive to task parameters (Salinius and Hari 2003). Higher cognitive processes such as selective attention are also known to affect oscillatory synchronization, as LFPs within a particular cortical area show increased synchronization in the gamma band, and decreased synchronization in the alpha band, when attention is directed to information represented by that cortical region (Fries et al. 2001).

Despite the propensity of recent research to focus on the integrative role of relatively high-frequency oscillations, it is clear that the relevance of oscillatory brain synchronization to brain function is much more varied and nuanced. Intracranial EEG (iEEG) recordings taken from humans show that cortical gamma-band responses vary greatly across brain loci during cognitive processing, and do not in all cases conform to rules such as "local gamma activation reflects active processing, and synchronization functionally couples regions that must cooperate for the performance of a given task" (Lachaux et al. 2005). Moreover it is becoming increasingly clear that equating oscillatory activations across different scales and methods of measurement cannot always be meaningfully accomplished in a straightforward way. Careful attention must also be devoted to the frequency and scale of oscillatory dynamics. Local synchronization of alpha rhythms, unlike gamma oscillations, typically reflects active inhibition of processing within a cortical area (Klimesch et al. 2007; Ward 2003). Synchronization of alpha oscillations across long distances, however, has been increasingly interpreted as an index of functional coupling much like long-range synchronization at higher frequencies (Palva and Palva 2007). It is a challenge for investigators in this field to interpret the complex relationship between oscillations in various frequency bands and their expression at various scales of measurement.

Functional Anatomy, Local Synchronization, EEG Potentials, and MEG Fields

Neuroimaging and lesion studies have shown that there is a substantial amount of functional specialization in particular regions of the human brain (Gazzaniga et al. 2002). Basic cognitive processes such as selective attention and object recognition, however, require coordinated activity within a distributed network of brain regions. Endogenous deployment of visual attention, for example, involves coordinated activation within a distributed set of cortical regions, including the primary visual cortex, superior parietal lobule, inferior parietal lobule, and frontal eye fields (Corbetta and Shulman 2002). Recognition of a familiar object would require activity in a separate but overlapping set of brain regions, including the superior parietal lobule, the inferior parietal lobule, and the inferior temporal cortex (Supp et al. 2007). Performance of a cognitive task requiring activation within such a distributed network generally entails changes in activation in each relevant area. These neuro-electric changes propagate through the volume of the brain and head and reach the scalp in the form of multi-determined, somewhat spatially overlapping electrical fields. To conceptually bridge the gap between activation of LFP and MUA oscillations and the large-scale population dynamics recorded by EEG, it would be useful to imagine the scenario indicated by the cumulative work of Wolf Singer's group, as described in the previous section. A visual object is represented by the synchronization of columns in primary visual cortex that code for and bind together various basic stimulus properties of the object, and this ensemble also synchronizes with cortical columns in secondary visual cortex, extra-striate motion areas, and presumably other regions representing other aspects of the viewed object such as its linguistic label, object category, and associated memories. Within each engaged region the co-activation of oscillations would sum to a dipolar source, and activation of multiple such dipolar sources would conduct throughout the volume of the head and sum to produce a specific topography of oscillatory activity on the scalp (figure 7.4).

Traditional EEG research has consisted largely of reporting changes of electrical activity at the scalp that are time-locked to a stimulus or response (event-related potentials, or ERPs), and the study of oscillatory synchronization is no exception. Brain oscillations recorded from the scalp are highly multi-determined and typically reflect the population dynamics of a large area of cortex (Nunez 1995). Activation in a cortical region is generally understood to yield increased synchronization of high-frequency oscillatory activity within that area, leading to a pronounced population dynamic in that frequency range (Varela et al. 2001). This view is supported by a number of human iEEG experiments reporting localized gamma-band spectral power modulations accompanying a variety of cognitive tasks, including memory, visual attention, perception, and language (Mainy et al. 2007; Tallon-Baudry et al. 2005; Tanji et al. 2005).

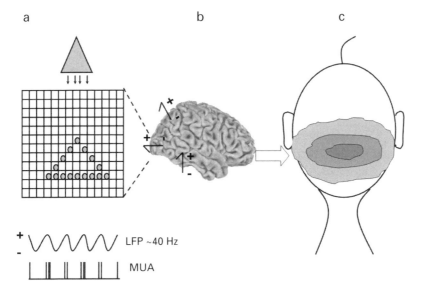

Figure 7.4
(a) Simple visual object and the resultant roughly 40 Hz synchronous oscillations of retinotopically organized cortical columns on the surface of primary visual cortex as shown in figure 7.3. (b) Coactivation of multiple roughly 40 Hz synchronous oscillations produces an additive effect, resulting in a local dipolar source of gamma-band activation, in this case from primary visual cortex and also from various other regions active in representing the higher order aspects of the viewed object. (c) Multiple dipolar sources of gamma-band activity propagate through the volume of the brain and head and produce a corresponding topography of gamma-band activity on the scalp, which can be recorded by EEG electrodes.

The culmination of multiple, more spatially restricted, modulations of oscillatory power constitutes a population dynamic and it is such summations of activity that are recorded at the scalp using EEG. Fourier analysis has been useful in characterizing such oscillatory activity by measuring the temporal dynamics of spectral power in each of several frequency bands for a variety of cognitive tasks. In particular, gamma-band spectral power increases on the scalp have been shown to accompany active cognitive processing across a wide variety of domains, including working memory, selective attention, the recognition of objects and faces, and long-term memory processing (for reviews, see Jensen, Kaiser, and Lachaux 2007; Kaiser and Lutzenberger 2005; Ward 2003). The application of source localization techniques to such effects generally reveals sources of oscillatory activation consistent with our existing knowledge of functional neuroanatomy. When the orientation of a face is held in working memory, for example, increased gamma-band oscillations are localized to the occipital lobe (Jokisch and Jensen 2007).

Even for relatively anatomically circumscribed changes in oscillatory power, however, it can be difficult to gain much insight into the location of brain generators by looking at scalp topography. The lateralized changes in alpha-band activity associated with the deployment of attention to one side of the visual field are a telling example of this. Studies measuring spectral power at the scalp show that these changes are maximal at parieto-temporal electrodes (Worden et al. 2000; Sauseng et al. 2005; Kelly et al. 2006). Localization of the generators of these rhythms using MEG and fMRI, however, reveal that they originate from the calcarine sulcus, which contains area V1 and is located some distance from the parieto-temporal cortex (Yamagishi et al. 2005).

Long-Distance Synchronization: Communication and Integration

As we discussed in the first section of this chapter, the newest and potentially most valuable application of synchronization measurement in the brain is to study communication between, and integration of activity in, brain regions that are fairly far away from each other. As we mentioned, communication between neurons is most efficient when it is synchronized so that inputs from one group of neurons arrive at their targets when those targets are most sensitive to such inputs (e.g., Fries 2005). In this section we discuss several of the most-used techniques for assessing synchronization among brain regions that are distant from one another. These techniques can be applied to records from either EEG or MEG sensors or to inferred activity of neural sources. Here we will focus on sensors, and in a later section we will illustrate applications to neural sources.

Several commercial or freeware computer programs are available to accomplish the analyses we describe, and more are being introduced in the near future. These include especially Matlab routines in the signal-processing toolbox, BESA, and EEGLAB (which runs in Matlab). BRAINSTORM and FIELDTRIP (both of which also run in Matlab) are two source localization programs that also include some frequency analysis routines, including especially filtering, and they can potentially be usefully employed in synchronization analyses. All of the last four additionally include source localization routines that can be used in concert with the synchronization analyses, both directly to obtain local synchronization measures (amplitude or spectral power) and indirectly to filter data for later analysis by other routines.

Phase and Amplitude via Wavelet Analysis

As we mentioned when discussing Fourier analysis, phase computed using the FFT, even the short-time FFT, is not very useful for studying long-distance synchronization. This is because the size of the time window selected affects both frequency and time resolution, but in opposite ways. In response to this difficulty the technique of multi-resolution analysis was invented. Here, instead of decomposing a signal into sine and cosine waves (or cosine waves with different phase offsets), the signal is decomposed into various versions of wavelets (little sections of waves), chirplets (wavelets that vary in frequency), or other components. Wavelets are the most used for EEG and MEG analysis. As in Fourier analysis, what is computed here is the similarity of a particular wavelet, usually the Morlet wavelet (which is the product of a sinusoidal wave with a Gaussian, or normal, probability density; see figure 7.5) to the signal at various times and in various relevant frequency bands. In most applications (e.g., Le Van Quyen et al. 2001) an EEG or MEG signal, $h(t)$, is filtered into small frequency ranges using a digital band-pass filter, and then the (complex) wavelet coefficients, $W_h(\tau, f)$, are computed as a function of time, τ, and center frequency of each band, f, from

$$W_h(\tau, f) = \int_{-\infty}^{\infty} h(t)\Psi_{\tau,f}^*(u)\,du, \tag{6}$$

where $\Psi_{\tau,f}^*(u)$ is the complex conjugate of the Morlet wavelet, which in turn is defined by

$$\Psi_{\tau,f}(u) = \sqrt{f}\,e^{i2\pi f(u-\tau)}e^{-(u-\tau)^2/2\sigma^2}. \tag{7}$$

Note that in equation (7) the first exponential represents a cosine wave as described in the section on Fourier analysis, and the second exponential is the Gaussian probability density function (figure 7.5). The complex conjugate of a complex number $z = x + iy$ is defined as $z^* = x - iy$. For a given time and frequency, $\Psi_{\tau,f}^*(u)$ is only a function of σ, the standard deviation of the Gaussian density function (proportional to the inverse of f), and it determines how many cycles of the wavelet are to be used. The number of cycles, $nc = 6f\sigma$. The frequency resolution of the analysis, namely the frequency range for which the phase is measured, is determined by σ because the range of frequencies analyzed is about from $f - 4f/nc$ to $f + 4f/nc$. For 40 Hz, for example, the frequency range would be from 20 to 60 Hz for $nc = 8$. This is despite the fact that we may have filtered so that the signal being analyzed is narrowband and only ranges

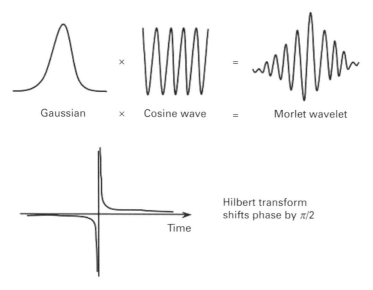

Gaussian   ×   Cosine wave   =   Morlet wavelet

Hilbert transform
shifts phase by $\pi/2$

Time

Figure 7.5
Representation of the envelope of a sinusoidal function whose amplitude is varying over time.
Also shown is a representation of instantaneous amplitude (envelope amplitude) and phase
(location on the time/phase axis) at a given time point.

from, say, 38 to 42 Hz. This result illustrates an important property of wavelet and
other multi-resolution analyses: at low frequencies the frequency resolution is good
but the time resolution is poor, whereas at high frequencies the time resolution is
good but the frequency resolution is poor. Note that the poorer the frequency resolution, the less meaningful is the phase. It is common practice (e.g., Delorme and Makeig
2004; Le Van Quyen et al. 2001) to use fewer cycles of the wavelet for lower frequencies (e.g., 3 cycles for 6 Hz) and more cycles for higher frequencies (e.g., 9 cycles for
35 Hz) with number of cycles increasing linearly with frequency between whatever
limits are used.

The wavelet transform supplies both the amplitude of the envelope of the signal
and the phase at each time point available (figure 7.6). This is because the wavelet is
passed along the signal from time point to time point, with the wavelet coefficient
for that time point being proportional to the match between the signal and the
wavelet in the vicinity of that time point; the wavelet-signal match is closely related
to the amplitude of the envelope of the signal at each analyzed time point. The
instantaneous phase at each time point, on the other hand, is the phase offset between
the natural oscillation of the wavelet and the oscillation of the signal, as in the
Fourier analysis described earlier (equation 5). Both of these are reflected in the wavelet
coefficients.

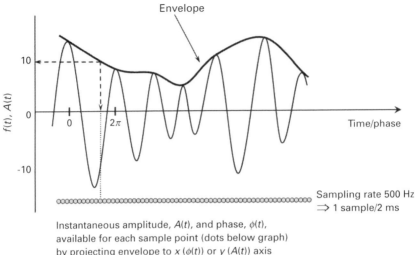

Instantaneous amplitude, $A(t)$, and phase, $\phi(t)$,
available for each sample point (dots below graph)
by projecting envelope to x ($\phi(t)$) or y ($A(t)$) axis

Figure 7.6
(*Top*) A cosine wave multiplied by a Gaussian probability density function yields a Morlet wavelet.
(*Bottom*) The Hilbert transform illustrated when convolved with the signal yields a phase shift
by $\pi/2$ radians.

The difference between the phases of two signals, j and k, say one from each of two
sensors or neural sources, can be computed directly from the wavelet coefficients for
each time and frequency point from

$$e^{i(\phi_j(\tau,f)-\phi_k(\tau,f))} = \frac{W_j(\tau,f)W_k^\star(\tau,f)}{|W_j(\tau,f)W_k(\tau,f)|}. \tag{8}$$

Relative stability of this phase difference across time represents stochastic phase
locking between the signals as described earlier.

Phase and Amplitude via Analytic Signal and Hilbert Transform
Another effective technique available for obtaining the instantaneous phase of a signal
is to use the Hilbert transform to obtain the analytic signal. Le Van Quyen et al. (2001)
directly compared the wavelet and Hilbert techniques for analysis of neural synchrony
in data from neuronal models, intracranial EEG, and scalp EEG, and they found these
techniques to be essentially equivalent across three different ways of assessing synchronization (described in the next subsection).
    The analytic signal, invented by Gabor (1946), is defined for a measured function
of time, $f(t)$, as

$$\varsigma(t) = f(t) + i\tilde{f}(t) = A(t)e^{i\phi(t)},$$ (9)

where $\tilde{f}(t)$ means the Hilbert transform of $f(t)$,

$$\tilde{f}(t) = \frac{1}{\pi} PV \int_{-\infty}^{\infty} \frac{f(t)}{t - \tau} d\tau,$$ (10)

$i = \sqrt{-1}$, and PV has a special meaning in regard to the improper integral that need not concern us (Pikovski et al. 2001). The Hilbert transform essentially shifts the signal's phase by $\pi/2$ (see figure 7.5), making the analytic signal analogous to Euler's identity (equation 3), with the real ($f(t)$) and imaginary ($i\tilde{f}(t)$) parts shifted by $\pi/2$ (as are the cosine and sine in Euler's identity). Indeed, when the signal is narrowband, as it must be for phase to have any meaning, then the analytic signal essentially *is* Euler's identity because $f(t)$ is sinusoidal and $i\tilde{f}(t)$ is $f(t)$ phase-shifted by $\pi/2$.

In equation (9) the instantaneous amplitude is $A(t)$, and the instantaneous phase is $\phi(t)$. $A(t)$ is the amplitude of the envelope of the signal (figure 7.6) and is closely related to the Fourier amplitude at the frequency of the signal, and $\phi(t)$, the instantaneous phase, is the quantity that would be entered into computations involving measurement of synchronization, as when two sources or two sensors are being compared. The Hilbert transform is computed across entire epochs, or even across an entire EEG or MEG record.

Again, instantaneous phase is only meaningful for narrowband signals, so filtering must be done before the analytic signal is computed. The filtering is usually accomplished, as for the wavelet analysis, by applying a digital bandpass filter to the recorded EEG or MEG signals. We have found that a filter having a passband of $f \pm 0.05f$ is effective. This means that the passband is narrow for low frequencies (e.g., for $f = 10$ it is 9.5–10.5 Hz) whereas for higher frequencies it is wider (e.g., for $f = 40$ Hz it is 38–42 Hz).

Both filtering and the Hilbert transform tend to distort results at the temporal boundaries of the signal because they are based on integrals taken from $-\infty$ to $+\infty$. The analyzed epochs should thus be extended so that the distortion does not intrude on meaningful time points. The distortion is worse for lower frequencies because more sampled time points are involved in each cycle, and so the extension should take into account the range of frequencies of interest. We find in practice that with meaningful epochs of around 1 s in duration sampled at 500 Hz, adding an additional 200 ms (100 sample points) to each end of the epoch avoids distortion from about 6 to 60 Hz. We simply throw away the amplitudes and phases for the added sample points and use only those from the sample points of interest. An alternative technique is to filter and transform the entire data set and extract epochs afterward. We have not tried this technique because of computational limitations. But it should yield equivalent results with less distortion for a wider frequency range.

Phase-Locking Value and Other Measures of Synchronization

Phase-Locking Value   We feel that the most useful measure of phase synchronization is phase locking value, or PLV (Lachaux et al. 1999). PLV measures the relative constancy of the difference of phases between two sensors or sources, as computed either by the wavelet transform or using the analytic signal, across the trials of an experiment (usually represented by epochs time-locked to a particular repetitive stimulus presentation). It is defined by

$$PLV_{j,k,t} = N^{-1} \left| \sum_N e^{i[\phi_j(t) - \phi_k(t)]} \right|, \tag{11}$$

where $\phi_j(t)$ and $\phi_k(t)$ are the phases of sensors or sources j and k at time point t for each of the N epochs considered (Lachaux et al. 1999). PLV ranges from a maximum of 1, when the phase differences are exactly the same across all N epochs, to a minimum of 0, when the phase differences vary randomly across the different epochs. Changes in PLV over time, in the absence of confounding factors such as volume conduction (see the next section) reflect changes in the synchronization of the neural activity in a particular frequency band recorded by the sensors or inferred from the sources. PLV is proportional to the standard deviation of the distribution of differences in phase, $\phi_j(t) - \phi_k(t)$, when each difference is transformed into a vector on the unit circle in the Argand plane, and can be represented by a resultant vector in that plane (see figure 7.7).

If the recorded EEG or MEG signal is filtered into several frequency ranges, and PLV is then calculated for each sample point available for a particular pair of sensors or sources, then a time–frequency plot of PLV can be made. Typically normalized PLVs rather than raw PLVs are plotted. This is done to remove the record of ongoing synchronization unrelated to task demands. Normalization of PLVs is accomplished by subtracting the mean baseline PLV from the PLV for every data point and dividing the difference by the standard deviation of the baseline PLV. The baseline is often selected to be the time period just before the presentation of the stimulus to which the epochs are time-locked. For example, in one study we used the 200 ms before a cue stimulus was presented as a baseline to study the changes in synchronization that happened after the cue onset (Doesburg, Roggeveen, et al. 2007). This normalized PLV, here labeled PLV_z, bears a resemblance to a z-score in statistics because it represents the number of baseline standard deviations a particular PLV value is from the baseline mean. Unfortunately, there is no developed statistical theory for such numbers (as there is for z-scores of sample data). Thus surrogate statistics must be used to ascertain statistical reliability. To this end, surrogate PLV_z distributions are created for each frequency and time point available by randomly shuffling the epochs for one or both of the sensors, and recomputing PLV_z for the scrambled data, a large number

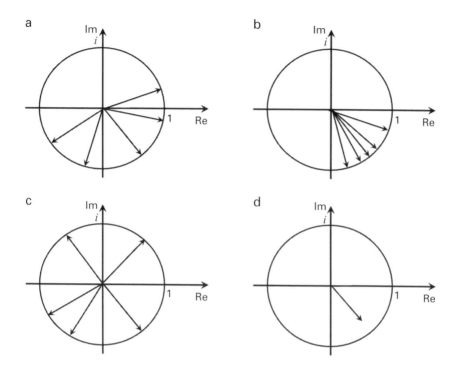

Figure 7.7

(a) Phase difference vectors at a given time point and frequency in the baseline for five trials.
(b) Phase difference vectors for the same five trials and frequency at a time point after a stimulus
where there is a relative increase in phase locking. (c) Phase difference vectors for the same five
trials and frequency at a time point after a stimulus where there is a relative decrease in phase
locking. (d) PLV vector for the phase differences in (b).

of times (in our work 200 times, following Le Van Quyen et al. 2001). As the temporal
relationships between pairs of sensors or sources are random in the shuffled data, the
surrogate distribution of PLV_z values represents a null distribution over the same actual
data. If a PLV_z value either exceeds the 97.5th (or higher if a more conservative test is
desired) percentile or is less than the 2.5th (or lower) percentile of the surrogate distribution, then the PLV_z is considered to represent a significant increase (resp. decrease)
in synchronization at an alpha level of 0.05. A decrease in synchronization is often
referred to as *phase scattering*.

The most meaningful time–frequency diagrams are probably those that plot significant PLV_z increases in one color, decreases in another color, and unchanged PLV_z in a
third color, as in figure 7.8. The black splotches in the figure represent increases in
phase synchronization in the gamma band during a time period from about 250 to
300 ms after stimulus onset (which occurred at 0 ms), and in the alpha band from

about 400 to 800 ms. The light-gray splotch represents significant phase scattering in the theta band from about 300 to 700 ms. No other PLV_z values are significant (represented by the medium gray background). The observation of significant changes across several frequencies and several time points is typical, and the recurrence of a pattern of synchronization/desynchronization across multiple adjacent data points is an effective criterion for confirming that observed effects are not spurious given the large number of data points analyzed (e.g., Doesburg, Roggeveen, et al. 2007 Doesburg, Kitajo, and Ward 2005; Doesburg, Emberson, et al. 2007; Kitajo et al. 2007; Le Van Quyen et al. 2001).

Information Measures PLV is an excellent measure of so-called 1:1 phase locking, where the oscillation frequencies being compared are close to the same at both sensors or sources. It so happens, however, that sometimes there is a wish to see whether there is a constant relationship between oscillations at different frequencies, or to test whether phase locking occurs for any combination of frequencies that can be related by $nf_1 = mf_2$. This situation is called $n:m$ *phase locking*, where n is the number of cycles of one oscillation that occur during m cycles of the other. Consider, for example, a 20 Hz (beta) oscillation and a 40 Hz (gamma) oscillation. In this case there are two cycles of the 40 Hz wave for every one cycle of the 20 Hz wave, a case of a 1:2 frequency relationship. In general, phase locking is difficult to observe when n and m are large. Nonetheless, a more general measure, based on information theory, can be used to detect such $n:m$ phase locking, and it also serves for 1:1 locking of course.

In general, a tendency toward phase locking is revealed by a clumping of the distribution of phase differences around a particular value (figure 7.8), as opposed to a uniform distribution of such differences when the phase relationship of two oscillators is random. The most general way, and that requiring the fewest assumptions statistically, to characterize deviation from a uniform distribution is to measure the Shannon entropy of the distribution. The Shannon entropy of a distribution of observations over a particular number, N, of intervals (or bins) is maximal when that distribution is uniform, and is equal to $\ln(N)$. Tass et al. (1998) defined an entropy synchronization index as

$$S = \frac{H_{\max} - H}{H_{\max}}, \tag{12}$$

where

$$H = -\sum_{m=1}^{N} p_m \ln p_m \tag{13}$$

and p_m is the relative frequency of phase differences being found in bin m. This index ranges from 0, for a completely uniform distribution (where $H = H_{\max}$), to 1, when all of the phase differences fall into the same bin (complete phase locking, at least with

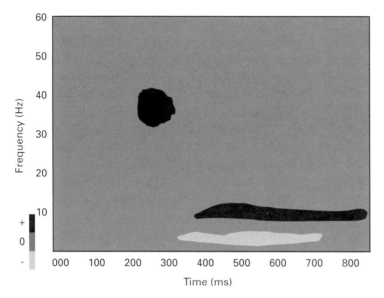

Figure 7.8
A time–frequency diagram of normalized PLV, PLV_z. The scale at lower left indicates which splotches represent increases and which represent decreases in phase locking from the baseline.

respect to the width of the bins, with $H = 0$). Tass et al. (1998) recommend choosing the number of equal-sized bins to be $N = \exp[0.626 + 0.4 \ln(M - 1)]$, where M is the number of samples available in each epoch.

Alternatively, we could use the mutual information, which measures the departure of two systems from complete independence. Mutual information is written as

$$MI = H(\phi_j) + H(\phi_k) - H(\phi_j, \phi_k). \tag{14}$$

$H(\phi_j)$, $H(\phi_k)$, and $H(\phi_j, \phi_k)$ are defined by equation (13) for $p_{j,m}$, $p_{k,m}$, and $p_{j,k,m}$, and the latter is the relative frequency of finding both ϕ_j and ϕ_k in bin m. Again, a normalized index is used: $S_{MI} = MI/MI_{\max}$, where $MI_{\max} = \ln(N)$, and S_{MI} ranges between 0 (no synchronization) and 1 (perfect synchronization).

Once again, there is no statistical theory for these information measures used this way, so surrogate statistics must be used. These can be computed the same way as for the PLV analyses, by shuffling the epochs to destroy the temporal structure of the original data. The results can be displayed and interpreted in a similar fashion to the PLV analyses, and as we mentioned, Le Van Quyen et al. (2001) found the results of PLV, Shannon entropy, and mutual information analyses all to be equivalent for simulated data, iEEG data, and scalp-recorded EEG data.

Coherence We do not recommend the use of the standard measure of source or sensor linear coherence,

$$LC_{1,2}(f,t) = \frac{\sum_{k=1}^{N} W_{1,k}(f,t)W_{2,k}^{\star}(f,t)}{\sqrt{\sum_{k=1}^{N}|W_{1,k}(f,t)|^2}\sqrt{\sum_{k=1}^{N}|W_{2,k}(f,t)|^2}}, \tag{15}$$

where $W_{1,k}(f,t)$ is the wavelet coefficient for sensor or source 1 at frequency f and time t, and $W_{2,k}^{\star}(f,t)$ is the complex conjugate of the corresponding wavelet coefficient for sensor or source 2. This is because linear coherence reflects both the correlation between the amplitudes of signals from sensors or sources and the relationship of their phases, thus confounding them. Indeed, as can be seen from equation (15), the form of the expression is that of a correlation coefficient, with a cross product in the numerator and the product of two standard-deviation-like quantities in the denominator. Instead a more useful way to use the phase information provided by a wavelet analysis is to compute phase cross-coherence between sensors or sources across trials, N,

$$CC_{1,2}(f,t) = \frac{1}{N}\sum_{k=1}^{N}\frac{W_{1,k}(f,t)W_{2,k}^{\star}(f,t)}{|W_{1,k}(f,t)W_{2,k}(f,t)|} \tag{16}$$

(e.g., Delorme and Makeig 2004). In equation (16) the denominator, which is the magnitude of the cross product of the wavelet coefficients, is responsible for canceling out the amplitude information and thus leaving only a function of the phase difference to be averaged across trials. This index too varies between 1 (for perfect phase locking) and 0 (for a random phase relationship). By the similarity between equations (16) and (8), it can be seen that the phase cross-coherence defined in this way is highly analogous to phase locking value defined in equation (11).

Synchronization Likelihood Another interesting suggested measure of synchronization generalizes the approaches already described to systems that cannot be characterized as consisting of oscillators (e.g., Stam and van Dijk 2002). Leaving aside the question of whether this applies to the brain, we will briefly describe this tool, which arises from the study of chaos theory. It applies to a set of M simultaneously recorded time series like those from EEG or MEG sensors. From these time series are constructed a set of vectors consisting of consecutive subsequences of a given length. For example, for two time series

$$X = x_1, x_2, x_3, x_4, x_5, x_6, \ldots, \quad \text{and} \quad Y = y_1, y_2, y_3, y_4, y_5, y_6, \ldots,$$

we could select subsequences x_1, x_2, x_3, and x_2, x_3, x_4, and so forth, from series X and y_1, y_2, y_3 and y_2, y_3, y_4, and so forth, from series Y. The essential idea is to define a probability that such subsequences over the interval of interest are closer together than a given small distance, ε. This is done by computing the Euclidean distance between the various comparable subsequences treated as vectors. The distance ε is selected by choosing a suitably small probability, p_{ref}, such that the probability of vectors being closer than ε for the first time point is equal to p_{ref}. Then that distance is used for the other time points in the series for that pair. This is repeated for the other pairings of sensors with respect to a given sensor, and then a normalized average is taken. The resulting index, called a "synchronization likelihood," or $S_{k,i}$, represents how strongly sensor k at time i is synchronized to all the other $M - 1$ sensors available; it ranges between p_{ref}, for no synchronization at all, and 1 for complete synchronization. $S_{k,i}$ can also be averaged across sensors and time when appropriate.

$S_{k,i}$ is related to mutual information (equation 14) and has been used to characterize aberrant sensor synchronization in EEG and MEG records in people with serious illnesses such as epilepsy and Alzheimer's disease (e.g., Stam and van Dijk 2002).

Spurious Synchronization

It is possible that what look like significant and functionally meaningful changes in phase locking between sources or sensors instead may be spurious; that is, they arise because of the noise in the brain or because electromagnetic fields from active regions propagate throughout the brain because of volume conduction. The main problem with noise is that it causes phase slips, and too many of these simply make it more difficult for a relatively constant phase difference between oscillators to persist for any length of time. Since the brain is always noisy, the solution to the noise problem is to increase signal-to-noise ratio, usually by accruing sufficient epochs that the periods of constant phase difference begin to stand out from the noise.

The volume conduction problem, which is conceptually more difficult, arises because impressed currents (movement of ions, or charged particles) in the dendrites of neurons in a particular brain area cause return currents to flow throughout the rest of the brain (see Wolters and de Munck 2007). EEG measures the potential differences between the return currents at various places on the scalp, and MEG measures the magnetic flux caused by both impressed and return currents near the scalp. These are the signals we have available from which to infer synchronization. Luckily for MEG, the magnetic field outside the head is independent of the conductivity of the brain, skull, and scalp tissue, except for deviations of the head from spherical symmetry (Wolters and de Munck 2007). Thus volume conduction is not considered to be a serious problem for MEG. EEG, however, is very much affected by volume conduction because the potential measured at the scalp depends on how easily the electrical field penetrates the brain, skull, and scalp tissue, in other words their conductivities as these vary with tissue type.

The volume conduction problem has been studied extensively in the context of neural source analysis. The task in that analysis is to reconstruct the primary (impressed) current distribution within the brain from the electric or magnetic fields measured on or near the scalp. This is called the inverse problem, and there is no unique solution for any given electrical or magnetic scalp topography. Complex models that incorporate the measured conductivities of the various tissue layers, however, can be used to infer the activities of various neural sources that optimize some measure of error or fit, and thus give a reasonable map of those primary current generators (see the next section). In the analysis of neural phase synchronization, however, much less work has been done. Thus the possibility of volume conduction creating spurious synchronies remains a serious consideration at present.

The most extensive work on this problem was done by Lachaux et al. (1999). They concluded that volume conduction is unlikely to cause spurious long-range synchronization as measured by PLV. They computed wavelet-based PLV from local field potentials recorded from intracranial electrodes spaced at 1 cm intervals in a human brain. In their analyses, volume-conduction-induced spurious synchrony extended no farther than 2 cm in normal brain tissue. They then used the same LFP recordings as theoretical dipole sources in a simulation study. Here they calculated the scalp potentials arising from the recorded activity of the dipoles using a standard three-layer spherical model of the head (called the forward solution). From the simulated scalp potentials they calculated PLVs for scalp potential, scalp current density (SCD, which is the spatial second derivative of the scalp potential; see Perrin, Bertrand, and Bernier 1987) and the electrocorticogram (ECoG; see Le and Gevins 1993). Both SCD and ECoG transforms reduce the overlap of the brain volumes recorded by different scalp electrodes, in particular, eliminating the contributions of deep sources and shrinking the scalp areas affected by shallow sources. Both the SCD and the ECoG sharpened synchronous regions and reduced spurious synchronization relative to the untransformed scalp potential. In another study Nunez et al. (1997) found that SCD and ECoG reduced the effects of volume conduction on coherence between scalp electrodes, with virtually no spurious coherence for separations of 4 cm or more between scalp electrodes. Therefore we recommend computing PLV on the SCD- or ECoG-transformed potentials as well as on the raw potentials when using EEG. Convergence between the results of the several analyses is a good indication that the synchronization observed is not spurious, especially for electrodes separated by 4 cm or more (e.g., see Doesburg, Kitajo, and Ward 2005).

More recently Doesburg, Roggeveen, et al. (2007) studied the relationship between instantaneous amplitude and phase locking of sensors when the sensors receive signals from more than a single source (see also Meinecke et al. 2005). They showed that the PLV measured between any two sensors depends on the constancy of the relative amplitudes of the sources from which they are receiving signals as well as on the constancy of their relative phases across trials. The standardized PLV_z eliminates volume conduction effects of sources whose amplitudes do not change from those in the baseline period. But even if PLV_z indicates that synchronization between two sources has increased ($PLV_z > 0$) or decreased ($PLV_z < 0$) from the baseline period, there could still be a problem with volume conduction. True changes in synchronization mean that the true phase difference between the sources must have become more (or less) constant across trials, regardless of changes in the amplitudes of the source activities. Spurious synchronization, on the other hand, could arise in the absence of a change in the difference between the true phases of the sources if the amplitude of one or the other source increases (or decreases) reliably across trials by enough that the measured phases at the two sensors now each contain significantly more (or less) contribution from a particular source, thus making the measured phases more (or less) constant across trials. The latter could happen either because a source that is already active becomes more (or less) active reliably across trials or because a source that is inactive during the baseline is reliably activated by the task during part of the analyzed epoch. This means that spurious, volume-conducted synchrony does not appear in the absence of correlated changes in amplitude (or power) at both sensors. For this reason we emphasize inspection of both PLV_z and amplitude in our interpretation of synchrony changes in analyses based on sensors alone.

Another way to discriminate between spurious synchronization caused by mixing of neural sources and real synchronization among them is to use a technique that locates the sources and generates their (inferred) signals, which can then be analyzed using the techniques just described. We discuss in the next section several such techniques, all of which require assumptions about the brain, conductivity, and so forth. It is also possible to use so-called blind source separation techniques like independent component analysis (ICA; see Delorme and Makeig 2004) to generate signals that, although not those of the actual sources, are a transform of them that preserves real synchrony but dispenses with spurious synchrony caused by mixing. A demonstration-in-principle of this approach was accomplished by Meinecke et al. (2005). They showed that PLV analyses of the independent components revealed true synchronization and suppressed spurious synchronization for both artificially mixed simulated signals and for real EEG signals. As EEGLAB can do ICA analysis, this is a promising approach, although ICA analysis is not without its difficulties.

Synchronization between Neural Sources

As evidence mounts that long-distance synchronization of human brain rhythms serves to functionally integrate distant neural populations into large-scale networks, increasing energy is being devoted to the combination of source localization techniques with synchronization and coherence analysis methods. This step is a necessary one if strong claims are to be made about the putative engagement of specific brain regions in large-scale, synchronous, oscillatory brain networks. At this early point of inquiry it appears that there are multiple viable methods for the localization of human brain rhythms that can be combined effectively with indexes of long-distance neural synchronization. These include at a minimum independent component analysis (ICA), beamformer analysis, minimum norm solutions, and autoregressive techniques.

Several plausible techniques have been developed for the estimation of synchronous oscillations across multiple localized sources of activity. The most prolific of these has been the dynamic imaging of coherent sources (DICS) approach, which has been principally employed in the study of functional networks in the motor system (e.g., Gross et al. 2001). Perhaps the most elegant technique for the determination of locally coherent oscillatory sources and the extraction of epoched signals for phase-locking analysis is one in which minimum norm current solutions are employed in an itera-tive sequence to determine intertrial coherence and coherence between adjacent voxels for source reconstruction (David and Garnero 2002; David et al. 2002, 2003). To date, however, this technique has only been used in the processing of brain responses entrained by flickering stimuli and has not been employed for the estima-tion of endogenous oscillatory activity (e.g., Cosmelli et al. 2004). More recently autoregressive techniques have been employed for the estimation of multiple sources of task-relevant oscillatory activation within a particular frequency band. Sources identified using this method can be successfully combined with PLV analysis, as has been eloquently demonstrated in the study of gamma oscillations in the human object recognition network (figure 7.8; see Supp et al. 2007). Two practical advantages to this approach should be noted: (1) such analyses can be performed using a freely available open source Matlab toolbox and (2) this technique has proved compatible with available methods for the calculation of Granger causality measures that index the causal direction of information flow between sources. This toolbox, BioSig (Version 1.95), an open source software library for biomedical signal processing, is available online at http://biosig.sourceforge.net/.

A technique for the localization of oscillatory sources in cognition that has borne increasingly promising fruit is beamformer analysis. Beamformer is able to produce an estimate of the contribution of each voxel in a source space to activity measured from the scalp by reducing correlations between voxels within a designated time–frequency window (Van Veen et al. 1997). Beamformer analysis can be implemented on EEG data using commercially available software such as the Brain Electrical Source Analysis suite (BESA 5.1; Megis Software, Germany). Such software applications have proved effective in revealing the sources and timing of oscillations relevant to cogni-tive processes such as endogenous attention control (Green and McDonald 2008; see their chapter in this volume for a detailed description). Another productive variant of beamformer analysis can be found in synthetic aperture magnetometry (SAM), a beamformer technique developed for MEG analysis (Vrba and Robinson 2001).

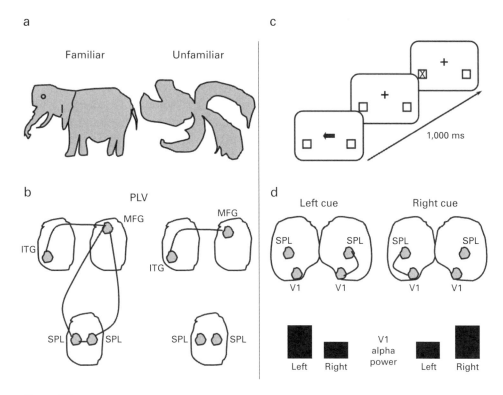

Figure 7.9

(a) Stimulus display of familiar and unfamiliar objects. (b) Sources of gamma-band activation and gamma-band phase locking, indicated by black lines. Increased gamma-band synchronization is interpreted as a "re-ignition" of a distributed Hebbian cell-assembly when the familiar object is recognized. (c) Lateralized visuospatial cueing paradigm. (d) Alpha-band activation and increased interregional synchronization (indicated by black lines). Increased occipitoparietal synchronization is interpreted as enhancing functional coupling between these regions, accounting for the enhanced processing of information appearing at attended locations. Note the reciprocal relationship of occipitoparietal synchronization and local V1 power. This underscores the complexity of interpreting oscillatory synchronization across various scales of cortical distance. In this case interregional synchronization in the alpha band indexes functional integration, whereas local alpha synchronization (local power) reflects inhibitory processes.

Event-related SAM (erSAM) has been effectively used to uncover sources of neuromagnetic activity associated with cognitive processing (Herdman et al. 2007). Studies employing a combination of the beamformer technique (using both BESA algorithms and SAM) with PLV analysis have proved to be effective for elucidation of large-scale oscillatory synchronous brain networks. An example of this can be found in the analysis of phase synchronization between reconstructed sources of oscillatory activation. Convergent results have been found using BESA beamformer algorithms (EEG) and SAM analysis (MEG) in conjunction with the PLV technique (analytic signal approach). In both cases, when attention is deployed to one visual hemifield, increased synchronization in the alpha band is observed between reconstructed occipital and parietal sources in the contralateral hemisphere (figure 7.9; see Doesburg, Herdman, and Ward 2007; Doesburg, Green, et al., submitted). Interestingly this lateralization of long-distance synchronization is inversely related to local occipital power measurements in the same frequency range, illustrating the complexity of the relationship between oscillatory synchronization and cognitive processing.

Postscript: Granger Causality and Other Exotica

Phase synchronization between two neural sources indicates that information is likely being exchanged between those sources. The timing of the synchronization can indicate when this information exchange is taking place and can contribute to a causal analysis of the operation of the neural network. Often this is not enough, however, to infer causality. Several techniques have been used in fMRI analysis to help make this inference, namely functional connectivity (temporal correlations between remote neurophysiological events) and effective connectivity (the influence of one neural system over another) analyses (e.g., Friston 1994). Functional connectivity is closely related to linear coherence analysis (equation 15). These techniques can be applied to EEG and MEG data, but they are more typically used for PET and fMRI studies. Our analysis of phase locking specializes functional connectivity to a particular form that is independent of oscillatory amplitude, namely that of oscillatory synchronization. Effective connectivity, on the other hand, attempts to describe the causal interaction of neural systems. Oscillatory synchronization could possibly be a necessary condition for a causal interaction between two neural sources, but it is silent on the direction of such an interaction. A measure that is more directly indicative of causal direction is that of Granger causality. Granger causality is an analysis of time series data based on the idea that the cause of something must precede the effect (e.g., Granger 1969). If the previous (to some time t) data points in one time series can provide an increment in predictability of subsequent data points in a second time series over that provided by the previous data points of the second time series, then the first time series is said to "Granger-cause" the second. Granger causality can be unidirectional or bidirectional. This analysis has been extended to multivariate time series and various frequency bands (see Ding et al. 2006 for a review of applications in neuroscience). It is already being used successfully, as mentioned in the previous section, to determine the causal direction of source interactions specified by synchronization analysis (e.g., Supp et al. 2007). Partial directed coherence (Baccala and Sameshima 2001) seems to be a particularly useful variant for time series data from neural sources. Additional applications and extensions of the technique should allow us to approach one significant goal of cognitive neuroscience: to describe the temporal dynamics of the causal interactions between brains areas involved in implementing cognitive processes.

Acknowledgments

This chapter was supported by a grant from the Natural Sciences and Engineering Research Council (NSERC) of Canada. We thank Stephanie Thái for help with the references.

References

Baccala LA, Sameshima K. 2001. Partial directed coherence: a new concept in neural structure determination. *Biol Cybern* 84:463–74.

Bhattacharya J, Petsche H, Feldmann U, Rescher B. 2001. EEG gamma-band phase synchronization between posterior and frontal cortex during mental rotation in humans. *Neurosci Lett* 311: 29–32.

Burgess AP, Ali L. 2002. Functional connectivity of gamma EEG activity is modulated at low frequency during conscious recollection. *Int J Psychophysiol* 46:91–100.

Canolty RT, Edwards E, Dalal SS, Soltani M, Nagarajan SS, Kirsch HE, Berger MS, Barbaro NM, Knight RT. 2006. High gamma power is phase locked to theta oscillations in human neocortex. *Science* 313:1626–8.

Corbetta M, Schulman GL. 2002. Control of goal-directed and stimulus-driven attention in the brain. *Nat Rev Neurosci* 3:201–15.

David O, Cosmelli D, Hasboun D, Garnero L. 2003. A multitrial analysis for revealing significant corticocortical networks in megnetoencephalography and electroencephalography. *NeuroImage* 20:186–201.

David O, Garnero L. 2002. Time-coherent expansion of MEG/EEG cortical sources. *NeuroImage* 17:1277–89.

David O, Garnero L, Cosmelli D, Varela FJ. 2002. Estimation of neural dynamics from MEG/EEG cortical current density maps: application to the reconstruction of large-scale cortical synchrony. *IEEE Trans Biomed Eng* 49:975–87.

Delorme A, Makeig S. 2004. EEGLAB: an open source toolbox for analysis of single-trial EEG dynamics. *J Neurosci Meth* 134:9–21.

Ding M, Chen Y, Bressler SL. 2006. Granger causality: basic theory and application to neuroscience. In: Schelter S, Winterhalder N, Timmer J, eds. *Handbook of Time Series Analysis*. Hoboken, NJ: Wiley, 451–74.

Doesburg SM, Emberson L, Rahi A, Cameron D, Ward LM. 2007. Asynchrony from synchrony: gamma-band neural synchrony and perception of audiovisual speech asynchrony. *Exp Brain Res* 185:11–20. doi: 10.1007/s00221-007-1127-5.

Doesburg SM, Green JJ, McDonald JJ, Ward LM. 2008. Occipital-parietal alpha-band synchronization and the maintenance of selective visuospatial attention. Unpublished manuscript.

Doesburg SM, Herdman AT, Ward LM. 2007. MEG reveals synchronous neural network for visuospatial attention. Poster presented at the 2007 Meeting of the Cognitive Neuroscience Society in New York City.

Doesburg SM, Kitajo K, Ward LM. 2005. Increased gamma-band synchrony precedes switching of conscious perceptual objects in binocular rivalry. *Neuroreport* 2:229–39.

Doesburg SM, Roggeveen AB, Kitajo K, Ward LM. 2007. Large-scale gamma-band phase synchronization and selective attention. *Cerebr Cortex* 18:386–96. doi: 10.1093/cercor/bhm073.

Doesburg SM, Ward LM. 2007. Long-distance alpha-band MEG synchronization maintains selective attention. In: Cheyne D, Ross B, Stroink G, Weinberg H, eds. *New Frontiers in Biomagnetism: Proceedings of the 15th International Conference on Biomagnetism (BIOMAG 2006)*. Burlington, MA: Elsevier, 551–4.

Engel AK, König P, Kreiter AK, Singer W. 1991. Interhemispheric synchronization of oscillatory neuronal responses in cat visual cortex. *Science* 252:1177–9.

Engel AK, König P, Singer W. 1991. Direct physiological evidence for scene segmentation by temporal coding. *Proc Natl Acad Sci USA* 88:9136–40.

Engel AK, Kreiter AK, König P, Singer W. 1991. Synchronization of oscillatory neuronal responses between oscillatory neural responses between striate and extrastriate visual cortical areas of the cat. *Proc Natl Acad Sci USA* 88:6048–52.

Engel AK, Singer W. 2001. Temporal binding and the neural correlates of sensory awareness. *Trends Cogn Sci* 5:16–25.

Fell J, Klaver P, Lehnertz K, Grunwald T, Schaller C, Elger CE, Fernández G. 2001. Human memory formation is accompanied by rhinal-hippocampal coupling and decoupling. *Nat Neurosci* 4:1259–164.

Frein A, Eckhorn R, Bauer R, Woelbern T, Kehr H. 1994. Stimulus-specific fast oscillations at zero phase between visual areas V1 and V2 of awake monkey. *Neuroreport* 5:2273–7.

Fries P. 2005. A mechanism for cognitive dynamics: neuronal communication through neuronal coherence. *Trends Cogn Sci* 9:474–9.

Fries P, Reynolds JH, Rorie AE, Desimone R. 2001. Modulation of oscillatory neuronal synchronization by selective visual attention. *Science* 291:1506–7.

Friston K. 1994. Functional and effective connectivity in neuroimaging: a synthesis. *Hum Brain Mapp* 2:56–78.

Gabor D. 1946. Theory of communication. *J IEE (London)* 93:429–57

Gazzaniga MS, Ivry RB, Mangun GR. 2002. *Cognitive Neuroscience,* 2d ed. New York: Norton.

Granger CWJ. 1969. Investigating causal relations by econometric models and cross-spectral methods. *Econometrica* 37:424–38.

Gray CM, König P, Engel AK, Singer W. 1989. Oscillatory responses in cat visual cortex exhibit inter-columnar synchronization which reflects global stimulus properties. *Nature* 338:334–7.

Gray CM, Singer W. 1989. Stimulus-specific neuronal oscillations in orientation columns of cat visual cortex. *Proc Natl Acad Sci USA* 86:1698–1702.

Green JJ, McDonald JJ. 2008. Electrical neuroimaging reveals timing of attentional control activity in human brain. *PLoS Biol* 6:e81.

Gross J, Kujala J, Hämäläinen M, Timmermann L, Schnitzler A, Salmelin R. 2001. Dynamic imaging of coherent sources: studying neural interactions in the human brain. *Proc Natl Acad Sci USA* 98:694–9.

Gruber T, Müller MM, Keil A. 2002. Modulation of induced gamma band responses in a perceptual learning task in the human EEG. *J Cogn Neurosci* 14:732–44.

Herdman AT, Pang AW, Ressel V, Gaetz W, Cheyne D. 2007. Task-related modulation of early cortical responses during language production: an event-related synthetic aperture magnetometry study. *Cerebr Cortex* 17:2536–43.

Jensen O, Kaiser J, Lachaux JP. 2007. Human gamma-frequency oscillations associated with attention and memory. *Trends Neurosci* 30:317–24.

Jokisch D, Jensen O. 2007. Modulation of gamma and alpha activity during a working memory task engaging the dorsal or ventral stream. *J Neurosci* 27:3244–51.

Kaiser J, Lutzenberger W. 2005. Human gamma-band activity: a window to cognitive processing. *NeuroReport* 16:207–11.

Kelly SP, Lalor EC, Reilly RB, Foxe JJ. 2006. Increases in alpha oscillatory power reflect an active retinotopic mechanism for distracter suppression during sustained visuospatial attention. *J Neurophysiol* 95:3844–51.

Kitajo K, Doesburg SM, Yamanaka K, Nozaki D, Ward LM, Yamamoto Y. 2007. Noise-driven large-scale synchronization of human brain activity enhances perception. *Europhys Lett* 80:40009p1–6.

Klimesch W, Sauseng P, Hanslmayr S. 2007. EEG alpha oscillations: the inhibition timing hypothesis. *Brain Res Rev* 53:63–88.

Lachaux JP, George N, Tallon-Baudry C, Martinerie J, et al. 2005. The many faces of the gamma-band response to complex visual stimuli. *NeuroImage* 25:491–501.

Lachaux JP, Rodriguez E, Martinerie J, Varela FJ. 1999. Measuring phase synchrony in brain signals. *Hum Brain Mapp* 8:94–208.

Le J, Gevins A. 1993. Method to reduce blur distortion from EEG's using a realistic head model. *IEEE Trans Biomed Eng* 40:517–28.

Le Van Quyen M, Foucher J, Lachaux JP, Rodriguez E, Lutz A, Martinerie J, Varela FJ. 2001. Comparison of Hilbert transform and wavelet methods for the analysis of neural synchrony. *J Neurosci Meth* 111:83–98.

Llinás R, Urbano FJ, Leznik E, Ramírez RR, van Marle HJF. 2005. Rhythmic and dysrhythmic thalamocortical dynamics: GABA systems and the edge effect. *Trends Neurosci* 28:325–33.

Mainy N, Kahane P, Minotti L, Hoffmann D, Bertrand O, et al. 2007. Neural correlates of consolidation in working memory. *Hum Brain Mapp* 28:183–93.

Meinecke FC, Ziehe A, Kurths J, Müller KR. 2005. Measuring phase synchronization of superimposed signals. *Phys Rev Lett* 94:84–102.

Miltner WH, Braun C, Arnold M, Witte H, Taub E. 1999. Coherence of gamma-band EEG activity as basis for associative learning. *Nature* 397:434–6.

Nunez P. 1995. *Neocortical Dynamics and Human EEG Rhythms*. Cambridge: Oxford University Press.

Nunez PL, Srinivasan R, Wetrdorp AF, Wijesinghe RS, Tucker DM, Silberstein RB, Cadusch PJ. 1997. EEG coherency. I: Statistics, reference electrode, volume conduction, Laplacians, cortical imaging and interpretation at multiple scales. *Electroencephalogr Clin Neurophysiol* 103:499–515.

Palva S, Palva JM. 2007. New vistas for alpha-frequency band oscillations. *Trends Neurosci* 30:150–8.

Perrin F, Bertrand O, Pernier J. 1987. Scalp current density mapping: value and estimation from potential data. *IEEE Trans Biomed Eng* 34:283–8.

Pikovsky A, Rosenblum M, Kurths J. 2001. *Synchronization: A Universal Concept in Nonlinear Sciences*. Cambridge: Cambridge University Press.

Press WH, Teuklosky SA, Vettering WT, Flannery BP. 1992. *Numerical Recipes in C: The Art of Scientific Computing*, 2d ed. Cambridge: Cambridge University Press.

Ramirez RW. 1985. *The FFT. Fundamentals and Concepts*. Upper Saddle River, NJ: Prentice-Hall.

Rodriguez E, George N, Lachaux JP, Martinirie J, Renault B, Varela FJ. 1999. Perception's shadow: long-distance synchronization of human brain activity. *Nature* 397:430–3.

Roelfsema PR, Engel AK, König P, Singer W. 1997. Visuomotor integration is associated with zero time-lag synchronization among cortical areas. *Nature* 385:157–61.

Salenius S, Hari R. 2003. Synchronous cortical oscillatory activity during motor action. *Curr Opin Neurobiol* 13:678–84.

Sauseng P, Klimesch W, Stadler W, Schabus M, Doppelmayr S, Gruber WR, Birbaumer N. 2005. A shift of visual spatial attention is selectively associated with human EEG alpha activity. *Eur J Neurosci* 22:2917–26.

Schnitzler A, Gross J. 2005. Normal and pathological oscillatory communication in the brain. *Nat Rev Neurosci* **6**:285–96.

Stam CJ, van Dijk BW. 2002. Synchronization likelihood: an unbiased measure of generalized synchronization in multivariate data sets. *Physica D*163:236–51.

Supp GG, Schlogl A, Trujillo-Barreto N, Muller M, Gruber T. 2007. Directed cortical information flow during human object recognition: analyzing induced gamma-band responses in brain's source space. *PLoS One* 8:e684 (1–11).

Tallon-Baudry C, Bertrand O, Peronet F, Pernier J. 1998. Induced γ-band activity during the delay of a visual short-term memory task in humans. *J Neurosci* 18:4244–54.

Tallon-Baudry C, Bertrand O. 1999. Oscillatory gamma activity in human and its role in object representation. *Trends Cogn Sci* 3:151–62.

Tallon-Baudry C, Bertrand O, Henaff MA, Isnard J, Fischer C. 2005. Attention modulates gamma-band oscillations differently in the human lateral occipital cortex and fusiform gyrus. *Cerebr Cortex* 15:654–62.

Tanji K, Suzuki K, Delorme A, Shamoto H, Nakasato N. 2005. High-frequency gamma-band activity in the basal temporal cortex during picture-naming and lexical-decision tasks. *J Neurosci* 25:3287–93.

Tass P, Rosenblum MG, Weule J, Kurths J, Pikovsky A, Volkmann J, et al. 1998. Detection of $n{:}m$ phase locking from noisy data: application to magnetoencephalography. *Phys Rev Lett* 81:3291–4.

Van Veen BD, van Drongelen W, Yuchtman M, Suzuki A. 1997. Localization of brainelectrical activity via linearly constrained minimum variance spatial filtering. *IEEE Trans Biomed Eng* 44:867–80.

Varela F, Lachaux JP, Rodriguez E, Martinerie J. 2001. The brainweb: phase synchronization and large-scale integration. *Nat Rev Neurosci* 2:229–39.

Vrba J, Robinson SE. 2001. Signal processing in magnetoencephalography. *Methods* 25:249–71.

Ward LM. 2003. Synchronous neural oscillations and cognitive processes. *Trends Cogn Sci* 17:553–9.

Wolters C, de Munck JC. 2007. Volume conduction. *Scholarpedia* 2(3):1738.

Worden MS, Foxe JJ, Wang N, Simpson GV. 2000. Anticipatory biasing of visuospatial attention indexed by retinotopically specific α-band electroencephalography increases over occipital cortex. *J Neurosci* 20-RC63:1–6.

Yamagishi N, Goda N, Callan DE, Anderson SJ, Kawato M. 2005. Attentional shifts toward an expected visual target alter the level of alpha-band oscillatory activity in the human calcarine cortex. *Brain Res Cogn Brain Res* 25(3):799–809.

8 Procedures and Strategies for Optimizing the Signal-to-Noise Ratio in Event-Related Potential Data

Durk Talsma and Anne-Laura van Harmelen

A predominant recurring issue in event-related potential (ERP) research concerns the trade-off between the number of conditions in the experiment, trial length, and recording time. In order to obtain a clean signal, it is necessary to collect a lot of data, typically meaning that a large number of stimuli have to be presented. While this is usually possible in simple experiments, the added complexities of more sophisticated experiments rise significantly to the total recording time. Given the number of stimuli presented, the final length of an experiment is also significantly influenced by the duration of each stimulus presentation. It is ultimately necessary to balance these requirements in order to come up with an experimental design that is of reasonable length yet is powerful enough to yield clean data. This chapter aims to provide some general guidelines for obtaining this goal.

ERPs are tiny electrical fluctuations that are elicited by the brain in response to sensory input, mental operations, or motor responses. These potential fluctuations are embedded in the ongoing electroencephalographic brain activity (EEG), and are an order of magnitude smaller in amplitude (about 5–15 µV) than the ongoing background EEG signal (typically about 50 µV of amplitude). Because ERP signals are so much smaller than the ongoing background EEG, they can typically not be observed in response to a single stimulus or other evoking event. Instead ERPs are estimated through the repeated presentation of a large ensemble of the evoking event of interest (henceforth referred to as "trial") and by averaging sweeps of EEG activity that are time-locked to such trials.

The averaging process causes random fluctuations to cancel out as more and more trials are added to the average, while the ERP signal itself remains more or less constant. It can be shown that the signal-to-noise ratio of ERPs improves by a factor of $\sqrt{N}$, where N indicates the number of trials included in the average (beim Graben 2001; Niedermeyer and Lopez-De Silva 1993). ERPs typically consist of a number of components, which are identified by their latencies, polarities, scalp topographies, and amplitudes (e.g., see Talsma 2008). In general, early components such as the P1 and N1 are of a much lower amplitude than longer latency components such as the P3. Consequently a much larger number of trials is needed to reliably estimate the early components than the late components. A component such as the P300 can typically be estimated using about 40 to 80 trials per condition (Bosch, Mecklinger, and Friederici 2001; Johnson and Donchin 1978; Pelosi and Blumhardt 1999; Ruchkin et al. 1997; Scheffers, Johnson, and Ruchkin 1991), whereas the early components require much higher numbers of trials (Hickey, McDonald, and Theeuwes 2006; Molholm et al. 2002; Talsma, Doty, and Woldorff 2007; Talsma and Woldorff 2005a; Yago et al. 2001).

The aim of this chapter is to discuss a variety of strategies to optimize the signal-to-noise ratio of ERPs, while keeping the length of the experiment down to a reasonable time. In part, this will be done by means of a formal discussion of available data optimization procedures. To a large degree, however, this chapter will also consist of a discussion of many laboratory procedures that we have established empirically, that is, through trial and error. We present these procedures in the hope that they will be useful to other researchers in the field as well.

Experiment Design

Most experienced ERP researchers will likely be familiar with the following scenario: An idea for a great ERP experiment presents itself. The proposed experiment, however, involves a multitude of conditions, each of which is supposed to be included as fully orthogonal factors, and lengthy trials that are in turn composed of a multitude of stimuli. On top of it all, the experiment is designed to investigate the existence of an amplitude modulation of the early latency C1 component, which is known to require a lot of trials.

In our experience many such ideas carry great promise, but they ultimately fail an initial plausibility check. This is because a simple multiplication of the above-mentioned factors (trial length by number of trials per cell by number of factors by levels per factor) results in an unyieldingly high number of seconds of pure recording time. Given these considerations, one of the major challenges of contemporary ERP research consists in redesigning such study proposals in such a way that they become plausible ERP designs. In terms of ERP signal-to-noise ratio this comes down to ensuring that enough trials are available for averaging, while keeping the recording time down to acceptable levels.

Possible strategies for achieving this goal consist of combining trial types, speeding up stimulus presentation rate, and splitting large experiments into multiple smaller, more manageable studies. The advantages and disadvantages of each of these strategies will be discussed below.

Combining Trial Types If Possible
One strategy to optimize signal-to-noise ratio is based on the fact that data from multiple conditions can oftentimes be collapsed. Consider, for example, a visual memory

experiment where the goal of the experiment is to relate the processes involved in memorization to the subsequent retrieval of the memorized stimuli. Typically a delayed match-to-sample task is used whereby participants are required to look at information for a few seconds before a test stimulus is presented, which they need to match with the memorized stimuli. Usually a limited number of memorization conditions are included in the experiment (memory load, location of memorized stimulus, etc.) and followed by a multitude of possible test stimuli (target/nontarget, same-hemisphere/opposite-hemisphere relative to the memorandum, etc.). With prolonged memorization processes this type of experiment is likely to yield a relatively high number of erroneous trials, due to eye movement artifacts. This, in turn, can lead to an insufficient number of trials in the conditions of interest. In such a case, one could opt for the strategy of analyzing the ERPs elicited by the memoranda and the ERPs elicited by the test stimuli separately. Take, for instance, a condition where the left hemisphere stimulus is memorized. Such a stimulus could be followed by a test stimulus that matches the memorized stimulus or by a test stimulus that does not match the memorized stimulus. However, up to the moment of the test stimulus presentation both stimuli are identical, and they can therefore be combined.

Although different trial types can be combined this way, one should be cautious of the fact that the ERPs in one data set are composed of a slightly different set of trials than those in the other data set. In our example, eye movements and blinks during a relatively lengthy memorization phase were given as the reason for losing a relatively high proportion of the trials. When trials that contain eye movements during memorization are excluded from the memory ERPs, but not from the test stimulus ERPs, there has to be a way to ensure that the process resulting in trial loss in one condition does not affect the processes in the other condition. It is probable that eye movements during memorization lead to an encoding difference and in turn affect the ERPs in the subsequent recall. Therefore, while it is possible to collapse ERPs across trial types, one should be aware of the differences in cognitive processes between the two sets of data, and keep these differences from affecting the outcome (see Talsma et al. 2001 for a discussion of this problem).

Optimize the Proportion of Stimuli of Interest

In many ERP studies the main condition of interest is presented with a relatively low probability. In the most classic of ERP paradigms, the oddball paradigm, the major stimulus of interest is a deviant that occurs relatively infrequently (e.g., see Debener et al. 2005). Likewise the mismatch negativity, an ERP reflection of the brain's response to deviant auditory stimuli, is elicited by a relatively infrequently occurring stimulus (e.g., Näätänen et al. 1989). Even in many attention studies frequent validly cued targets are contrasted with infrequent invalidly cued targets. Obviously the infrequent events need to be infrequent for a reason as many psychological processes depend on the relatively rare occurrence of these stimuli. For ERP purposes it might be possible to modify the relative frequency slightly so that a significant amount of trials will be gained. For instance, having a rare stimulus occur in of 25 percent of all trials will result in a requirement to present a total of 400 trials in order to get 100 observations of the event of interest, while having the rare event occur with a proportion of 20 percent will require a total of 500 trials to get the required 100 observations of the event of interest. Thus choosing this slightly higher proportion would reduce recording time to four-fifths of the experiment compared to using the lower proportion of infrequent stimuli.

In addition to gaining a quicker means of obtaining the required number of trials, adapting the proportion of infrequent trials can have additional advantages. For instance, a typical symbolic cueing task usually contains 60 percent valid cues, 20 percent noninformative cues, and 20 percent invalid cues (Posner 1980). Although these proportions work well in behavioral experiments, they might be somewhat less than optimal in ERP studies, in particular, when ERPs elicited by the attention directing cues (i.e., the valid and invalid cues) are compared to the noninformative cues. In this case the infrequent noninformative cue is not only reducing the amount of available trials, the relatively rare occurrence (20 percent of all trials) might make the ERP elicited by this trial type susceptible to contamination by ERP components that are purely related to stimulus frequency (e.g., the novelty P300; see Friedman and Simpson 1994). Although we initially ran studies using the original 60/20/20 percent proportion of trials (Talsma, Slagter, et al. 2005). We have subsequently adapted this proportion to 50 percent valid, 33.33 percent noninformative, and 16.67 percent invalid trials. Using these proportions, one is able to present 33.33 percent leftward directing cues, 33.33 percent rightward pointing cues, and 33.33 percent noninformative trials, with both the ERP and the behavioral data indicating that the required attention effects are still reliably present (Talsma, Mulckhuyse, et al. 2007).

Collapse across Hemispheres

Perhaps the most efficient way of saving recording time consists of collapsing data across conditions. In many ERP studies the stimuli are presented at left and right hemifield locations. Depending on the known lateralization of the component under investigation, one could decide to collapse the data across hemispheres. For instance, the visual P1 and N1 components are characterized by scalp topographies with a posterior maximum over the hemisphere contralateral to the location of the evoking stimulus, and amplitude modulations of these components by attention are also observed over the contralateral hemisphere (Heinze et al. 1994; Woldorff et al. 2002). That being the case, data from left and right visual field can be collapsed. It should be noted that before the data can be collapsed, a mirror image of the original electrode array needs to be created for one of the conditions. This way an ERP response evoked by a left hemifield stimulus occurring over the right hemisphere will be combined with a similar response that was triggered by a right hemifield response but occurring over the left hemisphere.

Optimize the Number of Conditions and Stimulus Positions

These days many experiments require fairly complex setups, utilizing many conditions and intricate sequences of stimuli. As described previously, in many studies the psychologically interesting conditions are the ones that occur relatively infrequently (e.g., Debener et al. 2005; Näätänen et al. 1989). Because stimuli are oftentimes presented from symmetrical left and right hemifield positions, one can oftentimes collapse across recording locations, as described above.

Instead of stimulating from symmetrical locations, and applying a post hoc collapsing of left and right hemifield data, it is in some cases a viable alternative to present stimuli from just one location. If the experimental design allows for such a stimulation protocol, this approach might actually be preferable to post hoc collapsing of data, since one does not need to consider a priori assumptions regarding the contralaterality of the effects under investigation. In particular, when early sensory components are investigated, this approach might be used in combination with optimizing the position of stimuli so as to generate the most optimal response. Foxe and colleagues pioneered this approach to demonstrate a possible involvement of the earliest visual component, the C1, in attention (Kelly, Gomez-Ramirez, and Foxe, 2008) or multisensory integration (Molholm et al. 2002). Foxe and colleagues typically run a short probe task, where stimuli are presented from a limited number of about eight locations. ERP responses to these probes are then averaged, and the location that elicits the largest C1 response is subsequently used in the main experiment. Obviously such an approach has its advantages: a relatively small number of stimuli can be used to determine the optimum position for the stimuli in the main experiment, after which a large number of stimuli is presented in each condition (typically on the order of a few hundred per condition; see Kelly et al., 2008; Molholm et al. 2002), thus yielding a high signal-to-noise ratio.

Optimize Trial Length

Having established the minimum number of conditions and trial types, determined which trial types can be collapsed, and how many locations should be used for stimulation, the final decision involves choosing how long a trial should be. As with all previous optimizations, the trial length is oftentimes determined by other experimental requirements. For instance, some attention experiments require a relatively fast stimulation protocol because otherwise one may find that participants have enough capacity to attend to the irrelevant stimuli as well (e.g., see Woldorff, Hackley, and Hillyard 1991; Woldorff and Hillyard 1991). In contrast, studies on working memory require a much slower pacing, as participants are required to hold stimuli in memory for seconds or more (Brisson and Jolicœur 2007; Klaver et al. 1999; Talsma et al. 2001; Vogel and Machizawa 2004). Despite these restrictions, optimizing the trial length is worth a careful consideration. For example, reducing the stimulus onset asynchrony from an average of 3 seconds to an average of 2 seconds will reduce the total length of an experiment to two-thirds of its original length and would therefore allow one to run 1.5 times as many trials in the same amount of time as would otherwise have been possible.

Determine the Maximum Recording Time and Number of Sessions

The maximally allowable recording time is probably one of the most debated issues in everyday lab practice that we are aware of. Most researchers will agree that a one-hour session is acceptable. Because of the amount of preparation time involved for most EEG systems, this is also oftentimes considered to be the minimum time that an experiment should last. When it comes to the maximally allowable recording time in one session, opinions differ considerably. In our experience, there are several factors influencing this number, including factors specific to the participant, such as age and state of mind. For instance, a well rested young adult will usually be able to comply with the experimental requirements for much longer periods of time than an older adult diagnosed with Parkinson's disease or a young child diagnosed with ADHD. Experimental requirements also weigh in here. Participants are usually much better able to comply with the requirements of an experiment when it is considered to be a challenging task than when it is considered to be a boring task. In particular, most ERP experiments consist of tasks that are mentally exhausting, yet at that same time these tasks are considered to be extremely boring by many participants. It is this combination of factors that is a limiting factor in prolonging recording time. In order to make the experimental session interesting and variable, we have recently adopted the procedure of intermixing the main experiment with shorter tasks. These tasks are either of an entirely different nature or just consist of passive stimulation so that participants are able to relax and take a break from the main experiment. Even though additional tasks raise the total time one is in the recording chamber, our experience is that the added variety helps keep participants motivated much longer, and thus adds to the overall quality of the data. A bonus of this approach is a more favorable preparation time to recording time ratio, which helps improve the overall efficiency of an ERP lab.

Finally, when it turns out to be impossible to fit the experiment into one session, one can always consider splitting the experiment into two separate sessions. There is, of course, overhead to this procedure, not only because it requires twice the preparation one would have to do for a regular session, it also requires considerable subject management time. However, the added session typically pays off in terms of the cleanliness resulting from collecting more data.

Data-Recording Procedures

The final quality of an ERP data set is predominantly determined by the quality of the originally recorded data. Therefore a few additional minutes spent verifying and ensuring good data quality during the recording phase can save hours of postprocessing later on. Although this sounds easy and obvious, this part of the EEG recording procedure is in our experience one of the harder parts to master. In particular, the following concerns have to be dealt with: (1) fixing the impedance/recording quality of a faulty electrode, (2) removing the contribution of an apparent artifact on the overall data set, and (3) determining whether to continue recording in the face of apparently poor data quality/performance.

At the time of writing, we conducted the majority of ERP experiments on one of two EEG recording systems. The first of these systems is a 64 Neuroscan Synamps recording system, and the second one is a 128 channel BioSemi active-2 system. In the following sections, examples of our recording experience of either one of these systems are highlighted.

The participant's state of mind is perhaps one among the most important factors influencing the quality of a recording session. We assume that the readers of this volume have experienced participating in experiments one way or another and can therefore recall their own first experience in participating in such experiments. In particular, to inexperienced freshmen the procedures can be intimidating, mostly due to the unfamiliar environment, equipment, and the apparent presence of the syringes and needles that are used for adding conductive gel into the recording electrodes. For this reason, getting to know the level of experience that a participant has and providing the appropriate level of explanation and comforting is a very important step toward obtaining good quality data. In this respect we always approach new participants in a serious and respectful, albeit informal manner. Notably, when running inexperienced participants, we avoid jokes, as we have witnessed that they may inadvertently be misinterpreted by a nervous participant and have a strong adverse effect in comforting them. For returning participants this is a different issue, but a good deal of common sense should still be employed in such cases.

In giving participants instructions, our experience is also that an informal approach works best in getting them to comply. Currently our practice is to let participants watch along as we conduct impedance checks (Neuroscan setup) or check electrode offsets while attaching the electrodes (BioSemi setup). Once the electrode preparation is finished, we typically take about 3 to 5 minutes to review the participant's own online EEG recordings. During this procedure we show the participants some of their own EEG data characteristics. We also explicitly ask the participants to make some eye movements, blink their eyes, frown, bite their teeth, and move around. We show them the effect of these artifacts on the EEG recordings, and then ask them to continue to be aware of the possible consequences of such actions on the EEG recordings, and ask them to try and refrain from performing these actions during the recording sessions. Our experience is that making participants aware of the possible EEG artifacts and asking them in an informal way to comply with the no-movement instructions is more effective in obtaining good quality data than not making participants aware and being very formal and pedantic about these instructions. Again, the latter approach may have an adverse effect on an already nervous participant.

Electrode Preparation

With the advent of actively shielded EEG systems and high-impedance amplifiers, electrode preparation has become a lot easier compared to about a decade ago. Yet, in the same period of time, the average number of electrodes used has drastically increased from about 32 to 128 or more. With this many electrodes the chances are that one or more electrodes yields poor quality data at any given time during the recording. Because of the increased number of electrodes, the demands of electrode preparation and online monitoring of the EEG signals has presumably increased instead of decreased, despite the increased ease of preparation. Even with modern systems that claim to be able to record with high electrode impedance, it is our experience that the traditional way of electrode preparation, that is, using a needle or wooden stick to scratch the skin, still yields the best result. In particular, we have observed many occasions where electrodes yield unpredictable results, despite having good impedances (on a Neuroscan system) or offset potentials (on a BioSemi system). Using the back end of a wooden stick to push the electrolyte firmly onto the skin works best to address these problems, and seems to yield better results than using a blunted needle does.

Online Filtering

The issues observed above can be particularly problematic when data are recorded in direct current (DC) mode, that is, without the application of any online high-pass filter. By the nature of this procedure, any offset potential that is present will be reflected in the recorded signal. Offset potentials can occur because of electrode polarization, which causes the electrode to act as a capacitor. In particular, tin (Sn) electrodes are sensitive to polarization, whereas sintered Ag/AgCl electrodes are very robust against polarization (Tallgren et al. 2005). Offset potentials can also result from poor electrode connections and changes in skin resistance (Fisch 1991). The increasing polarization that will then occur in electrodes will show a gradually increasing positive or negative offset potential. Offset potentials can eventually become so large that they saturate the hardware's dynamic range and produce a dead signal. It may, of course, seem logical to always employ an online high-pass filter, but there are many reasons not to employ such a filter. First, a filter not only can attenuate the drifting signal but also affect the part of the signal that is of interest. This is of particular concern when investigating slow wave potentials, such as the contingent negative variation (CNV; see Walter et al. 1964) or the contralateral negative slow wave (also known as the sustained posterior contralateral negativity, SPCN, or contralateral delay activity, CDA; see Klaver et al. 1999; Brisson et al. 2007; Vogel et al. 2004) related to visual working memory maintenance processes. That being the case, one should either record data in DC mode or opt for an online high-pass filter with a sufficiently low cutoff frequency. Since many commercially available systems have a fairly high cutoff frequency in their online high-pass filter, some researchers have chosen to use custom built recording equipment (Klaver et al. 1999; Talsma et al. 2001) or to have a custom built high-pass filter installed (e.g., Grent-'T-Jong and Woldorff 2007) in commercially available hardware.

Second, filters can introduce subtle latency shifts of ERP components. Conceptually an online hardware based filter works by integrating past and present input to determine the filtered output signal. This procedure inevitably results in some distortion of the recorded signal, in the case of an online filter resulting in a small delay of the observed peaks in the signal, compared to their true occurrence. The degree of distortion depends on many factors, including the cutoff frequency and the attenuation factor of the filter. Although these distortions are typically reasonably small, one could opt to not use an online filter when the precise timing is of concern.

Third, many modern systems are no longer shipped with the possibility of saving filtered data. Contemporary EEG systems have an extremely high dynamic input range, and therefore many of the amplifier saturation problems are largely attenuated. This being the case, one is able to store the raw, unfiltered signal and choose to conduct all the filtering offline during postprocessing. The obvious advantage of conducting the filtering during postprocessing is the largely unrestricted time period, and therefore a much wider range of filtering techniques are at the researcher's disposal.

To summarize, we would argue that when using a high-dynamic range EEG system, it is usually best not to apply any online filtering at all. However, should this result in serious problems during data acquisition, one should consider applying the use of an online filter. In such cases a filter should be chosen after investigating whether the filter in question has an adverse effect on the ERP component under investigation. In particular, strong filters can lead to serious distortions of the recorded signal, and one should at all times be aware of those consequences.

Online Monitoring during Recording

Even in optimal circumstances the signal quality of the recorded EEG will vary from participant to participant, from session to session, and within sessions, even from moment to moment. Some participants have more trouble complying with task instructions than others. During recording sessions even well complying participants may become so engaged in performing in the experiment that they lose sight of the secondary instructions (those related to blinking, movements, etc.). Even well attached electrodes may lose connections, and random equipment failures may occur. For these and other reasons it is important that the EEG signals be monitored constantly throughout the recording sessions. The timely detection of a faulty electrode, and a friendly reminder that the participant should comply with the instructions, can save many trials that would otherwise have been lost for the analysis. In addition during the recording a log book should be kept of channels that are deemed faulty in the recording process, so that these channels can be interpolated from surrounding channels if that is deemed necessary (Picton et al. 2000).

Although this may be obvious, considerable experience is required for the online monitoring of EEG signals and estimating the impact of the observed signal on the eventual ERP signal. A channel that is breaking contact is usually easy to spot, as are the obvious spike artifacts resulting from electrode pops or participant's muscle activity. Oftentimes, however, relatively large amplitude fluctuations can be seen on electrodes that are apparently still recording. In these situations the electrodes still show typical EEG-like fluctuations that are superimposed on an erratic periodic signal of generally a somewhat lower frequency and about a magnitude in amplitude larger than that of the EEG. In particular, when EEG is recorded using an electrocap, or equivalent elastic cap, the electrodes showing this type of erratic behavior are typically at locations where there is a considerable amount of space between the electrode and the scalp, making their impedance relatively sensitive to movement of the electrode. With electrocaps, these electrodes can usually be found near the medial temporal and medial central locations where the connecting wires enter the cap. Because this type of artifact is usually random, the averaging procedure would attenuate its presence in the ERP estimates (Talsma 2008). Nevertheless, this type of artifact can still be problematic. The occurrence of this artifact can be mitigated considerably by ensuring that all the electrodes are in close proximity to the scalp, by stretching the cap as far across the participant's head as possible, and by continuing to push the cap's fabric down until the central and temporal electrodes are firmly in contact with the scalp. When one has the option of using one of two possible cap sizes, we recommend using the smallest possible cap because the problems of loosely connected electrodes are magnitudes smaller as compared to using a larger sized cap. One should exercise extreme caution here, however, because a cap that is too small can lead to substantial discomfort on the participant's side, including headaches, dizziness, and nausea.

A somewhat related observation is that temporal electrodes can show signals that are apparently continuously artifactual. In particular, the lateral temporal electrodes, such as T7 and T8 can oftentimes show signals that bear little or no apparent EEG activity. These channels are also sensitive to small pulse artifacts. In addition, when participants are wearing glasses, the added proximity of the temples and the ear pieces to the electrodes may add more noise to the recordings. Although these electrodes yield apparently noisy EEG signals, it is our experience that these slightly deviant signals have a relatively low impact on the ERP averages, and should therefore not be of a high concern during monitoring.

Data Analysis

Artifact Detection Procedures

As we argued previously, in ERP data analysis one should strive to maximize signal-to-noise ratio. Although signal-to-noise ratio increases as a function of the number of trials included in the average (beim Graben 2001; Niedermeyer et al. 1993), one of the authors of this chapter has recently shown that this is not generally the case in the presence of trials containing artifacts (Talsma 2008). For this reason recording artifacts should be dealt with.

There are many automated procedures for identifying artifacts in EEG data. These methods are discussed extensively elsewhere (Croft and Barry 2000; Onton and Makeig 2006; Talsma and Woldorff 2005b), so we will not repeat these methods in detail here. Instead we will focus on discussing the problems related to adapting some of these procedures to meet one's needs. In this context a distinction can be made between methods that are based on intrinsic statistical properties of the data and and on methods that compare the actual data against arbitrary thresholds. Thresholding methods check the EEG signal against a set of user specified thresholds, and mark a trial as artifactual whenever one of the critical parameters exceeds the user-specified threshold. Since statistical methods are data driven, they do not typically require much user configuration. These statistical methods do, however, typically require considerably more computational resources than the threshold-based methods do.

Although statistical procedures appear to be more attractive than thresholding methods, the computational requirements cause the simpler thresholding methods to remain a relatively popular alternative. For instance, independent component analysis (Delorme, Sejnowski, and Makeig 2007) is well known to be able to separate the observed EEG into as many independent spatial patterns as there are recording sites, making it easy to identify those spatial patterns corresponding to brain activity and those related to artifacts, be it from eye movements, blinks, or recording artifacts. However, a full ICA analysis may easily take up several gigabytes of memory, making this type of analysis currently suitable only for high-end workstations. In addition, even though ICA is reasonably automated, the procedure still assigns brain wave activity and artifactual activity arbitrarily to its resulting components. So user intervention is required to reassemble the final signal. In the process, the decision whether to include a factor or not is still left to the human operator.

Other statistical methods are computationally less complex. For instance, many spike-like artifacts could be found by discarding portions of the EEG signal that exceed a predefined number of standard deviations of the mean of the EEG signal. Although statistical methods are based on intrinsic properties of the signal, the cutoff that is used to determine whether a trial is artifactual is still based on a rather arbitrary value. Moreover this cutoff value does not seem to necessarily relate to the intrinsic complexity of the underlying signal. This being the case, one may use the simpler threshold methods just as well.

Thresholding methods are described in Talsma and Woldorff (2005b). For instance, artifacts containing high-amplitude transients are found by shifting a moving window across the data set and determining whether the peak-to-peak amplitude of the EEG signal inside the window exceeds a predefined threshold. Although this is a relatively straightforward method of detecting large artifacts, it can be more problematic to detect smaller ones. For this reason oftentimes elaborate user configuration is needed to optimize the threshold settings. Once a reasonable set of parameters has been established, there is usually no reason to change the thresholds too drastically. It is a well-known problem, however, that a reasonable set of thresholds that work for one participant results in a rejection rate that would be considered to be far too high in another one. Because of such possible problems, the actual parameters should be chosen with care, and adapted where necessary.

An inherent problem with this type of method lies in the fact that the actual thresholds are chosen rather arbitrarily. One possible strategy of finding the optimal set of thresholds could consist of an iterative procedure that starts with two sets of thresholds, one that hardly rejects any trials and one that rejects many. The relevant thresholds are then iteratively fine-tuned by choosing intermediate values and evaluating the resulting ERPs. Although we are currently not aware of any implementation of such a method, it could easily be automated, and if combined with an actual calculation of the observed signal-to-noise ratio (e.g., using the equations described by Möcks, Gasser, and Tuan 1984), there could result a set of threshold parameters that are ideally tuned for each individual data set.

This idea formed the basis for a new approach that was recently published by one of the authors of this chapter, and that combines the automatic determination of the ERP's signal-to-noise ratio using the intrinsic statistical signal properties (Talsma 2008). This method, labeled "auto-adaptive averaging," combines many of the advantages of statistics-based artifact classification methods with a relatively low computational footprint. In addition the method is completely user independent, so it is ideal for inclusion in large-scale batch operations. The auto-adaptive averaging method is not a separate step prior to signal averaging but is an integrated, multi-pass signal averaging procedure. Instead of determining a fixed set of parameters for each type of artifact, the auto-adaptive averaging method operates on the basis of the assumption that artifact-bearing trials will sufficiently distort the observed ERP. In other words, trials containing artifacts have a relatively high impact on the observed ERP signal. Auto-adaptive averaging therefore first classifies the impact of each trial on the average and then rank-orders trials in order of increasing impact. Next, based on the rule that signal-to-noise ratio of artifact-free trials increases as a function of N, though may actually decrease in the presence of artifact bearing trials (Talsma 2008), trials of increasing impact are added to a running estimate of the average. After each addition an estimate of the signal-to-noise ratio of this running estimate is computed. Because low impact trials (and therefore relatively artifact-free) trials are initially added to the running estimate, this running estimate of the average's signal-to-noise ratio will initially increase. This will eventually no longer be the case, however, when higher impact trials are added. Finally, in the presence of clear artifacts, signal-to-noise ratio will decrease again. Consequently the estimated maximum in signal-to-noise ratio is taken as the cutoff point that determines which trials are included in the final averages and which ones are not.

As was mentioned above, this method has its advantages: it is based on the statistical properties of the data, requires no user intervention, and places a relatively low demand on computing power. It should be cautioned, however, that the method is relatively insensitive to artifacts that are more or less time-locked to the trial of interest or in situations where the majority of trials contain artifacts. For these situations the auto-adaptive averaging methods is best used in combination with traditional threshold-based methods to remove those huge artifacts that may cause systematic distortions time-locked to the trial of interest. In addition the general recommendations provided in the beginning of this chapter should also be followed so that a large pool of trials is available for averaging.

Order of Operations

Many of the above-described signal-processing operations are linear. Therefore the exact order of operations should not matter greatly. There are some subtle nonlinearities involved in ERP analysis that make it worthwhile to consider the effect of the exact order of operations on the final ERP estimate. For instance, running a digital filter before checking for artifacts may cause some trials to pass the artifact detection thresholds that might have been rejected if no filtering had been applied. Therefore inverting the order of operations between digital filtering and artifact detection will almost certainly result in ERP averages that are composed of slightly different trial ensembles. In particular, when analyzing linear drift bearing signals, and applying a relatively strong high-pass filter, inverting the order of operations can have a relatively high impact on the final number of trials that is available for inclusion. Likewise reconstructing faulty channels, by interpolating neighboring ones (Picton et al. 2000), before conducting artifact detection should be preferred over reconstructing these channels after conducting artifact detection.

A similar effect of the order of operations can be found between the averaging stage and the stage at which data are collapsed across categories. This effect is most notable in two cases: (1) when an ERP postprocessing procedure such as the adjacent response (ADJAR) overlap estimation procedure is used (Woldorff 1993) and (2) when using the above-described auto-adaptive averaging procedure. ADJAR, is a postexperimental procedure that estimates the degree of overlap resulting from the previous trials, as is present in the signal. The ADJAR procedure estimates this overlap by convolving the original ERP estimate (i.e., the ERP that is obtained after averaging) with the event distribution of all the preceding events. The resulting overlap estimate is then subtracted from the original ERP, and the accordingly cleaned up ERPs are used to make a better estimate of the overlap by iteratively deconvolving these cleaned-up ERPs with the event-distribution of the previous events. One requirement for this procedure is that the original data are reasonably noise free, since the noise residue in the original ERPs will otherwise contribute to the overlap estimates. For this reason too it is usually better to collapse trials across categories before averaging, since the a priori collapsing yields a data set with only a few categories that are composed of many trials and therefore relatively free of noise. The alternative would have been to average all the original trial types separately, which would have resulted in a data set consisting of many categories that would each be composed of just a few trials and in a relatively noisy data set to be used in the ADJAR procedure. It should be noted that in this case one could also have opted for a more complex approach by first averaging all the individual trials according to their original trial type categorization and then collapsing these data across categories before applying the ADJAR procedure.

When using the ADJAR procedure, it is also important to evaluate any possible processing step that might influence the relative baseline of the ERP averages. Although ERPs are typically baselined on a short period of time before stimulus onset, it is important to note that any modifications to the mean amplitude value of the ERP averages might seriously distort the outcome of the ADJAR procedure. The rationale behind this is that the ADJAR procedure needs to read the original data in such a way that the relative voltage of the latter part of the preceding stimulus ERP matches that of the earlier part of the succeeding stimulus ERPs. When this assumption is violated (e.g., by employing a prestimulus baseline correction to the data), nonoverlapping components of the data will be considered overlap, and vice versa, and cause the iterative convergence of the overlap estimates to fail (see Woldorff 1993). Again, for this reason it is usually better to digitally filter the raw EEG data before averaging, to ensure that the aforementioned relative amplitudes remain intact. Filtering the ERPs after averaging, in contrast, may result in a differential adjustment of the mean amplitude of each ERP wave, and therefore disrupt the matching of the aforementioned relative amplitudes.

Somewhat similar logic holds when using the auto-adaptive averaging procedure (Talsma 2008). Even though the auto-adaptive averaging procedure is capable of determining the optimal signal-to-noise ratio in ERPs, this procedure works best when a large ensemble of trials is available for averaging in any one given condition. When many trials are available, small changes in signal-to-noise ratio can be tracked very accurately, whereas this is to a much lesser degree the case when only a limited number of trials are available.

Although there is still considerable flexibility in the order of operations, the consequences of the above-described order have resulted in a sequence of processing steps that we now more or less consistently apply in our lab. This sequence is typically run using two sets of batched operations. The first of these takes care of data conversion and clean-up of the raw EEG data. The second of these takes care of the signal averaging. Then additional postprocessing scripts can be run as necessary.

In the first batch all EEG data are converted to a generic data format, channels are referenced against the two mastoids, and in the case of our BioSemi setup, bipolar channels are created by subtracting the relevant external channels from each other (i.e., by subtracting the left and right ocular channels from each other as well as subtracting the upper and lower ocular channels from each other, separately for the left and right eye). When processing our BioSemi data, we also create six additional EEG channels that are derived from the external channels that are placed around the eyes by subtracting the combined mastoid recordings from the raw signals recorded on these external channels. The additional EEG channels can be used to improve dipole source estimations, since the addition of more distant recording sites may improve the quality of the dipole fits. Also during the channel referencing stage the channels that were denoted as artifactual during recording are reconstructed on the basis of their neighboring channels by using an interpolation procedure (Picton et al. 2000). Digital filtering comprises the last step in this sequence of procedures that clean up the raw data files. In our appraisal, even though filtering the raw data is computationally much more intensive than filtering only the ERP averages, the advantage of being able to use the cleaned-up data as input to the next processing steps outweighs the added computational disadvantage. Next we construct lists of trials for each condition in the experiment. During this stage as many trial types as possible are collapsed into their respective categories.

Once the trial lists are completed, the ERP averages are created. The averaging process consists of two steps. First, a generic threshold-based artifact detection procedure is run to remove the largest artifacts, and also identify trials that contain eye movements and/or blinks. Next, after these artifact-bearing trials are excluded from the trial lists, the auto-adaptive averaging procedure is run, which further fine-tunes the signal-to-noise ratio of the final data set. Once these two basic steps are completed, a number of additional analyses can be conducted, among these the process of estimating and removing overlap from the data as well as a further collapsing of trial types if needed, or the subtraction of ERP data to create difference waves of the conditions of interest.

The Grand Average

Having constructed ERP averages for each single subject, the final step—save for statistics—consists of computing a grand average. The grand average typically consists of an unweighted average of all the individual subject's ERPs. Occasionally one will be confronted with a grand average that is suboptimal. When this occurs, the poor quality of the final grand average can oftentimes be attributed to just a few participants with disproportionally large noise levels in the grand average. So the need arises to discard these participants from the grand average, and hence from any further analysis. A major problem in this respect is that heretofore no, or a most only few, formal criteria have been established that can be used to determine whether a single subject's data can be deemed as being "too noisy." Occasionally the logbook entries made during the recording phase may help identify the underlying cause for a noisy data set. Likewise a record of the number of trials rejected due to recording artifacts, or eye movements, may be indicative of potential problems. One can decide to discard a subject from further analysis on the basis of any of these three criteria. In the case of eye movements or artifacts, again the problem is that no firm criteria are established that can be used to determine whether a subject's data should be removed from the analysis altogether.

We recently adopted a new procedure for estimating the noise levels in single-subject ERP data. This procedure consists of computing the root mean square (RMS) of the residual power in the prestimulus baseline period of the ERP waveform. Since it is, with the exception of anticipatory activity, a theoretical impossibility that stimulus-locked ERP activity starts before the onset of the triggering stimulus, deflections from zero during the prestimulus baseline period can be interpreted as residual background EEG activity and/or other sources of noise. Although we typically use this noise estimate to identify participants with high levels of residual noise in their data, just using this method alone to discard participants from further analysis presents the same problems as the eye movement or artifact count methods described above. Currently no objective criterion exists that will allow us to determine at what noise levels the inclusion of a single subject's ERP data becomes problematic.

One solution to this problem may be in extending the noise level calculation with an auto-adaptive averaging approach. As with constructing a single-subject ERP, the grand average creation process could be conducted after rank-ordering the data according to increasing noise levels and then evaluating the signal-to-noise ratio of a running estimate of the grand average once each single subject's data has been added. Again, the assumption here is that the signal-to-noise ratio of the grand average should increase after the addition of each single subject's data set. However, with really noisy data the signal-to-noise ratio should decrease again. The set of participants that result in an optimal signal-to-noise ratio should then be used, and participants that cause a decrease of the signal-to-noise ratio could be discarded. More research along with more formal evaluation of this method is needed before it can be applied in practice, however.

Summary

This chapter discusses a variety of methods and procedures that can be used to optimize the signal-to-noise ratio in event-related potential data. These methods range from decisions regarding the experimental design to automated procedures for optimizing artifact detection during data analysis. Methods to optimize the experimental design consist of optimizing the number of conditions in the experiment, making a priori decisions on collapsing data across conditions, optimizing the proportion of frequent and infrequent trials, and optimizing the length of each individual trial. During recording, signal quality can be optimized by careful online monitoring of the incoming EEG signals, and knowing when and how to fix faulty EEG channels. Also providing the appropriate level of comforting to novice participants can help to drastically improve the quality of the recorded data. During offline analysis, several methods are available that can help in removing large recording artifacts from the data. The relative advantages and disadvantages of each of these methods is presented, along with a brief description of a new method, recently developed by one of the authors of this chapter, that optimizes signal-to-noise ratio of ERP data. The possibility is suggested of using this method in developing similar methods that help determine whether participants should be discarded from further analysis.

References

Beim Graben P. 2001. Estimating and improving signal-to-noise ratio of time series by symbolic dynamics. *Phys Rev* E64:1–15.

Bosch V, Mecklinger A, Friederici AD. 2001. Slow cortical potentials during retention of object, spatial, and verbal information. *Cogn Brain Res* 10:219–37.

Brisson B, Jolicœur P. 2007. A psychological refractory period in access to visual short-term memory and the deployment of visual-spatial attention: multitasking processing deficits revealed by event-related potentials. *Psychophysiology* 44:323–33.

Croft RJ, Barry RJ. 2000. Removal of ocular artifact from the EEG: a review. *Neurophysiol Clinique-Clinical Neurophysiol* 30:5–19.

Debener S, Makeig S, Delorme A, Engel AK. 2005. What is novel in the novelty oddball paradigm? Functional significance of the novelty P3 event-related potential as revealed by independent component analysis. *Cogn Brain Res* 22:309–21.

Delorme A, Sejnowski T, Makeig S. 2007. Enhanced detection of artifacts in EEG data using higher-order statistics and independent component analysis. *Neuroimage* 34:1443–9.

Fisch BJ. 1991. *Spehlman's EEG primer*, 2nd ed. Amsterdam: Elsevier.

Friedman D, Simpson GV. 1994. ERP amplitude and scalp distribution to target and novel events: effects of temporal-order in young, middle-aged and older adults. *Cogn Brain Res* 2:49–63.

Grent-'T-Jong T, Woldorff MG. 2007. Timing and sequence of brain activity in top-down control of visual-spatial attention. *Plos Biol* 5:114–26.

Heinze HJ, Mangun GR, Burchert W, Hinrichs H, Scholz M, Münte TF, et al. 1994. Combined spatial and temporal imaging of brain activity during visual selective attention in humans. *Nature* 372:543–6.

Hickey C, McDonald JJ, Theeuwes J. 2006. Electrophysiological evidence of the capture of visual attention. *J Cogn Neurosci* 18:604–13.

Johnson R, Donchin E. 1978. Does P300 amplitude depend on expectancy for physical stimuli or for stimulus categories. *Psychophysiology* 15:262.

Kelly SP, Gomez-Ramirez M, Foxe JJ. 2008. Spatial attention modulates initial afferent activity in human primary visual cortex. *Cerebr Cortex* 18:2629–36. doi: 10.1093/cercor/bhn022.

Klaver P, Talsma D, Wijers AA, Heinze HJ, Mulder G. 1999. An event-related brain potential correlate of visual short-term memory. *Neuroreport* 10:2001–5.

Möcks J, Gasser T, Tuan PD. 1984. Variability of single visual evoked-potentials evaluated by 2 new statistical tests. *Electroencephalogr Clin Neurophysiol* 57:571–80.

Molholm S, Ritter W, Murray MM, Javitt DC, Schroeder CE, Foxe JJ. 2002. Multisensory auditory-visual interactions during early sensory processing in humans: a high-density electrical mapping study. *Cogn Brain Res* 14:115–28.

Näätänen R, Paavilainen P, Alho K, Reinikainen K, Sams M. 1989. Do event-related potentials reveal the mechanism of the auditory sensory memory in the human-brain. *Neurosci Lett* 98: 217–21.

Niedermeyer E, Lopez-De Silva F. 1993. *Electroencephalography. Basic Principles, Clinical Applications, and Related Fields*, 3d ed. Baltimore: Williams and Wilkins.

Onton J, Makeig S. 2006. Information-based modeling of event-related brain dynamics. *Event-Rel Dyn Brain Oscillations* 159:99–120.

Pelosi L, Blumhardt LD. 1999. Effects of age on working memory: an event-related potential study. *Cogn Brain Res* 7:321–34.

Picton TW, Bentin S, Berg P, Donchin E, Hillyard SA, Johnson R, et al. 2000. Guidelines for using human event-related potentials to study cognition: recording standards and publication criteria. *Psychophysiology* 37:127–52.

Posner MI. 1980. Orienting of attention. *Quart J Exp Psychol* 32:3–25.

Ruchkin DS, Berndt RS, Johnson R, Ritter W, Grafman J, Canoune HL. 1997. Modality-specific processing streams in verbal working memory: evidence from spatio-temporal patterns of brain activity. *Cogn Brain Res* 6:95–113.

Scheffers MK, Johnson R, Ruchkin DS. 1991. P300 in patients with unilateral temporal lobectomies: the effects of reduced stimulus quality. *Psychophysiology* 28:274–84.

Tallgren P, Vanhatalo S, Kaila K, Voipio J. 2005. Evaluation of commercially available electrodes and gels for recording of slow EEG potentials. *Clin Neurophysiol* 116:799–806.

Talsma D. 2008. Auto-adaptive averaging: detecting artifacts in event-related potential data using a fully automated procedure. *Psychophysiology* 45:216–28.

Talsma D, Doty TJ, Woldorff MG. 2007. Selective attention and audiovisual integration: is attending to both modalities a prerequisite for early integration? *Cerebr Cortex* 17: 679–90.

Talsma D, Mulckhuyse M, Slagter HA, Theeuwes J. 2007. Faster, more intense! The relation between electrophysiological reflections of attentional orienting, sensory gain control, and speed of responding. *Brain Res* 1178:92–105.

Talsma D, Slagter HA, Nieuwenhuis S, Hage J, Kok A. 2005. The orienting of visuospatial attention: an event-related brain potential study. *Cogn Brain Res* 25, 117–129.

Talsma D, Wijers AA, Klaver P, Mulder G. 2001. Working memory processes show different degrees of lateralization: evidence from event-related potentials. *Psychophysiology* 38:425–39.

Talsma D, Woldorff MG. 2005a. Attention and multisensory integration: multiple phases of effects on the evoked brain activity. *J Cogn Neurosci* 17:1098–114.

Talsma D, Woldorff MG. 2005b. Methods for the estimation and removal of artifacts and overlap in ERP waveforms. In: Handy TC, ed. *Event-Related Potentials: A Methods Handbook*. Cambridge: MIT Press, 115–48.

Vogel EK, Machizawa MG. 2004. Neural activity predicts individual differences in visual working memory capacity. *Nature* 428:748–51.

Walter WG, Cooper R, Aldridge VJ, McCallum WC, Winter CV. 1964. Contingent negative variation: an electric sign of sensorimotor association and expectancy in the human brain. *Nature* 203:380–4.

Woldorff MG. 1993. Distortion of Erp averages due to overlap from temporally adjacent ERPs: analysis and correction. *Psychophysiology* 30:98–119.

Woldorff MG, Hackley SA, Hillyard SA. 1991. The effects of channel-selective attention on the mismatch negativity wave elicited by deviant tones. *Psychophysiology* 28:30–42.

Woldorff MG, Hillyard SA. 1991. Modulation of early auditory processing during selective listening to rapidly presented tones. *Electroencephalogr Clin Neurophysiol* 79:170–91.

Woldorff MG, Liotti M, Seabolt M, Busse L, Lancaster JL, Fox PT. 2002. The temporal dynamics of the effects in occipital cortex of visual-spatial selective attention. *Cogn Brain Res* 15:1–15.

Yago E, Escera C, Alho K, Giard MH. 2001. Cerebral mechanisms underlying orienting of attention towards auditory frequency changes. *Neuroreport* 12:2583–7.

9 Statistical Strategies for Translational ERP Studies

Todd C. Handy, Lindsay S. Nagamatsu, Marla J. S. Mickleborough and
Teresa Y. L. Liu-Ambrose

Over the past half decade, one of the more notable trends in event-related potential (ERP) research has been the increasing prevalence of translational investigations, or studies designed to apply basic research findings in the medical and clinical domain. Fueling the trend have been several key factors, including the financial and accessibility advantages of ERPs as a clinical tool relative to neuroimaging technologies, such as PET and fMRI, and large increases in the size of age-related clinical populations, such as Alzheimer's and Parkinson's disease patients. The hope is that by improving our understanding of how neurocognitive systems are impaired in clinical populations, we may improve on our ability to diagnose and treat clinical disorders that are neurocognitive in origin.

For example, falls by the elderly are the leading cause of accidental death in those 65 years and older. Central among the factors contributing to falls risk are impairments in cognitive function, yet little is known about the specific nature of these deficits (Lord et al. 2007). Toward addressing this lacuna, we are now using ERPs to investigate whether impairments in visual spatial attention—which is integral to normal visuoperceptual (e.g., Mangun and Hillyard 1991) and visuomotor (e.g., Handy et al. 2003) functions—may be associated with falls among the elderly (Nagamatsu, Liu-Ambrose, and Handy 2008). The potential clinical benefits of this research program are twofold. First, if visual-spatial attention is indeed impaired in fallers, the ability to detect these impairments via ERPs may provide a more sensitive diagnostic measure than those currently available. Second, the knowledge that impairments in visual spatial attention are contributing to falls risk may provide insight into the design of novel, more effective intervention strategies.

Translational research itself does not come without its own unique set of challenges for the researcher. For one, it's not just academic theory that's at stake in study outcomes. Rather, findings may play a direct and essential role in the development of clinical practices. For another, the stationarity of the brain's event-related response over repeated trials tends to be decreased in clinical populations. As a consequence this introduces a systematic source of variance into one's data set that is not present when testing young, healthy populations. In turn these twin challenges speak to a common concern, which serves as the nexus for our chapter: the clinical implications of translational research magnifies the need for accuracy in one's statistical analysis, yet the accuracy of one's statistical analysis is jeopardized by the increased measurement variability characteristic of ERP data sets obtained from clinical populations. In essence, in this chapter we ask: Given these opponent pressures, what is one to do?

The solutions presented here are inherently statistical in nature, focusing on the traditional least squares approach to equal means testing in general, and univariate repeated-measures ANOVA as typically applied to ERP data sets in particular (e.g., Dien and Santuzzi 2005). The chapter itself is built around understanding the adaptations that can be made to univariate repeated-measures ANOVAs when the two key assumptions underlying this statistical approach are violated—the assumptions of homogeneity of covariance and a normal sampling distribution. The statistical strategies that we discuss have all been developed to overcome the biases that arise in both type I and type II error rates when one's data fail to conform to these assumptions.

Our reasons for this focus are somewhat pragmatic. First, repeated-measures ANOVAs are by far the dominant statistical approach taken when analyzing ERP time series data, and measures of component amplitude in particular. The value and importance of using these tools in an informed manner thus cannot be overstated. Second, ERP data sets in healthy young participants are already well known to violate the covariance and normality assumptions underlying repeated-measures ANOVAs (e.g., Keselman 1998; Vasey and Thayer 1987). Studying clinical populations—with their increased temporal variability of within- and between-subjects responses—will only exacerbate the biases in type I and type II error rates typically present in ERP data sets. Our goal is thus to help the reader appreciate the nature of these problems, and what can be done to produce more reliable and valid statistical outcomes.

Background Issues

Our chapter is written with two distinct audiences in mind: (1) experienced ERP researchers coming from a background in basic ERP research in healthy young participants, who may be familiar with equal means statistical tests but unfamiliar with issues arising from clinical populations, and (2) experienced ERP researchers coming from a medical ERP background, where there is familiarity with the idiosyncrasies of clinical populations, but the typical statistical concern is identifying how a single individual compares to a normative population, rather than performing equal means testing between groups (e.g., Chiappa 1997).

Throughout, our intention is to provide a conceptual introduction to the reader and point toward the primary sources of more technically minded statistical information, rather than presenting a rigorous mathematical treatment or a general tutorial with specific recommendations. Our reasons for this focus are again somewhat pragmatic. For one, we are applied researchers, not formal statisticians. For another, what may be the optimal statistical approach to take with any given data set will depend on the particulars of the data themselves, and practically speaking, will be constrained by the statistical software actually available to the given researcher.

Before we get to the main issues at hand, however, there are several key background points to make regarding the material we present and its organization.

Chapter Structure

For ease of discussion our chapter separates discussions of variance and normality. Nevertheless, variance and departures from normality are highly (and positively) correlated in repeated-measures ERP data sets (e.g., Vasey and Thayer 1987; Wasserman and Bockenholt 1989). Thus, in separating our discussion of variance versus normality, some readers may find this to be an arbitrary or awkward distinction to make. For example, those factors discussed as influencing variance are often the same as those factors discussed as influencing normality and the shape of distributional curves. The reader should thus be aware of this strong overlap in issues, and that the optimal strategies for dealing with violations of variance and normality in many cases favorably affect both at once.

Background Sources

There are several background sources that may be useful for some readers. First, all the statistical strategies that we discuss arise from the inherent limitations of repeated-measures ANOVAs, and these strategies can thus be viewed as variants or "tweaks" to the canonical ANOVA approach to ERP data sets. For those readers who may wish to have a refresher on this essential topic, Luck (2005) provides a good general introduction to ANOVAs as applied to ERPs, while Dien and Santuzzi (2005) provide a more extensive tutorial that includes basic between-groups considerations and comparisons with multivariate statistical approaches. Second, the validity of ERP statistical analyses directly depends on the accuracy of the measurement or quantification of the ERP waveforms involved. Introductions to ERP measurement can be found in both Handy (2005) and Luck (2005). Third, for those looking for a more extensive treatment of group assignment and the underlying issues of control involved when testing clinical populations, an excellent source can be found in Swick (2005). Finally, and more generally speaking, Wilcox (2001) presents an outstanding nontechnical introduction to the statistical issues discussed in our chapter, and his book is highly recommended for those wishing to ground themselves in a firm understanding of modern approaches to equal means testing.

Generalizability

Our chapter is written as if the main goal of one's analysis is to compare measures of ERP component amplitude (e.g., mean or peak amplitude) between conditions of interest. At the outset, however, there are at least two important ways in which the material we introduce here generalizes beyond equal means testing of ERP amplitude measures. First, the methods we introduce here are by no means limited to equal means testing. For example, outliers can produce strong biases into measures of association (i.e., correlations). While traditional approaches for dealing with outlier biases in correlations have been to use Spearman's rho or Kendall's tau (correlation coefficients which rank order observations to mitigate outlier magnitudes), the boot-strapping procedures we discuss can be applied to correlation analyses—a strategy that can surmount inherent limitations in rank-ordered measures of association (e.g., Wasserman and Bockenholt 1989). Second, in terms of what data are interrogated via the methods presented here, the basic issues and ideas discussed apply to any data sets that are appropriate for equal means testing via ANOVAs, MANOVAs, and *t*-tests. For example, we consider several different approaches to removing and/or correcting for outliers in one's data set. For cognitively oriented researchers these principles may be equally useful for examining performance data (e.g., reaction times and response accuracy) or measures of hemodynamic signal intensity (e.g., fMRI or PET). Likewise, although we have written the chapter as if one's analysis goal is to compare measures of ERP component amplitude, the principles covered in our chapter can be easily applied to other forms of ERP component analysis, including component latency comparisons and spatiotemporal analyses.

Assumptions of Covariance

From a statistics perspective, variance is a measure of the spread or dispersion of a random variable. As noted above, univariate ANOVAs are predicated on the assumption that the variances of all groups and levels are equivalent—that is, the assumption of *homogeneity of variance*. Fortunately, violations of this assumption are commonly viewed as being nonproblematic for ERP data (e.g., Luck 2005) in that ANOVAs tend to be robust to violations of this assumption. Specifically, the probablity values returned by an ANOVA remain reasonably accurate when there is heterogeneity of variance.

Unfortunately, the accuracy of *repeated-measures* ANOVAs depend on a second and much more critical variance-related assumption, and one that is typically violated by ERP data sets: within-subjects, the *covariances* between each participants' set of repeated measurements within a given factor must be approximately equivalent. This is known as the *assumption of sphericity*, and it can be illustrated as follows: Suppose that we measure the mean amplitude of the P3 ERP component elicited by visual oddballs at electrode site PZ while a group of participants is placed under three different levels of cognitive load: low, medium, and high. Given that cognitive load is a factor with three levels, we can compute three different pairwise correlations between these repeated measures: low versus medium, medium versus high, and low versus high. If the assumption of sphericity is to be met, these three pairwise correlations need to be approximately equivalent.

The reason that sphericity is a critical assumption to meet is that the accuracy of the probability estimate (or P value) returned by a repeated-measures ANOVA depends on individual differences in mean responses remaining constant across all levels of a factor. For example, if participant 1 in the oddball study above elicits larger amplitude P3s relative to participant 2, then in general, we would expect participant 1 to have a larger P3 relative to participant 2 across all three levels of cognitive load (i.e., the individual difference in mean P3 amplitude should be a constant across repeated measurements). The trouble for repeated-measures ANOVAs is that if these individual differences fail to remain constant across levels of a repeated factor, the statistic can confuse changes in individual variability for effects of the treatment condition, thereby inflating the actual type I error rate. If so, the P value returned by the test will be smaller than the actual probability value (e.g., Jennings and Wood 1976; Keselman and Rogan 1980; Vasey and Thayer 1987; Wilson 1967).

Provided this understanding of sphericity, the problem of sphericity violations is particularly acute for translational ERP studies for two central reasons. The first concerns the *between-groups* covariance structure. Specifically, in addition to the sphericity assumption (which concerns within-groups covariance structure), one must also satisfy the assumption of *multisample sphericity*, or the requirement that the between-groups covariance matrices should manifest a similar level of equality (e.g., Mendoza 1980). The second concerns sources of variance intrinsic to clinical populations. In addition to decreased stability of event-related responses over time (as discussed above), one can expect variance stemming from clinical diagnoses themselves. In short, there is often some heterogeneity in the actual deficits and/or impairments included within the given clinically defined group.

The upshot is that translational ERP research only increases the odds of sphericity-related violations. Accordingly here we briefly review the common tests used to assess sphericity, followed by a consideration of the different strategic approaches that can be taken in order to safeguard against the biases in type I error rates introduced by sphericity violations.

Tests of Sphericity

In statistics the most commonly referenced test for sphericity or its absence is Mauchly's W, which returns a P value indicating whether or not sphericity has been violated by the given set of repeated measurements. If the P value of the test is <0.05, then a violation of sphericity is indicated. While Mauchly's test can be found in many commercial software packages, the value of the test has been questioned on the grounds that it is sensitive to—or is biased by—even small violations of normality in the sample distributions involved (e.g., Keselman et al. 1980). In other words, a significant P value may reflect a departure from normality rather than a violation of sphericity.

The more useful index of sphericity for electrophysiologists instead tends to be *epsilon*, which is a parameter capturing a population's departure from sphericity first developed by Box (1954). Like the population mean and variance, epsilon must be estimated from one's population sample, and over the years there have been a variety of different estimates derived. Not only does an epsilon estimate provide insight into the extent of a sample's sphericity violation, but as discussed below, it can also be used as a correction factor to adjust the degrees of freedom within the given F ratio (when a violation of sphericity is indicated). When the epsilon value is 1 (the maximum it can be), it indicates that the assumption of sphericity is tenable. As epsilon becomes increasingly less than 1, it indicates an increasing likelihood that the assumption of sphericity is untenable. The minimum possible value (or maximal sphericity violation) is defined as $1/(k-1)$, where k is the number of levels in the given repeated-measures factor.

Design Strategies

The general experimental strategies designed to combat sphericity violations can be dichotomized into two overarching categories: those strategies associated with experimental design (or "front-end" strategies), and those strategies associated with data analysis (or "back-end" strategies). Notably the design and analysis strategies presented here are by no means mutually exclusive of each other, and adopting both are essential for obtaining reliable and conclusive results. Here we discuss three specific strategies relevant to the design phase of an experiment. The first concerns how one sets up the levels of each independent variable to be manipulated, the second and third concern how to help reduce variance within and between sampled populations respectively.

Factor Levels

The one absolute strategy for avoiding concerns over sphericity is to have no more than two levels of any repeated-measures factor. Why? In the condition of only two levels (e.g., A and B) there is only one possible correlation between factor levels (A × B) and sphericity by definition cannot be violated. Thus, in deciding how to set up factors and levels in an experiment, all else equal, there is always an advantage from a sphericity perspective to keep any given factor to two levels. While some treatment conditions may not lend themselves to this strategy, it can certainly be a wise option when considering how to group or arrange electrode-related factors in one's ANOVA. Indeed, given that the independence between electrode sites increases with their spatial distance (i.e., covariance is greater for near vs. far electrode pairings), electrode factors are particularly vulnerable to sphericity violations if not carefully considered (for a review, see Dien 2005).

Within-group Controls

In translational research one is often faced with testing a population that has clearly defined subpopulations (or *strata*) of different sizes that can be potentially important sources of variance. For example, autism is more prevalent in males than females by a ratio of greater than 4 to 1. In such situations it may be helpful to account for the unequal sizes of strata by adopting *stratified sampling* procedures, which have two different variants, both designed to minimize the variance of one's sample from the given population. *Proportionate allocation* dictates that one samples from each strata in ratios equivalent to strata size. For example, if we assume a male-to-female ratio of 4 to 1 in autism, then if using proportionate allocation we would sample autistics at a ratio of 4 males for every 1 female. The idea here is that random sampling may deviate from this proportion by chance, and thus if gender does have some influence on the measure(s) taken in autistics, chance deviations from the 4-to-1 ratio of males to females would introduce a source of error in the sample variance, relative to the actual population variance. In contrast to proportionate allocation, which focuses on strata size as the factor determining sample sizes, *optimum allocation* is predicated on selecting sample sizes based on the known or expected variance within each strata on the measure(s) of interest. In short, one takes a larger sample from the strata having the larger known or expected variance regardless of the actual strata sizes per se. The notion here is that by weighting the sample size of each strata based on expected/ known variance, one can effectively minimize the sampling variance from each strata. In terms of the pros and cons of these sampling strategies, while it can be a critical way in which to reduce or control sample variance within a population of interest, it may not always be clear as to what the study-relevant strata are within a population, their relative proportions, and/or the degree of variance to expect on a measure within the strata of interest.

Between-group Controls

A third design consideration centers on controlling variance between-groups, an issue that is particularly germane to translational studies. The focus here is on how individuals are assigned to the group conditions—that is, grouping protocols. Depending on the type of study, one is conducting, controlling variance levels between groups may or may not be a significant point of concern.

In *randomized control trials* (RCTs) one randomly assigns participants to the different treatment (or intervention) and control conditions. The randomization process is assumed to equally distribute all known and unknown covariates between the groups in the study, meaning that the entire range of each covariates' distribution is represented within each group. Given that multisample sphericity depends on approximate equivalence of between-group's covariance matrices, RCTs by design help to counteract against violations of this assumption. However, for key covariates, one may want to control the amount of variance within the groups by adopting specific inclusion or exclusion criteria. For example, in a recent fMRI-based RCT study examining how weight training affects executive neurocognitive function in older individuals, we limited participation to a single gender (female) while setting minimum cutoffs for participants' physiological falls-risk profile and mini-mental state examination (MMSE) scores (Nagamatsu, Handy, and Liu-Ambrose 2008). In this manner our inclusion/exclusion criteria served to minimize the odds of residual systematic variance between-groups on at least three key neurocognitive factors.

In *cross-sectional studies*, one takes measures on one or more groups at a single point in time. Accordingly grouping factors are predetermined by the experimenter and each participant's status at the time of testing determines group assignment. For example, Curran and colleagues recently used ERPs to examine the effects of aging on visual spatial attention, with two groups of participants being studied: those younger (18–36 years old) and those older (57–84 years old) (Curran et al. 2001). Likewise we have been investigating whether migraineurs (or people who get migraine headaches) show impaired abilities to attentionally modulate visual sensory processing in cortex (Mickleborough and Handy 2008). In turn we have been testing four different groups, based on headache classification: migraine with aura, migraine without aura, tension-type headache, and non–headache controls. In designs such as these, one thus cannot rely on randomization as a means of stratifying confounding covariates within each group. In addition the need to determine participants' grouping status can be problematic when that status is less than certain, such as when using clinical diagnoses as per mentioned above. However, grouping protocols for cross-sectional studies can nevertheless combat sphericity violations in at least two important ways. First, one can attempt to match groups on as many parameters as possible, such as age, gender, education, and MMSE score. Second, when grouping based on diagnositc criteria, those criteria should be as clear as possible, including efforts to homogenize the clinical groups by controlling for subtypes of a disorder, its duration and severity (Picton et al. 2000).

In *prospective studies* one's goal is to follow participants' behavioral or clinical history over time, an experimental design that can be optimal for helping to identify potential predictors of clinical outcomes. In one variant the approach is akin to a cross-sectional study, where two or more groups may be predefined (e.g., participants with and without Alzheimer's disease), and then one compares whether the groups differ in their prospective histories on one or more metrics (e.g., number of falls). The considerations outlined above for participant grouping would then be essential for controlling variance. In another variant, however, rather than predefining one's groups of interest, one may test a single group of participants on some measure, and then group participants at a later point in time based on their prospective behavioral/clinical history *after* the initial testing session. For example, in a recent fMRI study, in looking at issues of cognitive impairment in risk of falls among older individuals, we scanned a large number of participants in a basic executive cognitive functioning task, and we followed their falls history forward in time (Liu-Ambrose et al. 2008). We then compared brain activation patterns between participants who had falls and participants who had not had one or more falls in the intervening time since the original scanning session, with the goal of determining whether there were any aspects of executive cognitive functioning predictive of subsequent falling episodes (i.e., were there any differences between the prospectively defined fallers and nonfallers groups). As with RCTs one can certainly apply specific inclusion or exclusion criteria in prospective studies to help control key covariates, but the participants' posttesting history determines the actual grouping factor.

Analysis Strategies

There are at least three basic strategies that are used to account for violations of sphericity when comparing means across repeated measures in both within- and between-groups analyses: data transformations, corrections to the probability values and/or degrees of freedom within a statistical test, and the use of *unpooled* error terms.

Data Transforms

The first analysis strategy to consider concerns the use of various data transformations in order to reduce the inequality of covariance between the pairwise repeated measures comparisons. In short, one simply applies a transform of some sort to each observation in one's data set prior to any statistical hypothesis testing. For example, one might apply a rank transform, where the data values within each set of measures are (1) ordinally ranked and then (2) the actual data values are replaced with the rank value. In this manner one can reduce inequalities in the variability or spread of the data themselves. Other options would include *z-score* transforms (replacing each actual data value within a measure with its *z*-score) or a loglinear transform (replacing each actual data value with its log equivalent). Which to choose, however, will depend on the nature of the data themselves. Indeed one might apply several transforms to one's data set and then identify which to select based on which produces the best (largest) epsilon estimate. The downside to transform strategies is that depending on the specific transform used, it can complicate interpretation of the data given that one may no longer be dealing with the same units that were actually measured.

Statistical Corrections

The more traditional approach to sphericity violations is to use an epsilon estimate (described above) as a correction factor. By far the two most prevalent epsilon estimates are the *Greenhouse–Geisser estimate* (1959) and the *Huynh–Feldt estimate* (1976), both commonly included in commercial statistical software. While the differences in how these estimates are calculated is beyond the scope of our chapter, the common recommendation regarding their use is that when the estimates are comparatively low (i.e., when the sphericity assumption is clearly violated), the Greenhouse–Geisser estimate provides the more accurate correction. Conversely, when the estimate is closer to one and thus there is a more minor violation of the sphericity assumption, the Huynh-Feldt tends to be more accurate (e.g., Levine 1991). When it may be ambiguous as to whether there has been a large or small departure from sphericity, one may instead choose to take the average of the two estimates as the correction factor (e.g., Stevens 1992). Regardless of which epsilon estimate is used, the degrees of freedom in both the numerator and denominator of the F statistic are multiplied by the epsilon estimate, and the F statistic is then recomputed accordingly (fractional values of each are rounded to the nearest integer value.) The idea here is that type I error rates are inflated beyond the given P value in an ANOVA when sphericity is violated, and thus these corrections are designed to be conservative (i.e., reduce/eliminate the type I error inflation).

However, there are also two important concerns about these corrections that should also be noted. First, they are often viewed as being overly-conservative in nature, thereby inflating the type II error rate as an artifactual consequence of controlling the type I error rate. Second, it has been demonstrated that they are overly sensitive to between-group designs with unequal groups sizes (or N), producing either increased or decreased type I error rates depending on the dynamics of how the group sizes and covariance matrices differ (Keselman, Keselman, and Lix 1995; Keselman and Keselman 1990). If the largest group also has the largest values within their covariance matrix, then it will produce a conservative bias in the degrees of freedom adjustment. Alternatively, if the largest group has the smallest values within their covariance matrix, it will produce a liberal bias in the correction (Keselman 1998). This makes the Greenhouse–Geisser and Huynh–Feldt epsilon estimates particularly unsuited for many translational studies, where unequal group sizes—or *unbalanced designs*—may often be the norm rather than the exception.

Unpooled Error Terms

There has been growing recognition that perhaps the most optimal strategy for dealing with violations of sphericity in psychophysiological data is to adopt a *multivariate* approach (e.g., Dien and Santuzzi 2005; Keselman, Wilcox, and Lix 2003; Vasey and Thayer 1987; Wheldon, Anderson, and Johnson 2007). While multivariate statistics such as MANOVA are traditionally applied in situations where one wants to include multiple dependent measures within a single statistical test, less commonly appreciated is that they can also be used with univariate data (e.g., Keppel and Wickens 2004). At issue is how error terms are calculated in the multivariate approach, and how the same calculations can be used with univariate data.

To the point, univariate ANOVAs rely on *pooled* error terms, where the variance (or sum of squares, in the least squares approach) is calculated across all observations in the given data set. In contrast, multivariate statistics such as MANOVA rely on *unpooled* error terms, or error terms that restrict variance calculations to the observations within the given factor(s) of interest. When the assumption of sphericity holds in a data set, the general advantage of a pooled error term is that because the degrees of freedom are higher relative the unpooled term, it will produce an overall smaller denominator in the subsequent *F* test and thus provide more power (because in ANOVAs, error terms are based on dividing the sum of squared errors by the degrees of freedom). However, the problem with pooled error terms from a sphericity standpoint is that when sphericity doesn't hold, the actual type I error rate will be inflated relative to the probability value returned by the statistical test. When using an unpooled error term in the identical situation, not only will the test return an unbiased probability value but the approach does not introduce the inflated type II error rate characteristic of epsilon-based corrections (i.e., it is not overly conservative).

Conclusions: Covariance

The preceding section can be summarized as suggesting that there is an advantage to using a multivariate, unpooled error approach to repeated measures ERP data sets. The advantage is borne of the need to account for heterogeneity of covariance in a manner that doesn't suffer from the overly conservative nature of Greenhouse-Geisser and Huynh-Feldt epsilon corrections. Accordingly many researchers are now recommending the use of multivariate statistics as a default for ERP analysis (e.g., Dien and Santuzzi 2005; Keselman 1998). As well, it will always be advantageous to carefully consider how front-end strategies invoked during experimental design stage can also be used to help mitigate problematic covariance structure.

Assumptions of Normality

From a statistical perspective, normality concerns whether or not the frequency distribution of a given parameter conforms to the classic normal, Gaussian curve, The assumption of normality in statistical tests like ANOVAs are predicated on the idea that the probability of the given statistical outcome—such as a sample mean taken from some defined population—can be accurately described by a normal curve. The basis for this assumption stems from the *central limit theorem*, which stipulates that regardless of what the shape of the population distribution looks like (e.g., normal, lognormal, or uniform), the distribution of sample means drawn from that population will approximate a normal curve centered around the actual population mean.

For example, suppose that we draw a large number of samples of the same size from the same population (e.g., 1,000 samples of $N = 40$) and then plot the frequency of the means of each of these samples. The central limit theorem dictates that this *sampling distribution* will approximate a normal curve regardless of the shape of the underlying population distribution from which our samples were taken. Accordingly inferences of probability regarding one's sample mean can then drawn based on the assumed normal distribution of the sampling means.

Given this assumption of sampling distribution normality, modern statistical methods have highlighted two fundamental and interrelated problems with the assumption, as detailed in Wilcox (2001). First, the sampling distribution will only approximate normal if the sample size is sufficiently large. Second, even very small deviations from normality in the sampling distribution can lead to grossly inaccurate probability inferences. While it can be a matter of debate as to how large a sample size must be for the normality assumption to be viable, the size of the samples typical of most ERP studies ($n < 20$ or so) universally fail to be sufficient (e.g., Vassey and Thayer 1987; Wasserman and Bockenholt 1989). Compounding the problem for translational ERP studies, the greater the overall variance in the population of interest, the greater the risk of deviation from normality and the larger the sample size must be in order to meet the normality assumption.

Why are even small deviations from normality such a problem? The issue stems from outliers and how they can adversely bias the sampling mean and variance. In the general linear model, variance is calculated based on summing the squared distance of each observation in a sample from the sample mean. As a result outliers have a disproportionate influence on the variance of the sample that only increases with the size of the outlier. Likewise even a single outlier can cause a nontrivial shift in the sample mean toward the tail of the sampling distribution containing the outlier. The problem here is that the underlying "normal" probability distribution used to draw inferences from one's data (i.e., the normal distribution that one must assume for equal means hypothesis testing) is defined in relation to the sample mean and standard deviation. When these sample statistics are biased by the presence of one or more outliers, one is making probability inferences from a distribution that can significantly deviate from the actual distribution, in relation to both location (where the mean is located) and *kurtosis* (it's overall breadth). The end result are statistical tests that may result in grossly inflated type I or type II error rates, depending on the particulars of one's data set and the questions being asked.

Given the problematic nature of the central limit theorem for making probability inferences, our goal here is to outline two key statistical advances that can improve the accuracy and power of repeated-measures tests under conditions where the assumption of normality is untenable. The first concerns the use of data resampling strategies, which take outliers into account by defining the shape of one's probability distribution based on the actual observations in one's data set, rather than assuming a normal distribution based on the sample's mean and standard deviation. The second concerns what are called *robust* measures of central tendency, which deal with outliers by either removing them from the data set or by correcting them. Collectively these strategies have been deliberately developed to mitigate the inaccuracy of probability estimates that arise with undersized samples and when dealing with populations that deviate in any way from normal. We begin, however, by first briefly discussing tests of normality.

Tests of Normality

There are a number of tests—often referred to as goodness-of-fit tests—available for assessing whether a sample distribution is normal. In essence, most tests take into account the *skewness* of the sample (whether it's asymmetrically shifted to the right or left) and the kurtosis, and then compare these to what would be expected if the data were indeed normal. Of these the Kolmogorov-Smirnov test is by far the most frequently encountered, and returns a *P* value indicating the probability that the sampling distribution is in fact normal. From the perspective of discussion here, the utility of these tests are less than certain: not only may the tests be insensitive to small deviations of normality, but the strategies we present are designed to improve statistical accuracy regardless of whether or not normality holds. Researchers may thus not want to concern themselves with normality testing as a means of deciding whether to use resampling methods, robust measures of central tendency, or both. Rather, the advantage in terms of maximizing statistical power may reside with the researcher who simply invokes both strategies as a default (e.g., Keselman et al. 2003; Wilcox 2001).

Resampling Strategies

Data resampling strategies are designed to provide more exact *P* values than is possible when estimating critical values based on the assumed normal shape of a sampling distribution. The procedures are instead based on using the observations that one has actually taken to specify the actual probability value for the obtained result. In this regard resampling procedures can be considered as *parametric-free* approaches to least squares statistical analysis, in that they rely on no assumptions regarding distribution shapes. Here we consider the two most prevalent forms of resampling, *permutation tests* and *bootstrapping*.

Permutation Tests

As applied to repeated-measures analysis of ERP data sets, permutation tests are based on the idea that if the null hypothesis is in fact true, then the actual repeated measurements within each participant only differ due to measurement error (e.g., Blair and Karniski 1993). In other words, under the null hypothesis the mapping between each participants' repeated observations and the treatment conditions to which each

of those repeated measures can be assumed to be arbitrary. Leveraging this consequence of a true null hypothesis, permutation methods are based on comparing the
magnitude of one's actual inferential test statistic (e.g., a t value or F ratio), relative to
the magnitudes of the same statistic calculated for each possible reordering of the
observation-condition mappings. In this manner one can calculate the exact probability of obtaining a test statistic as large as the one returned by the original (or actual)
observation-condition mappings by simply rank-ordering the statistic calculated for
each mapping.

For example, consider the simple case where two participants (1 and 2) have the
mean amplitude of their P3 ERP component measured at a single electrode site in each
of two conditions (A and B), with the analysis goal is to compare the means for conditions A and B via a paired t-test. Here are the P3 measures (in μv) in their original (or
actual) observation-condition mappings:

	Condition	
	A	B
Participant 1	6.2	8.9
Participant 2	8.6	10.2

For this data set there are three permutations possible, on the condition that observations are only permutated within each participant (i.e., that only repeated-measures
within a subject are reordered)—the pair of observations for participant 1 can be
flipped, the pair of observations for participant 2 can be flipped, and the observations
for both participants can be flipped:

	A	B		A	B		A	B
Subject 1	8.9	6.2	and	6.2	8.9	and	8.9	6.2
Subject 2	8.6	10.2		10.2	8.6		10.2	8.6

For each of these four orderings of the data (the actual ordering and the three per-
muatations), a paired t statistic would be computed. The four resulting t values would
then be rank-ordered from lowest to highest. Based on this ordinal ranking, one can
then compute the exact probability of obtaining a t value as large as the one provided
by the data in their original (or actual) observation-condition mapping. Here, if the
actual obtained t value was the largest, relative to the t values calculated in the three
possible permutations, then the probability value of the statistical outcome based on
the null hypothesis being true would be 0.25. That is, based on a true null hypothesis,
one would expect a t value as large as the one obtained with the original data orderings 1 in 4 times. This is then used as the type I error rate and is considered to be
exact (e.g., Blair and Karnisky 1993).

Obviously permutation methods have little utility with such small permutation
numbers, but as the sample sizes and number of repeated-measures treatment con-

ditions increase, the precision or resolution of the exact probability value increases. For example, if one wants to have a type I error rate of at least 0.05, then at least 20 permutations must be available. Likewise a level of 0.01 would require at least 100 permutations. Notably permutation tests are also easily exported to between-groups and mixed-model designs, where one simply computes the relevant statistic (e.g., F) for each possible permutation of each participant's repeated measures, regardless of group. There is also no limit on which statistics can or cannot be used with permutation tests—the same basic principle applies regardless of what is calculated for each permutation. While computationally intense for large data sets, permutation tests are now easily handled by modern desktop computers. On the downside, however, permutation tests require an assumption of equal variance and distributional shape (e.g., Nichols and Holmes 2001; Wilcox 2001), thereby limiting their utility for ERP data.

Bootstrapping

Like permutation tests, bootstrapping involves the resampling of data, yet unlike permutation tests, there is no need for assumptions of equal variance. As a consequence bootstrapping has been a popular nonparametric approach to analyzing ERP data sets (e.g., Keselman et al. 2003; Wasserman and Bockenholt 1989). The bootstrap procedure itself can be broken down into three steps or stages.

First, one randomly samples—with replacement—a subset of the original observations in the data set. This is referred to as a *bootstrap sample* and rests on the idea that the values measured in one's original sample can be seen as representing the actual probabilities of obtaining each measured value. For example, if one has the sample

2, 2, 4, 5, 5, 5, 6, 8, 8, and 9,

bootstrapping considers the probability of obtaining a 5 to be 0.3, the probability of obtaining a 2 to be 0.2, the probabilities of obtaining a 4, 6, or 9 to be 0.1. The probability of any other values is 0. Because sampling is done with replacement, these probability values are preserved for all samples taken.

The second step is to compute one's statistic(s) of interest from the bootstrap sample, such as a mean or, if used for hypothesis testing, a t value or F ratio. This is referred to as the *bootstrap mean* or *bootstrap t/F value*.

The third step is to repeat the first two steps a large number of times (e.g., 3,000–4,000) and then generate a frequency plot of all the bootstrap means, t/F values, or other bootstrap statistics calculated. These frequency plots then serve as the *bootstrapped sample distribution* for each statistic of interest. One then uses this bootstrapped sample distribution to calculate the probability of the actual sample obtained. In this sense the frequency plot is an estimate of the probability distribution from which one's original sample was taken, and the probability value returned is a relatively accurate, unbiased estimate of the actual probability (e.g., Wilcox 2001).

Strategies of Robust Measures

Whereas resampling strategies take into account outliers and their effect on probability estimates, strategies involving robust measures deal with outliers by either removing them from one's data set (as in the case of trimmed means) or correcting for them (as in the case of Winsorized means and M-estimators). The term *robust* refers to the fact that by removing or correcting outliers, the measures remain relatively uninfluenced—or unbiased—by these extreme values. Here we consider three different robust measures of location (or central tendency), measures that have become essential for dealing with departures from normality in sampling distributions (e.g., Keselman 1998; Keselman et al. 2003).

Trimmed Means

The simplest approach to dealing with outliers in one's sample is to remove or "trim off" the observations falling in the two tails of the distribution. While traditional approaches in this domain have relied on using a standard deviation (or SD) criteria for what observations to remove from one's data set (e.g., remove any values more than 2 or 2.5 sds from the sample mean), the problem with this kind approach is that even a single extreme outlier can increase the sd to such a level that less extreme outliers may not be removed. The question then becomes how much to trim, with recommendations converging on a value of 20 percent on each tail end—that is, one removes the lowest 20 percent of the observations within the sample, and the highest 20 percent of the observations within the sample (e.g., Wilcox 2001; Wilcox and Keselman 2001). The downside to trimmed means is that it can be difficult to select how to treat repeated-measures data, as one must keep each individual's set of paired measures in tact. For example, in a study having three levels of a repeated measure, one subject may be an outlier in the first level only, a second subject may be an outlier in the second level only, and a third subject may be an outlier in the third level only. How best to proceed under such circumstances is less than clear. For any number of reasons, it may also be less than optimal to decrease one's N.

Winsorized Means

Winsorizing the observations in one's data sample solves the problem of outliers by correcting extreme values rather than removing them. The procedure itself is fairly simple. One first decides on how many values to correct, with the upper and lower 20 percent of the distribution being a typical value (Wilcox 2001). One then multiplies this percentage value by N, and rounds down to the nearest integer in order to determine how many observations on each end of the distribution will be corrected. The correction is made on each end of the distribution by simply replacing each outlier observation with the next least extreme value in that end of the sample. In this manner one establishes what is essentially a bandpass limit on how large and small values can be; any values exceeding the bandpass limit on either end of the distribution are set at (or corrected to) the bandpass limit for that end of the tail.

For example, suppose a sample contains the following $N = 12$ observations, arranged from lowest to highest value:

2 10 12 16 18 19 22 28 31 40 45 68.

To perform a 20 percent Winsorizing, we compute $0.2N$, which in this case would be $(0.2)(12) = 2.4$. Rounding down, this would give us 2, indicating that we should replace the two most extreme values on each end of the distribution. Given that the third smallest value is 12 and the third largest value is 40, the two smallest values in the distrbution would be corrected to 12, and the two largest values would be corrected to 40. This then creates the 0.2 Winsorized distribution

12 12 12 16 18 19 22 28 31 40 40 40.

Desired descriptive and/or inferential statistics are then computed based on this Winsorized sample.

Importantly for ERPs, the logic of Winsorizing easily generalizes to repeated-measures situations. For example, suppose that a sample contains the following $N = 12$ paired or repeated-measures observations on variable X under two different levels, X_1 and X_2:

X_1: 15 49 25 28 46 5 44 75 25 35 53 24,

X_2: 44 36 75 30 7 32 43 9 3 0 46 14 64.

And suppose again that we want to perform a 20 percent Winsorizing. Calculating $0.2N$ again gives us 2.4, rounded down to 2. For each of the two variables X_1 and X_2 we then simply Winsorize within that distribution:

X_1: 24 49 25 28 46 24 44 49 25 35 49 24

X_2: 44 36 46 30 14 32 43 14 30 46 14 64.

For X_1 the corrected lower end value is 24 (which was the third smallest value in the distribution), and the corrected upper end value is 49 (which was the third largest value in the distribution). For X_2, the corrected lower end value is 14, and the corrected upper end value is 46. This procedure thus allows a subject's observation on one variable to be corrected (if it's one of the extreme values), while leaving that subject's paired observation on the other variable unchanged (unless it too is an extreme value in that distribution as well).

M-Estimators
Like Winsorized means, M-estimators are based on correcting extreme values in a distribution rather than eliminating them. Likewise they are also easily applied to

repeated-measures data where one value in a paired set of observations can be corrected without affecting any other paired values. Where they differ from Winsorizing is in the nature of the correction itself and how it's computed; however, an explanation of the computations themselves is beyond the scope of our chapter (for reviews, see Wilcox 2001; Wilcox and Keselman 2003). That said, M-estimators can be understood at a conceptual level as a downweighting of extreme values in one's distribution, but the downweighting itself is less severe than in Winsorizing. Given this context, there are any number of different M-estimators available, each differing in the downweighting function applied to a sample's outliers and the bandpass range of values in the middle of the distribution that are not subject to correction.

Conclusions: Normality

Violations of normality introduced by outliers can be addressed in at least two fundamental ways: using resampling-based nonparametric approaches to estimating probability distributions, and using robust measures of central tendency in order to mute the biasing influence of outlier values. Because use of either or both strategies produces accurate probability inferences regardless of whether or not one's data set actually violates the normality assumption, it has been suggested that one may be at an advantage in using the approaches as a default (e.g., Keselman 1998; Keselman et al. 2003).

Concluding Issues

Our chapter has introduced the problems that arise for equal means testing when the assumptions of sphericity and normality are violated, and the various strategies that can be employed to help improve the accuracy of statistical inferences—issues that are particularly germane to translational studies due to the increased magnitude/risk of sphericity and normality violations. In closing, there are several additional points to make that follow from our discussion.

Unbalanced Designs

In between-groups experiments a *balanced* design refers to the case where the groups sizes are equivalent, and an *unbalanced* design refers to the case where the group sizes differ. One consequence of pursuing translational studies is that one is often faced with unbalanced designs. For example, in RCTs, treatment conditions may stretch out over time, leading some participants to drop out for any number of reasons. Inevitably the dropout rate will not be equal between groups. Likewise, in prospective studies, there will rarely if ever be equality in the numbers of people showing different posttesting behavioral/clinical trajectories. Again, the result is that one will inevitably end up with different group sizes. In cross-sectional studies, there are several factors working against group equality. For some clinical populations it may be difficult to test sufficient numbers, relative to how many control participants can be tested. Rather than limit the size of the control group to match the size of the clinical group, researchers may be interested in including all control data in the analyses conducted. Similarly there is often greater rejection of clinical as compared to control participants during ERP data analysis due to residual noise in the participants' data sets, increased blinking, reduced ocular control, and the like. Under such situations, if the experimenter wishes to include all "good" participants in analysis as a way of leveraging power but is not in a position to correct for unequal rejection rates by running more participants from the clinical group(s), this can again lead to unbalanced designs.

From a statistical perspective, the problem with unequal group sizes is that unbalanced designs exacerbate the statistical biases described above for violations of sphericity and normality assumptions, in that they increase the magnitude of heterogeneity of covariance and deviations from normality. Toward addressing these concerns, Keselman and colleagues have developed a Welch–James (WJ) statistic for ERP data that uses unpooled error terms and that estimates the degrees of freedom for an accurate probablity inference via data resampling procedures (Keselman, Carriere, and Lix 1993). This makes the statistic robust to violations of sphericity and normality, and it is singled out by the authors as being particularly useful for analyzing data from unbalanced designs (e.g., Keselman 1998; Keselman, Algina, and Kowalchuk 2001; for a SAS/IML program implementing this statistic, see Keselman et al. 2003).

Multiple Comparisons

One point of concern in any statistical analysis centers on the problem of multiple comparisons, and in particular, whether one needs to control familywise type I error rates. In this regard there are two points of issue to consider from the perspective of modern approaches to equal means testing of ERP data. First, researchers have long stressed that violations of sphericity are particularly prevalent in follow-up statistical tests that examine the specific sub-effects and interactions arising in one's initial omnibus statistical analysis (e.g., Boik 1981). This only increases the likelihood of type I errors at the familywise level, especially when dealing with clinical or medical populations typical of translational studies. While one may consider using a Bonferonni-type correction, these are typically overly conservative, inflating the type II error rate as an unintended consequence of gaining control of the type I error rate. While it can be useful to preplan specific contrasts and thus not perform all possible combinations of comparisons, it may nevertheless be critical to account for multiple comparisons. In this regard, adopting unpooled error terms and nonparametric approaches to probabability estimates during all planned and unplanned follow-up testing can be critical for returning accurate probability values while controlling for familywise error rates (e.g., Vasey and Thayer 1987).

Resampling Revisited

While we discussed data resampling procedures as a strategy for dealing with violations of normality in one's data set during equal means testing, there are a number of additional usages for these procedures that may be of interest for translational ERP research. First, under some circumstances it may be of interest to compute confidence intervals for one's sample means rather than performing traditional equal means hypothesis testing. If so, bootstrapping can be used to produce more accurate confidence intervals when assumptions of sphericity and normality are violated (Wasswerman and Bockenholt 1989).

Second, our discussion has implicitly assumed that one's analysis goal is to compare the mean or peak latency of some ERP component across multiple electrode sites and conditions of interest. However, in some cases one may be interested in increasing the temporal resolution of component analysis, such as including each time point as a factor. This type of analysis strategy can be useful for identifying when in time effects of interest begin to emerge and/or dissipate. Under such situations, however, there is also an extreme need to control the familywise error, given that hundreds of time points may be involved. To control for type I error, permutation-based approaches have been developed that can be used when including time points within the given statistical analysis (Wheldon et al. 2007).

Finally, our chapter is premised on the point that studying populations of interest in translational studies necessarily dictates that there will be increased variability in event-related responses both within subjects and between subjects. Throughout, however, we have emphasized statistical strategies designed to combat between-participant sources of variance. In terms of within-participant sources of variance, one way to conceptualize this form of error is from a signal-to-noise (SNR) perspective. In essence, given that deriving ERPs depends on the stationarity of the brain's event-related response over time, the SNR of an ERP will decrease with increasing temporal variability in the given participant's event-related response. For situations where the SNR of an ERP may be of concern, bootstrapping procedures have now been applied to the problem of improving the accuracy of the estimated event-related responses in populations that are characteristic of reduced SNRs (McCubbin et al. 2008).

Conclusions

Our chapter stresses that studying the clinical populations typical of translational research places one at increased risk for biased statistical tests when using general linear approaches to equal means testing. In so doing, the challenge we face is that researchers can hold strong prejudices about what is and what is not appropriate to do with such data. For example, in suggesting that it may be helpful (if not imperative) to correct for outliers, an oft-heard response against such practices is: Well, these outliers may be telling us something important. We couldn't agree more. But our point is that to learn what they may be telling us requires us to account for them in our statistical analyses, not ignore them. Indeed the deeper theme here is that for translational studies, equal means testing—even when adopting the strategies discussed above—may only be giving us part of the critical picture. If outliers are of increased concern or in fact characteristic of a given population, then we may want to begin considering the *shape* of a population's distribution to be a metric of interest, in addition to any measures of central tendency. As translational ERP studies become ever more prevalent, it is precisely these kinds of advances we will need to be making in order to maximally leverage our understanding of neurocognitive function in the clinical domain.

References

Blair RC, Karniski W. 1993. An alternative method for significance testing of waveform difference potentials. *Psychophysiology* 30:518–24.

Boik RJ. 1981. A priori tests in repeated measures designs: effects of nonsphericity. *Psychometrika* 46:241–55.

Box GEP. 1954. Some theorems on quadratic forms applied in the study of analysis of variance problems: I. Effects of inequality of variance in the one-way classification. *An Math Stat* 25:290–302.

Chiappa, KH, ed. 1997. *Evoked Potentials in Clinical Medicine,* 3d ed. Philadelphia: Lippincott-Raven.

Curran T, Hills A, Patterson MB, Strauss ME. 2001. Effects of aging on visuospatial attention: an ERP study. *Neuropsychologia* 39:288–301.

Dien J, Santuzzi AM. 2005. Application of repeated measures ANOVA to high-density ERP datasets: a review and tutorial. In: Handy TC, ed. *Event-Related Potentials: A Methods Handbook.* Cambridge: MIT Press, 57–82.

Greenhouse SW, Geisser S. 1959. On methods in the analysis of profile data. *Psychometrika* 24: 95–112.

Handy TC. 2005. Basic principles of ERP quantification. In: Handy TC, ed. *Event-Related Potentials: A Methods Handbook.* Cambridge: MIT Press, 33–55.

Handy TC, Grafton ST, Shroff NM, Ketay S, Gazzaniga MS. 2003. Graspable objects grab attention with the potential for action is recognized. *Nat Neurosci* 6:421–7.

Huynh H, Feldt LS. 1976. Estimation of the box correction for degrees of freedom from sample data in randomized block and split-plot designs. *J Educ Stat* 1:69–82.

Jennings JR, Wood CC. 1976. The epsilon-adjusted procedure for repeated measures analysis of variance. *Psychophysiology* 13:277–8.

Keppel G, Wickens TD. 2004. *Design and Analysis: A Researcher's Handbook*, 4th ed. New York: Pearson.

Keselman HJ. 1998. Testing treatment effects in repeated measures designs: an update for psychophysiological researchers. *Psychophysiology* 35:470–8.

Keselman HJ, Algina J, Kowalchuk RK. 2001. The analysis of repeated measures designs: a review. *Brit J Math Stat Psychol* 54:1–20.

Keselman HJ, Carriere KC, Lix LM. 1993. Testing repeated measures hypotheses when covariance matrices are heterogeneous. *J Educ Stat* 18:305–19.

Keselman HJ, Keselman JC, Lix LM. 1995. The analysis of repeated measurements: univariate tests, multivariate tests, or both? *Brit J Math Stat Psychol* 48:319–38.

Keselman HJ, Rogan JC. 1980. Repeated measures *F* tests and psychophysiological research: controlling the number of false positives. *Psychophysiol* 17:499–503.

Keselman HJ, Rogan JC, Mendoza JL, Breen LJ. 1980. Testing the validity conditions of repeated measures *F* tests. *Psychol Bull* 87:479–81.

Keselman HJ, Wilcox RR, Lix LM. 2003. A generally robust approach to hypothesis testing in independent and correlated group designs. *Psychophysiol* 40:586–96.

Keselman JC, Keselman HJ. 1990. Analysing unbalanced repeated measures designs. *Brit J Math Stat Psychol* 43:265–82.

Levine G. 1991. *A Guide to SPSS for Analysis of Variance*. Hillsdale, NJ: Erlbaum.

Liu-Ambrose TYL, Nagamatsu L, Leghari MA, Handy, TC. 2008. Does impaired cerebellar function contribute to risk of falls in seniors? A pilot study using functional magnetic resonance imaging. *J Am Geriatr Soc 56:* 2153–55.

Lord S, Sherrington C, Menz H, Close J. 2007. *Falls in Older People: Risk Factors and Strategies for Prevention*. New York: Cambridge University Press.

Luck SJ. 2005. *An Introduction to the Event-Related Potential Technique*. Cambridge: MIT Press.

Mangun GR, Hillyard SA. 1991. Modulations of sensory-evoked brain potentials indicate changes in perceptual processing during visual-spatial priming. *J Exp Psychol Hum Percept Perform* 17:1057–74.

McCubbin J, Yee T, Vrba J, Robinson SE, Murphy P, Eswaran H, Preissl H. 2008. Bootstrap significance of low SNR evoked response. *J Neurosci Meth* 168:265–72.

Mendoza JL. 1980. A significance test for multisample sphericity. *Psychometrika* 45:495–8.

Mickleborough MJS, Truong G, Holditch L, Handy TC. 2008. Poster presented at the Cognitive Neuroscience Society Annual Meeting.

Nagamatsu LS, Liu-Ambrose TYL, Carolan P, Handy TC. 2009. Are impairments in visual-spatial attention a critical factor for increased falls risk in seniors? an event-related potential study. *Neuropsychologia* (under review).

Nichols TE, Holmes AP. 2001. Nonparametric permutation tests for functional neuroimaging: a primer with examples. *Hum Brain Mapp* 15:1–25.

Picton TW, Bentin S, Berg P, Donchin E, Hillyard SA, Johnson R Jr, Miller GA, Ritter W, Ruchkin DS, Rugg MD, Taylor MJ. 2000. Guidelines for using human event-related potentials to study cognition: recording standards and publication criteria. *Psychophysiology* 37:127–52.

Stevens JP. 1992. *Applied Multivariate Statistcs for the Social Sciences*, 2d ed. HIllsdale, NJ: Erlbaum.

Swick D. 2005. ERP's in neuropsychological populations. In: Handy TC, ed. *Event-Related Potentials: A Methods Handbook*. Cambridge: MIT Press, 299–321.

Vasey MW, Thayer JF. 1987. The continuing problem of false positives in repeated measures ANOVA in psychophysiology: a multivariate solution. *Psychophysiology* 24:479–86.

Wasserman S, Bockenholt U. 1989. Bootstrapping: applications to psychophysiology. *Psychophysiology* 26:208–21.

Wheldon MC, Anderson MJ, Johnson BW. 2007. Identifying treatment effects in multi-channel measurements in electroencephalographic studies: multivariate permutation tests and multiple comparisons. *Austr N Zealand J Stat* 49:397–413.

Wilcox RR. 2001. *Fundamentals of Modern Statistical Methods: Substantially Improving Power and Accuracy*. New York: Springer.

Wilcox RR, Keselman HJ. 2001. Using trimmed means to compare K measures corresponding to two independent groups. *Multivar Behav Res* 36:421–44.

Wilcox RR, Keselman HJ. 2003. Repeated measures one-way ANOVA based on a modified one-step M-estimator. *Brit J Math Stat Psychol* 56:15–25.

Wilson RS. 1967. Analysis of automatic reaction patterns. *Psychophysiology* 4:125–42.

Index

AAHC (atomized and agglomerate hierarchical clustering), 37–38
and Krzanowski–Lai criterion, 39
for VEPs, 40, 41
Action potentials, synchronization of, 179–81
Adaptation hypothesis, 154
Adaptive beamforming, 124
Adjacent response (ADJAR) overlap estimation procedure, 218
Aliasing, 176
Alzheimer's disease, 172
and synchronization likelihood, 192–93
Amplitude
via analytic signal and Hilbert transform, 186–87
and volume conduction problem, 194
via wavelet analysis, 184–86
Analytic signal, 186–87, 188
ANOVA, 228
assumption of normality in, 235
and clustering, 41, 42
error rates in (type I), 234
repeated-measures, 226, 227, 228
topographic (TANOVA), 31–32, 42
and translational research, 226
Argand plane, 176, 177
Artifact(s), 26–27
in EEG, 214–15
and beamforming, 89
and data recording, 211, 220

detection procedures for, 215–17, 219
and instructions to participants, 212
in MEG, 106, 115–18
and memorization processes, 207
Assumptions of covariance, in translational research, 228–29
Assumptions of normality, in translational research, 235–37
Assumption of sphericity, 228–29
in translational research, 228–29
Atomized and agglomerate hierarchical clustering. See AAHC
Attention, and MEG response amplitude, 115
Attention, visual
and falls by elderly, 225
and VESPA method, 12, 13
Attention search network, 171
Autism
and sampling for translational research, 231
and synchronization disturbance, 172
Auto-adaptive averaging, 216–17, 218, 219–20, 220
Autoregressive techniques, 196
Average reference, 26–27
Averaging, 205–206, 219
auto-adaptive, 216–17, 218, 219–20, 220
grand average, 220–21
group-averaging, 43–44, 130–131
and signal-to-noise ratio, 113–114, 205–206